BARKER PLAYS SIX

Howard Barker

PLAYS SIX

(UNCLE) VANYA
A HOUSE OF CORRECTION
LET ME
JUDITH
LOT AND HIS GOD

OBERON BOOKS
LONDON

First published in this collection in 2010 by Oberon Books Ltd
521 Caledonian Road, London N7 9RH
Tel: 020 7607 3637 / Fax: 020 7607 3629
e-mail: info@oberonbooks.com
www.oberonbooks.com

ISBN: 978-1-84002-961-1

Cover photography by Eduardo Houth

Printed in Great Britain by CPI Antony Rowe, Chippenham.

Contents

(UNCLE) VANYA

Notes on the Necessity for a Version of Chekhov's *Uncle Vanya*

Chekhov's *Uncle Vanya* is a *danse macabre*. Its charm lies in its appeal to the death wish in ourselves. In its melancholy celebration of paralysis and spiritual vacuity it makes theatre an art of consolation, a funerary chant for unlived life.

By the power of his pity Chekhov subdues our innate sense of other life and innoculates us against the desire to become ourselves. Vanya, the greatest of his characterizations, is the apotheosis of self-denial. In this broken soul the audience is enabled to pity itself. It is necessary for our own spiritual health to know Vanya need not be Vanya.

We love Vanya, but it is a love born of contempt. It is Chekhov's bad faith to induce in his audience an adoration of the broken will. In this he invites us to collude in our own despair.

When we approach a great writer, we come naked, with a certain innocence and fear. We fear what subtle damage might be done to a carefully-constructed life. In Chekhov, this painful exposure is not satisfied by what might be experienced as an act of love. Rather he sends us away more than ever bound in our own clothes. And we are gratified, with the sick gratification that attends on a seduction which is abandoned. Is it not too much trouble to seduce?

It is necessary therefore to demonstrate the existence of will in a world where will is relegated to the comic or the inept.

Chekhov's apologists argue his contempt is concentrated on a class, but we know that in diminishing the lives of a class he bleeds the will of his entire audience, making them collaborators in a cult of futility and impotence. Can the individual not burst the barriers of class and repudiate decay?

I remade Vanya because I loved his anger, which Chekhov allows to dissipate in toxic resentment. In doing this I denied the misery of the Chekhovian world, where love falters in self-loathing and desire is petulance.

In rescuing Vanya from resentment I lent him no solution, since there is no solution to a life. My Vanya is however, cleansed of bad blood, his actions liberated from the sterile calculation of the pleasure-principle, and his will to self-creation triumphant over guilt. In making him anew, I seized on the single instrument Chekhov had, as it were, left lying idly in his own text. Vanya's quitting of the Chekhovian madhouse became a metaphor for the potential of art to point heroically, if blindly, to the open door...

Characters

SEREBRYAKOV
A Genius in Decay

HELENA
A Woman in Search of Experience

SONYA
A Spinster with Powerful Arms

VANYA
An Undefeated Man

MARYIA
A Widow Inclined to Forgive

ASTROV
A Conscience Without Power

TELYEGHIN
An Apologist for Himself

MARINA
A Discriminating Servant

CHEKHOV
A Loved Dramatist

Act One

A MAN appears.

VANYA: Unc – le
    Van – ya *(Pause.)*
    Unc – le
    Unc – le
    Van – ya

    (Pause. A guitar is strummed..)

    STOP STRUMMING STOP THAT IDLE FUTILE STRUMMING
    YOU STOP IT.

    (It ceases, then continues.)

    I'LL KILL YOU.
    I'LL

    (It ceases. ASTROV enters.)

ASTROV: Man is endowed with reason and creative power so
    that he can enhance what he has been endowed with but
    up till now he has been destroying and not creating there
    are fewer and fewer forests the rivers are drying up the
    wild creatures are almost exterminated the climate is being
    ruined the land is becoming poorer and more hideous
    every day when I hear the rustling of the young saplings I
    planted with my own hands I

    (Pause.)

VANYA: Unc – le
    Unc – le *(Pause.)*
    Van – ya

ASTROV: I'm conscious of the fact that the climate is to some extent in my own power too and that if mankind is happy in a thousand years I will be responsible when I plant a little birch tree I.

(Pause. The guitar begins again.)

VANYA: KILL YOU I SAID

(An old SERVANT crosses the stage.)

MARINA: Shh…

VANYA: ABSOLUTELY KILL

MARINA: Shh…

(She goes out. The guitar stops.)

VANYA: I detest your futile and transparent attempts to suffocate my hatred in what you call love what you call compassion what you call what you call your absurd maternal and anodyne endearments what you call what you call

(The music begins.)

WHO IS THAT GUITARIST STOP HIM

ASTROV: Stop him yourself.

VANYA: The very sound of life-loathing
SHUDDUP

(It ceases. A wind blows.)

I have a gun. For so long now I have had a gun. This gun I clean most nights. I clean it with oil in the light of the moon. This is certainly the habit of an assassin.

ASTROV: Vanya.

VANYA: Unc – le
Unc – le
Unc – le

Unc – le

Van – ya

(Pause.)

ASTROV: I think you should give me the gun.

VANYA: Never. But do go on. I detest your views but do go on. The trees and so on. I detest your selflessness your abnegation your love of unborn generations which is simply an excuse to avoid living yourself I KNOW ALL THAT'S WRONG THE WHOLE OF IT but knowing is insufficient hence the uselessness of all criticism but but but YOU HIDE IN CRITICISM LIKE A LITTLE BOY WHO MURDERERS ARE SEEKING your caring your concern your

(The guitar begins.)

ALL RIGHT
TELYEGHIN
YOU ASKED FOR IT

(It ceases.)

is impotence admit it admit it why don't you?

ASTROV: It is you who is impotent.

VANYA: It is me who is impotent and that is how I am able to recognize the condition in you.

ASTROV: So what if I were? If women loved men for the dimensions of their

VANYA: They do

ASTROV: The dimensions and mechanical reactions of

VANYA: They do

ASTROV: Their phallic

VANYA: PRECISELY THEY DO

Pause.

ASTROV: I can't talk to you, Vanya, I really cannot talk

VANYA: You are so modern
  SO
  VERY
  PAINFULLY
  AND
  MISERABLY
  MODERN

(HELENA enters. VANYA intercepts her.)

It's true, confirm it please.

HELENA: What?

VANYA: The phallus.

ASTROV: Oh…!

VANYA: Its energy is

ASTROV: Stop trying to exercise power by –

(VANYA lets out a long cry.)

VANYA: I was
  I was

ASRTOV: Bullying young women

VANYA: TRYING TO TAKE POWER I WAS I WAS

(MARINA crosses the stage.)

MARINA: Shh…

VANYA: I was

MARINA: Shh… *(She goes out.)*

VANYA: Because I love you.

HELENA: Love!

VANYA: Yes, love. Love, yes. Love. Love. Why not love? That is the thing I mean, the word is certainly adequate, and though I dislike you I most cogently affirm love is what I mean and love is what I intend and no other synonym will suffice neither lust nor desire DON'T GO OUT OF THE ROOM I'M TALKING

(HELENA stops.)

HELENA: You are most exasperating and I must tell you I am not interested in you in that regard so please

VANYA: IN THIS REGARD
IN THAT REGARD
IN THIS REGARD
IN THAT REGARD

ASTROV: Vanya…

HELENA: On the other hand –

(She stops. The guitar is plucked.)

I don't know who I am interested in.

VANYA: *(Going to HELENA.)* You will be interested in the man who forces you to be interested in him.

(Pause. The guitar stops.)

HELENA: Yes.
Obviously.

ASTROV: You see the forests are diminishing at such a rate that

HELENA: My husband look.
I
YOUNG WOMAN OF PERFECT FECUNDITY
MY HUSBAND LOOK.
NAKED HE IS
Comes into my room at night and *(Pause.)*
Into my room and

(An old MAN appears.)

17

SEREBRYAKOV: I ache today.

HELENA: Yes.

SEREBRYAKOV: So much of me is aching.

HELENA: Yes.

SEREBRYAKOV: That only a little part of consciousness is left
    to me. Pain invades the little territory of self. The shrinking
    territory of self. Is anyone interested in pain?

VANYA: No. *(Pause.)*
    Well, are we? *(Pause.)*
    No!

   (MARYIA enters, kisses SEREBRYAKOV'S hand.)

    Oh God
    My mother
    Oh God
    My utterly and incurably

HELENA: FUCKS ME HARD

VANYA: Radical and progressive mother so full of life so full of
    vigour demonstrating with the workers paying the fines of
    anarchists and sewing banners her convictions are so
    (He lets out a howl.)
    She loves the primitive and disappearing tribesmen of the
    outer territories and thinks the weak are wonderful and on
    her blouse she wears the badges of the badges of so many
    badges
    (And howls again.)

MARYIA: Forgive me for saying so, Jean, but you have
    changed so much in the last year I positively don't
    recognize you –

VANYA: I HAVE A GUN

MARYIA: You were a man of positive convictions, an inspiring
    personality and now –

VANYA: THIS GUN

ASTROV: Oh, shut up about your silly gun –

VANYA: WAS GIVEN ME BY CHEKHOV. *(Pause.)* And having
given it to me, he was profoundly sorry…

(He sobs. SONYA enters.)

SONYA: Why are you weeping? Uncle? *(She goes to him.)*
Uncle…
Uncle…
Vanya…

(VANYA spontaneously recovers.)

SCENE TWO

VANYA: You love me.
You love to love me.
You love me more than anyone.
I am the so-loved.
I am your alibi.
I am your pretext for.
PITY RUNS FROM YOU LIKE SNOT FROM THE NOSE OF A
SICK CHILD.
Or vagrant thawing over soup.

(SEREBRYAKOV moans.)

SEREBRYAKOV: Pain – is – invasion

VANYA: Do you agree the professor is vile or do I slander him
am I correct or extreme HE GOES TO BED WITH SUCH A
YOUNG WOMAN am I poisoned by sexual jealousy or HE
PUTS HIS FLESH INSIDE HER BODY or or or AND THIS
SUCCESS WITH WOMEN HE ENJOYED FROM INFANCY
yes INFANCY my sister his first wife a beautiful woman
of sky-blue innocence had more admirers than she could
count and loved him with such ABSOLUTE as for my
mother she dotes on him and spent her perfect years in
writing envelopes for his campaigns THESE ABSURD

CAMPAIGNS what happens in their bedroom and naked he must be naked imagine the collision of her white skin and the

SEREBRYAKOV: I dozed off just now and imagined my left leg didn't belong to me

HELENA: Shh…

SEREBRYAKOV: I am disgusting even to myself.

HELENA: Shh…

(The SERVANT crosses the stage.)

MARINA: Shh… *(She goes out.)*

SEREBRYAKOV: You find me repulsive, admit it.

HELENA: If you wish me to.

SEREBRYAKOV: I wish you to.

HELENA: I admit it.

SEREBRYAKOV: I am a monster of egotism and self-regard I am a savage of acquisitiveness and gratification but I deserve it aren't I talented aren't I rare?

MARYIA: You are talented. You are rare.

VANYA: *(To HELENA.)* You are in the room next to me. I can hear you breathe at night.

HELENA: Shh.

VANYA: ALL THIS SHHHING!
Your empty thighs, I adore you. But are they empty? I am only forty-four and not dead yet
NOT DEAD
NOT DEAD
YET.

MARYIA: Shh.

VANYA: These thighs I think of day and night.

HELENA: Really.

VANYA: Yes. And if I talk ridiculously it is the fault of your thighs. You make me talk gibberish but if I talked sensibly nothing would change either. Give me your underwear I will treasure it.

HELENA: Shh.

VANYA: I AM NOT A DOG.

HELENA: Everyone is so stupid, so utterly stupid.

VANYA: It is not stupid to want – no – to CRAVE – your underwear, on the contrary it is you who is stupid to describe it so. It is yet another sign of your shallowness.

SONYA: I love the doctor. But could he love me?

VANYA: No. He also is too shallow to reciprocate your love. He has the appalling shallowness of the idealist whereas Helena at least is shallow in a thoroughly introspective way. Astrov's shallowness is that of the idealist with whom it is impossible to disagree. In your case it is better to pine than suffer the appalling bathos of fulfilment, believe me.

SONYA: Why should I believe you?

VANYA: No reason! You have spent a lifetime translating the professor's shallow books and consequently I know nothing but I do have these darts, these arrows of intuitive perception one of which is sticking in the doctor's heart and there is no blood, just ideas you cannot disagree with, trickling, trickling out *(He suddenly gasps.)* I KNOW CHEKHOV'S FEAR! I KNOW HIS TERRIBLE FEAR!

SEREBRYAKOV: You are insane.

VANYA: Yes.

SEREBRYAKOV: I am ill and you are insane.

VANYA: Possibly.

ASTROV: The ignorant are dull and the educated are boring. That is my conclusion. Nanny, bring me a drink!

SONYA: Don't drink.

ASTROV: Don't drink? Why not?

SONYA: Because you are beautiful.

ASTROV: Am I? Am I beautiful? I think I could never love a human being. Though what does still affect me is beauty. I think if Helena wanted to, for example, she might turn my head…

VANYA: Fancy! Fancy, for all his terrible decline which is our fault, for his tragic loss of hope, which is our fault, he could just – he might just manage –
TO FUCK HELENA!

SONYA: Stop it, Uncle!

VANYA: Unc – le
Unc – le
Unc – le
Unc – le
Van – ya
I'm going in the garden I'm going in the garden the garden the garden fewer liars in the garden… *(He goes out.)*

SEREBRYAKOV: Mad.

HELENA: He asked me for my underwear!

ASTROV: Come to the plantation tomorrow. About two o'clock.

HELENA: I can't possibly.

ASTROV: I will wait for you.

HELENA: Out of the question.

ASTROV: Two o'clock.

HELENA: No.
    Yes.
    No.

SEREBRYAKOV: Meet him. See what he can do for you. And
    then tell me.

(HELEN looks at SEREBRYAKOV.)

    Maryia, I must hold a meeting here tonight.

MARYIA: Whatever you say.

SEREBRYAKOV: I am not a practical man.

MARYIA: No.

SEREBRYAKOV: I am a man of the mind.

MARYIA: I have studied your mind. I have scoured your mind.
    I have stood in teeming rain beneath platforms in parks
    and squares listening to the treasures of your mind – spill…
    spill… fragile with concentration, the audience was like
    an egg, a single egg in your hand, and you made this egg
    vibrate with truth! What a truth teller! His shock of white
    hair fell across his brow, Peace, he said, PEACE IS YOUR

ASTROV: Naked
    Naked
    Naked

VANYA: *(Entering with the gun loosely in his hand.)* Oh metal
    thing which moonlight clings to, which starlight occupies…

ASTROV: Put it away, Uncle…

VANYA: Listen, it is the lever of my life. AND CHEKHOV
    HATED IT!

    (Pause.)

SONYA: Uncle… you are not… you are absolutely never to
    take your own life with that thing…

VANYA: Sonya, I haven't the courage to commit suicide.

ASTROV: Then what do you want it for?

VANYA: To coerce others with. What else? *(He examines it.)* It has a number on… *(He drifts out again.)*

SEREBRYAKOV: This meeting is to discuss the property and the management of my remaining years.

VANYA: *(Coming back in.)* Let me clear about one thing. The professor is not worse than other men. Not actually worse than others similarly endowed with greatness. It is true he has access to the body of a young woman to which he has no natural right, but what is a natural right? It's true this offends me, but so what? No, my offence is neither here nor there, what disgusts one about the great is the AND WE WILL CALL HIM GREAT I AM HAPPY TO APPLY THE TERM TO HIM is their KNOWLEDGE of their greatness which is inescapable which is endemic to greatness itself, what use would modesty be to greatness, it would be absurd, offensive in itself, no it is the self-awareness that is unforgivable, whilst being simultaneously inevitable. *(Pause.)* The serial number is 7786955797. *(Pause.)* What meeting is this anyway? I DON'T THINK CHEKHOV IS CLEAN. NOT CLEAN. *(He shoves the gun in his pocket.)* I'll put it away because whilst I want to coerce I cannot coerce and that is surely the worst condition that surely is the death of my soul, what meeting?

MARINA: *(Passing.)* No one cares for the old!

SEREBRYAKOV: How true…

MARINA: *(Leaving.)* No one pities the old!

VANYA: And how correct they are you would bend our backs if you could, no, this meeting, what is it? *(He pulls the gun out again.)* I haven't lived! Oh, I have not lived, I have annihilated the best years of my life!

ASTROV: Do stop waving that gun about!

HELENA: You should stop grumbling and reconcile people to one another, that's what you should do, there is so much petty enmity about and all you do is –

VANYA: Be quiet, you are idle and shallow.

HELENA: Yes, I am idle and I hate it.

Pause.

VANYA: No! No, you should be idle!

MARYIA: Oh, do stop offending everyone, it is so pitiful and –

SEREBRYAKOV: He can't help himself –

VANYA: She should be idle. Her terrible power is the product of her idleness. You know it as well as I do. Stay idle, for God's sake. An idle woman has the ripe smell of unplucked fruit, please be idle, refuse all labour, I beg you.

ASTROV: That is ridiculous – *(He moves the barrel of VANYA's gun, which is held loosely in his direction.)* She could do such –

VANYA: Who is interested in what she could do? We are interested in what she is. Let her be. Essence.

ASTROV: Rubbish.

VANYA: You would not want her if she were a whit less idle that she is. Hypocrite. *(He looks at the gun.)* The handle is ivory, why is that?

MARYIA: To beautify an evil purpose.

VANYA: It must be that!

ASTROV: Think of the elephants that die in order to –

HELENA: Yes!

ASTROV: Conceal with arabesques a monstrous design of human barbarity. The weapon pretends not to be a weapon. Vile.

VANYA: Vile? It's human greatness, surely?

HELENA: It is sin.

VANYA: IT IS NOT SIN IT'S HUMAN. HUMANS SIN. IT IS THE
ESSENCE OF THEIR BEAUTY. I'M GOING OUT.

SONYA: Uncle Vanya will be happy one day, won't you Uncle,
happy one day?

VANYA: Unc – le
Unc – le
Unc – le
Unc – le
Van – ya

He stands, swaying for an inordinate length of time, then goes out.

SEREBRYAKOV: I am an academic, bookish man and have
never had to do with practical life, and it is impossible for
me to remain living here, we are not made for the country
life. On the other hand –

SONYA: Papa, Uncle Vanya is not here –

SEREBRYAKOV: To live in town on the income we are
receiving from this estate is out of the question, therefore I
propose –

SONYA: Papa, Uncle is not here –

MARYIA: Shh –

HELENA: Shh –

SEREBRYAKOV: We sell the estate and invest the capital in
suitable securities, thereby raising four or five per cent,
which will enable us to buy a villa, say in Finland –

VANYA: *(Entering.)* What was that?

SEREBRYAKOV: Finland.

VANYA: Finland? What about Finland?

SONYA: Papa is selling the estate.

(A pause. A wind.)

HELENA: The madman wants my underwear!

(A pause.)

VANYA: Now wait a
Wait a
Wait

MARYIA: Shh –

VANYA: Wait because –

MARYIA: Don't contradict the professor –

VANYA: Because –

SONYA: Shh –

VANYA: I HAVE BEEN RUNNING THIS ESTATE FOR TWENTY-
FIVE YEARS

MARYIA: Don't shout.

VANYA: TWENTY-FIVE –

MARYIA: Don't –

VANYA: Mummy I am not shouting –
YEARS
SENDING HIM MONEY
READING HIS ARTICLES

HELENA: *(Rising to her feet.)* I am not sitting here –

VANYA: QUOTING HIS PAMPHLETS AND

HELENA: Listening to this –

VANYA: I could have been an architect, Helena!

(Pause. She looks at him.)

I have such a such a such a clever brain…

SEREBRYAKOV: You are a nonentity. *(Pause.)* I have no wish to be offensive, but you are. *(Pause.)* Isn't he?

SONYA: *(Through tears.)* Please, Papa, Uncle Vanya and I are so unhappy...

MARINA: Shh!

SONYA: *(Opening her arms.)* Nanny!

(VANYA drifts out. Pause.)

SEREBRYAKOV: I was unkind.

MARYIA: He does provoke the most –

SEREBRYAKOV: I was unkind. *(Pause.)* When you are famous, when you are in demand, how little you observe the pains of those who cluster at your feet...

MARYIA: You need not justify a single action. You have articulated the hope of all good people who –

SEREBRYAKOV: I'll talk to him. *(He gets up.)*

MARYIA: No need! No need! *(He goes out.)*

ASTROV: *(To HELENA.)* Come to my room.

HELENA: Which room is that?

ASTROV: You know perfectly well which room is –

(A shot. They are silent. Suddenly SONYA gets to her feet.)

SONYA: Our paralysis is nothing more than the reflection of our economic crisis the decline of rents and the aggressive style of capitalism in a backward economy we –

(Another shot. Pause.)

The rise of the proletariat and the exploitation of rural labour by –

(And another.)

Interest rates which –

(And another…)

STOP! STOP!

(Pause. At last VANYA enters, with the gun.)

MARYIA: Who gave you that gun…?

VANYA: Chekhov. Chekhov did.

(They stare at him.)

SONYA: Uncle Vanya, what have you –

VANYA: *(Quietly.)* Ivan.

SONYA: Have you hurt anyone, have you –

VANYA: Ivan. *(Pause.)*
     Hatred.
     Hatred.
     How perfectly it guided me.

(Pause. ASTROV goes to move.)

ASTROV: Oh, God, he's –

VANYA: *(Levelling the gun at ASTROV.)* Don't go.

(ASTROV stops.)

SONYA: Uncle, have you –

VANYA: Ivan. *(Pause.)* The word uncle castrated me. I forbid
     the word.

SONYA: *(Defiantly.)* You are my uncle and I'll –

(VANYA slaps SONYA's face. She reels.)

MARYIA: Jean!

VANYA: No, that's French. And Vanya is diminutive.
     No more diminutives, or endearments, abbreviations or
     THINGS TO HANG YOURSELF ON
     IVAN IS THE NAME.

MARYIA: Oh, pathetic man, who thinks the act of violence will –

VANYA: Yes, violence is the door OH BEAUTIFUL IVORY GUN OF IVORY MY DOORWAY MY BIRTHPLACE *(To HELENA.)* Get undressed.

MARYIA/SONYA: Certainly not!

ASTROV: She will do no such thing you are out of your –

VANYA: It was not enough to kill him. I disfigured him as well.

(HELENA lets out a cry.)

See for yourself!

(Pause. HELENA starts to unbutton her dress.)

ASTROV: No need for that –

MARYIA: Helena, no need to –

HELENA: No, I –

ASTROV: Please don't concede to his –

MARYIA: Quite unnecessary –

HELENA: What's nakedness anyway? It's only nakedness –

ASTROV: Please, I love you and –

VANYA: Stop there. *(Pause.)*

HELENA: Stop, but I've only just –

(VANYA silences her by a look.)

VANYA: I am surrounded by such poor minds, such educated and poor minds. My mother and her causes, my sister and her modesty, the doctor and his forests, and this immaculate object whose very nothingness is her potential to inflame our minds, such thin dreams, and such an ache for pain NOT TOO MUCH PAIN HOWEVER NOT TRAGEDY just an odour of deep-seated harmlessness, you all smell bad and yet…

(Pause.)

MARYIA: I hate you. You have murdered the greatest man of our time.

VANYA: Exuberance!

MARYIA: The hope of generations…

VANYA: Ebullience!

MARYIA: The voice of sanity…

VANYA: Ecstasy! And I am so calm. Have I, the eternal apologizer, ever been so calm? I am a lake among crags, dark, deep, and not toxic. Not toxic any more. Drink me. I'm sweet.

(Pause.)

HELENA: Serebryakov was…

(Pause.)

ASTROV: Shh…

HELENA: I WANT TO SPEAK.

(Pause.)

VANYA: *(Taking his own pulse.)* My pulse is –

HELENA: WANT TO SPEAK.

VANYA: Normal.

HELENA: A liar in some way. In his handling of my body.

ASTROV: Yes. Yes…

HELENA: A liar, yes. The hands lied.

(ASTROV nods seriously.)

They were skilful, but –

ASTROV: I know what you're saying –

HELENA: YOU DON'T KNOW. I must talk about his way of
fucking –

MARYIA: Don't please, he's lying out there in a –

HELENA: They moved, his hands, like those of a priest at mass
– that practised and swift covering of ground – so expert
and –

MARYIA: Please,
Please,
Helena

HELENA: AND HE WAS POTENT GOD HE WAS FOR ALL HIS
SIXTY-SEVEN *(She stops.)* Did you shoot him in the face?

VANYA: Yes.

HELENA: And I wanted him, am I lucid enough? I did. It
made me shudder when he walked into my room naked
and vaguely ugly yet he –

(ASTROV impetuously kisses HELENA on the mouth.)

VANYA: The face yes, I obliterated it, I think because it
was in his face the genius lay, I also had a face from
which my character peered, this way and that, as if from
curtained windows and afraid to walk the street, whereas
he WALKED OUT OF HIS FACE LIKE AN INDUSTRIALIST,
AN EMPEROR, A BRIDEGROOM! No, not a bridegroom,
they're afraid, no, A PAMPHLETEER ON THE MORNING
OF THE REVOLUTION.

(ASTROV parts from HELENA's mouth.)

MARYIA: We must have geniuses, Jean, and swallow all their
truths, Jean, and you want to substitute your temper for
their truth, your envy for their –

VANYA: NOT ENVY
NO

NOT
ENVY

(The sound of the guitar is heard. Then it stops. There is a scream offstage. TELYEGHIN enters, aghast.)

TELYEGHIN: I –
   I –
   I –

VANYA: Yes, I did it, shut up and sit down –

TELYEGHIN: I –
   I –

(He points offstage. VANYA pushes him in the chest so he falls into a chair. HELENA bursts out laughing.)

VANYA: My name is Ivan. That is how my father christened me. In that christening was hope, which every abbreviation chewed to dust… *(He turns to TELYEGHIN.)* Chekhov supplied the gun. I only used it.

HELENA: *(To ASTROV.)* I can't desire you. You want me to go into the homes of the poor and sacrifice my body in kind labour. Then you could say, how kind Helena is! How useful is her life! But would you want me? No. You suffocate your manliness in pity, I think you are dirty in some way and it comes off. *(She spits in her hands and rubs them together. She turns to VANYA.)* How long before you turn yourself in?

VANYA: Turn myself in?

HELENA: Yes. Saying God knows what came over me I was. We drove each other to the brink etcetera.
   How long?

ASTROV: Helena –

HELENA: Helena? You don't say it properly. *(She looks at VANYA.)* You must command me with your voice…

ASTROV: *(Defiantly.)* I am going to the police –

(VANYA stops him with the gun.)

Nevertheless I am going to the police –

HELENA: Mikhail, you are ridiculous and he will shoot you.

ASTROV: He will not shoot me because –

VANYA: I will –

ASTROV: You will not because –

VANYA: ALL RIGHT YOU ASKED FOR IT –

MARYIA: SIT DOWN, MIKHAIL

(ASTROV stops in his tracks. Pause. The figure of SEREBRYAKOV enters, with a hood, or bandaged face. He sits in a chair. He lights a cigarette.)

SEREBRYAKOV: Chekhov says put the gun away before it leads to

VANYA: No

SEREBRYAKOV: More trouble and

VANYA: No

SEREBRYAKOV: Disturbs the fragile

VANYA: No
No
No

SEREBRYAKOV: Balance of characters and

VANYA: HE GAVE ME THE GUN HE SUPPLIED ME WITH THE MEANS

SEREBRYAKOV: He knows this perfectly well.

VANYA: HE PROVIDED ME.

SEREBRYAKOV: He profoundly regrets this.

VANYA: DOES HE NOW

SEREBRYAKOV: Melodramatic interlude

VANYA: TOO BAD TOO LATE TOO EVERYTHING

(Pause.)

HELENA: I loved old men. Old men excited me. I wanted them to handle me intimately in public places. Doorways, for example, in wet weather. Train corridors on sunny afternoons. Department stores among the furnishings. Say you understand me.

MARYIA: No one understands you!

HELENA: No one?
No one?
No one undestands me?

SONYA: You see we are a dying class who cannot actually control our destiny because of the high level of inflation.

VANYA: SHUT UP

SONYA: The marginalisation of the intelligentsia is

VANYA: SONYA SHUT UP

ASTROV: Helena –

HELENA: No one says my name properly –

ASTROV: (Bitterly.) HOW DO YOU WANT IT SAID. (Pause.) You do not want to be respected, do you? Quite simply, you do not want to be respected, you are –

HELENA: IT IS RESPECT TO BE COMMANDED. (Pause.) But you can't.

(Pause.)

SEREBRYAKOV: The problem with an action Chekhov says is that it leads to others.

VANYA: I do not wish to know what he says

SEREBRYAKOV: Each action more ridiculous than the last

VANYA: So be it

SEREBRYAKOV: Ramifications of such outlandish character the perpitrator forfeits every sympathy

VANYA: I DON'T REQUIRE SYMPATHY TELL HIM. *(Pause.)* It is possible I am not human. I was comic and now I am inhuman. The comic, the pathetic, the impotence made me lovable, but underneath I was not human. And nor is anyone. Underneath. Human. TELL CHEKHOV!

SEREBRYAKOV: He knows.

VANYA: Does he? He knows everything, then! *(He turns away.)* It is me Helena loves. I murdered her husband in pursuance of a theft. The theft was her. We have nothing in common but a certain brutality. But that is sufficient for love. Helena, I must see you naked. Here or elsewhere.

HELENA: If you insist.

ASTROV: *(Horrified.)* IF HE INSISTS! IF HE INSISTS!

MARYIA: Poor Helena... Oh, poor Helena...

HELENA: It is you who is pitiful, Maryia Vassilievna.

MARYIA: Is it, why, my dear?

HELENA: Smothering all your aches in works, works, and more works. I anaesthetize nothing. The ache cries out.

MARYIA: What ache is this?

HELENA: My need cries out.

MARYIA: What need? What need? Aches and needs, what does she mean? Look for the truth in a man.

HELENA: The truth? THE TRUTH IN A MAN? Oh, God spare me the truth in him, the terrible transparency that shows him thin and stooping, lying and banal. *(She turns to VANYA.)* I do understand! I DO SO CLEARLY UNDERSTAND!

VANYA: What?

HELENA: Why you required my underwear. *(Pause.)* Worship it.

VANYA: I will.

HELENA: My relic. Treasure it.

VANYA: I will. Obviously I will.

(She laughs, with delight, staring at VANYA, then stops, breathless. Pause.)

ASTROV: We must protect ourselves from this. We really must protect ourselves – *(He goes to move.)*

SONYA: YOU ALL ADORE HER
OH YOU ALL
CRAZED FOR HER EVERY ONE *(Pause. She indicates VANYA.)*

I want this man
My uncle
Down the police station
In the cells
The prisoner transport
All of it
Rotting in a pit
Chains and frostbite
Cossacks' whips etcetera
WE COULD HAVE LIVED AT SUCH A LOW, SLOW PULSE
LIKE TOADS IN WINTER WAITING FOR GOD TO LIFT US
OFF THE LANDSCAPE *(Pause.)* I do want you to suffer.
Telyeghin, get down to the police post, my uncle yearns for
his first interrogation. *(Pause.)* I haven't been so animated
for years! *(Pause.)* It's hatred, isn't it? Animates me so?
Telyeghin.

TELYEGHIN: I'm sorry, no.

SONYA: Do as your told.

TELYEGHIN: *(Looking at HELENA.)* She'll hit me.

SONYA: All right, I will. *(She gets up.)*

VANYA: Sonya, I will put a bullet in your back.

(She stops.)

SONYA: Yes, I think you might. *(Pause.)* This is a long way from knitting. *(Pause. She turns on VANYA and hugs him, laughing.)*

SEREBRYAKOV: Chekhov says –

(SONYA and VANYA turn and hug, round and round.)

Chekhov says –

SONYA: Iv – an!
Iv – an Voi – nit – sky!

ASTROV: Don't call him Ivan, that's what he wants!

SEREBRYAKOV: Art is similar to medicine.

(VANYA turns on ASTROV. Pause. Then he tosses him the gun. ASTROV catches it. A void.)

But what sort of medecine?

VANYA: Mikhail, you drape your sensitivity like a dying cat hauls its entrails over the floor.

(ASTROV holds the gun. Suddenly he sits, as if broken.)

SEREBRYAKOV: We reverence him because
We reverence Chekhov
Because in such a confined space the melancholy of
Not tragedy
The melancholy of
Our unlived life is exquisitely redeemed
We are forgiven
We are forgiven
We
Do
So
Need
To

Be
Forgiven
Why
Is
That?

(Pause. Suddenly TELYEGHIN begins to stamp his guitar into fragments, with the routine thoroughness of a farm-hand treading grapes. When it is reduced to splinters, he stops, a smile on his face.)

VANYA: I've saved you from dying.
 Congratulate me then!
 Express your gratitude!

(The sound of splintering wood and breaking glass. Part of the verandah slips. They freeze in terror. A wind is heard. Pause.)

SONYA: It's Chekhov.

VANYA: Shut up.

SONYA: IT'S CHEKHOV, IVAN, CHEKHOV WANTS TO

VANYA: Shut up, Sonya

SONYA: PUNISH US...!

(Pause. SEREBRYAKOV laughs.)

VANYA: Thirty minutes since the murder. Thirty minutes and no regrets.

(Pause.)

HELENA: I'll go upstairs. I'll lie down and you.

VANYA: No, don't lie down.

(Pause.)

HELENA: Not lie down…? What, then?

VANYA: Stand up –

HELENA: Stand up, yes, and then –

VANYA: Wait –

HELENA: Wait, yes –

VANYA: Impatiently –

HELENA: Impatiently, yes, I adore you, Ivan Petrovich –

VANYA: I know you do –

HELENA: Not love – not love, but –

VANYA: Who cares what you call it?

HELENA: Who cares, yes!

VANYA: First, I am burying your husband –

HELENA: If you wish –

VANYA: Deep graves take time –

HELENA: And we –

VANYA: Lack time –

HELENA: Yes –

VANYA: So little time I cannot hope to wash my hands –

HELENA: No –

VANYA: But must come dirty-handed –

HELENA: Yes –

VANYA: Helena –

HELENA: Yes –

VANYA: Helena –

(The wind blows through the broken windows.)

SONYA: And I
    And I *(She gets up as if inspired.)*
    You see, the world is sad! Sad, oh, very sad and this
    sadness is the precondition of all action not the end of it.

This sadness is the climate of and not the prison of, the world. Sadness is not a shroud. It is not the end, but the beginning. *(She laughs.)* I lecture! I lecture you! *(She turns to ASTROV.)* I want a child and you must give it to me.

ASTROV: I –

SONYA: Now, yes. I love you, I always have loved you, and I insist.

ASTROV: *(Bewildered.)* Give you a –

SONYA: Yes. I'm fertile. Give me one.

(HELENA bursts out laughing.)

VANYA: Where are the shovels? *(He turns to go.)*

SONYA: I know you can do it, Mikhail Lvovich, you are potentially magnificent, you possess all the ingredients of masculinity but in the wrong order, I will help you, it's only a matter of WHY SHOULDN'T I HAVE WHAT I WANT?

(Pause. HELENA goes to leave.)

HELENA: Not deep… Ivan… *(She goes out.)*

SEREBRYAKOV: This is precisely the degeneration of the inevitable corruption of

VANYA: *(To MARYIA.)* Where are the shovels?

MARYIA: How should I know?

SEREBRYAKOV: Human decency that Chekhov anticipated once melancholy was usurped

VANYA: Telyeghin, get up and find a shovel!

TELYEGHIN: Yes! Yes, of course, Ivan Petrovich! *(He jumps up, goes out.)*

MARYIA: *(To VANYA.)* You've never dug a hole in your life.

VANYA: How you hate me…

MARYIA: Hate you? You're my son!

VANYA: Hate me, yes. And always did. Hated me for being nothing, and hated me for being something. Hated and hated even while words of charity cascaded from your mouth. *(Pause.)*

MARYIA: I don't know.
I don't know, Ivan, I'll think about that

SONYA: These arms are very strong. I was born with strong arms. I did not know until today the reason for these strong arms, which often I have felt ashamed of, felt to be unwomanly or mishapen. I denied myself a proper love of my anatomy. But now it's clear! These arms were granted me – yes – I was FAVOURED with these arms – to seize Mikhail Lvovich in a terrible embrace! *(She laughs.)*

ASTROV: For God' sake, Sonya –

SONYA: DON'T PREVARICATE.

(ASTROV shakes his head at MARYIA, who shrugs, wearily.)

MARYIA: You will make him hate you, Sonya, which can't be what you –

SONYA: IT IS WHAT I INTEND. *(Pause.)*

MARYIA: I don't understand… I don't understand!

(TELYEGHIN enters with a shovel.)

TELYEGHIN: I'll dig! *(Pause.)*

VANYA: All right, dig.

(TELYEGHIN goes out and begins on the ground outside the windows.)

SONYA: You see, what is terrible, what is unforgiveable, what is PURE TOXIN is – resentment, isn't it? And we all – oh we all RESENTED EVERYTHING! *(Pause.)* Which was comic. Which was pitiful. Which was utterly demeaning and hateful of mankind GET YOUR CLOTHES OFF, MIKHAIL.

ASTROV: Certainly not.

TELYEGHIN: *(Calling.)* This ground is hard as iron, Ivan..!

SONYA: Or will I take them off.

ASTROV: This is outrageous…!

SONYA: Isn't it?

ASTROV: And you are a bully! One day you are a Christian and the next day a bully, STAY AWAY FROM ME, SONYA! *(He aims the pistol clumsily, then, seeing himself, tosses it away, stands up in frustration.)* THIS IS SO –

TELYEGHIN: Ivan –

(VANYA is watching SONYA and ASTROV with fascination.)

Ivan –

(Pause.)

ASTROV: You – *(Pause.)*
There is – *(Pause.)*
I must admit something in you –

SONYA: Quick, then, before Chekhov comes –

ASTROV: That I – had never – *(Pause.)*
A CHILD… *(Pause.)*
YES!

(A sudden sound of further collapse, both masonry and splintering wood. TELYEGHIN ducks. This shock is followed by a surge of sound as waves break and flow with the appearance of the sea. TELYEGHIN points, in dumb astonishment, to the spectacle.)

MARYIA: Oh, look, a view!

SONYA: The sea!

VANYA: THE SEA! THE SEA! *(They gawp, rejoice.)* Chekhov won't come now…

MARINA: *(Entering.)* The tea urn's gone! Look, the tea urn's in the sea!

(They laugh. MARINA picks up random small objects and pelts the urn. SONYA joins her.)

SONYA: Got it!

MARINA: No, that was me!

SONYA: Sorry!

MARINA: *(Throwing again.)* Got it!

SEREBRYAKOV: Chekhov knows the brevity of pleasure
The insubstantiality of

MARYIA: I'M PADDLING!
Anyone?
I'M PADDLING!

(She rolls up her skirts. She sees VANYA throw off his jacket and go upstairs to HELENA. She hesitates.)

My son is going upstairs. To fuck. With a woman whose husband he has killed. Naked him And naked her. *(She turns, inspired.)*
Look at the waves! *(She skips out to bathe in the sea.)*

SEREBRYAKOV: All euphoria he knows to be merely the prelude
All ecstasy the mere preparation for
Inevitable

MARINA: *(Throwing an ashtray.)* Got it!

SONYA: It's sinking! The tea urn's sinking, nanny!

MARINA: I am not your nanny.

(SONYA looks at her.)

SONYA: No. *(She laughs.)* No, you're not!

SEREBRYAKOV: Inevitable.
   SOLITUDE.

SONYA: You were. And now. You're not.

(She laughs. TELYEGHIN comes in, throwing down his spade. He goes to ASTROV.)

TELYEGHIN: Mikhail Lvovich, we are not within a thousand miles of sea…

(ASTROV ignores him. He turns to MARINA.)

Marina, can you explain –

MARINA: Be quiet, you are a bore –

(SONYA laughs.)

He is! He is a bore! *(She goes out.)*

SONYA: If you don't believe it, stand in it.

TELYEGHIN: I wasn't intending to –

SONYA: If you let Chekhov in it's silence and the ticking of the clock – do you understand me – it's your guitar, it's emptiness and infertility, DO YOU WANT THAT!

TELYEGHIN: No.

SONYA: I am fertile and I will not be robbed! You are not to abort me, do you understand, Telyeghin…!

(He stares at her, appalled.)

TELYEGHIN: Abort? I wouldn't abort a – abort? All I want is –

SONYA: *(To VANYA, who enters.)* Ivan –

TELYEGHIN: *(Seeing VANYA, going to him.)* Excuse me, Ivan Petrovich, the sea is not there, is it? Not really there?

SONYA: Ivan, I want you to tie up Telyeghin

TELYEGHIN: TIE ME UP, WHAT FOR!

SONYA: Please, it is crucial Telyeghin is tied up and gagged.

TELYEGHIN: Gagged!

SONYA: Yes.

MARINA: I'll do it.

TELYEGHIN: PLEASE, I AM ONLY ASKING FOR A – *(He appeals to VANYA, who goes to a chair and sits.)*

VANYA: Let us talk about impotence.

(Pause. The sea washes. SEREBRYAKOV chuckles.)

Yes.
Let us talk about this thing.

(SEREBRYAKOV chuckles more.)

Yes.
We mustn't be afraid of it because

(SEREBRYAKOV stops.)

It is a god. I declare it to be. A god. *(Pause.)*
A god who brings you to the very rim of the world and
shows you – for those with eyes to see – such an expanse
of clear, translucent light. It is transfiguration. *(He gets up.)*
Listen, he who refuses shame becomes a master I DID
NOT LET CHEKHOV KILL MY PRIDE I DID NOT LET HIS
FINGERS THROTTLE MY DESIRE

(A sound of a new born child is heard.)

Tie him up if you want to, listen, listen I never wanted
a single thing, one thing, more in my life than the
nakedness of Helena and she also had me in her arteries,
I INHABITED HELENA I was the skin under her skin I
was the tenant of her brain and backbone and she undid
her clothes not me she Astrov would have burned whole
forests to have witnessed it –

ASTROV: Yes –

VANYA: Wonderful, he confesses –

ASTROV: Yes –

VANYA: Whole wards of patients could expire of neglect –

ASTROV: Oh, yes!

VANYA: Wonderful, he admits it – undid her clothes and I –

(A pause. HELENA enters. She takes VANYA's hand in hers, squeezes it powerfully, then wanders out towards the sea. Pause.)

It's true, I experienced the beginnings of a profound horror. A howling night which came down on my eyes and she was by no means charitiable THANK GOD HELENA IS NOT CHARITABLE
Not
One
Word
Of
Comfort
And in the wilderness I came to myself. I met myself. Between such wanting and such failing was – *(Pause.)* Truth… *(Suddenly, with passion.)* I don't like the word, either! I scorn it I assure you! *(He laughs.)* Truth! What's that? And I left the room.

ASTROV: I must talk with Helena…

SONYA: Why?

ASTROV: Where is she? *(He calls.)* Helena!

SONYA: Why must you?

VANYA: He thinks he is my rival. He thinks to compensate her with his ever-ready flesh, I HAVE NO RIVAL. He thinks she aches for his prosthesis, IT'S ME SHE WANTS.

(ASTROV goes out.)

I will kill Astrov. His superficiality enrages me.

SONYA: *(Looking after ASTROV.)* Yes…

VANYA: *(Going to SONYA.)* Sonya, I triumphed. I did not submit. I turned shame inside out and silenced his contempt. The laughter died in Chekhov's mouth.

SONYA: Yes…

VANYA: I SMOTHERED HIM.

SONYA: Yes… *(She kisses him.)*

TELYEGHIN: Don't tie me up, Ivan Petrovich. Please. If you say the sea's outside the door, then I'll…

VANYA: *(Taking him by the shoulders.)* Walk in it. Go on, walk in it…

(He propels TELYEGHIN out of the room and returns. MARYIA comes in, her clothes wet from the waves. She looks at SONYA, then at VANYA.)

MARYIA: If the sea is there… we can…

VANYA: Sail on it?

MARYIA: Yes.

SEREBRYAKOV: This
    Pathos
    Of

VANYA: Sail where, however?

SEREBRYAKOV: This
    Formless
    Urgency

MARYIA: I don't know where but

VANYA: Exactly

SEREBRYAKOV: Undirected
    Aspiration
    For

VANYA: HERE

SEREBRYAKOV: Meaningless
    Mobility

VANYA: AND ONLY HERE CAN WE BE FREE *(Pause.)* You must
    look without wanting. You must see without trying.

MARYIA: But it exists, therefore…

VANYA: It is a mirror on which you will discover only more
    of yourself. Self and more self. This self you must attend to
    and not attempt to evade by flight. There! I have advised
    you. Look at the sea by all means, but you will achieve
    precisely nothing by trying to cross it. You have so little
    time. You are old and Chekhov lies in wait for you. You
    more than anyone, perhaps…

    (ASTROV enters. He hesitates in the doorway.)

    Mikhail! You have the appearance of a man who thinks he
    might have sinned!

    (ASTROV ignores VANYA. He sits.)

    And this would haunt you. This would certainly make
    you tremble in your reed-bed of a soul… *(Pause. He looks
    at ASTROV.)* A breeze is blowing through the reed-bed of
    Mikhail's soul… I hear it… listen… flutter, rustle, crackle
    WHAT HAVE YOU DONE TO HELENA YOU BIGOT?

    (ASTROV leans forward on his knees, weeping.)

    You see? One act leads to another, everything is a
    consequence of everything else, like puppies pouring from
    the belly of a bitch, the room is filled with births –

    (MARYIA goes to assist ASTROV.)

    DON'T COMFORT HIM!

    (Pause.)

MARYIA: Ivan
    I think you are
    Ivan

As you call yourself
I think you are

VANYA: Yes –

MARYIA: The most –

SONYA: *(To ASTROV.)* Get up.

VANYA: Yes, I am –

SONYA: Get up, I said –

VANYA: Implacably unkind and heartless man...

MARYIA: *(Holding VANYA.)* Save yourself! Save yourself dear Jean, it is not too late!

(HELENA enters. She stands in the doorway. MARYIA abandons VANYA. Pause.)

What do you expect? All this. What do you expect? This. Nakedness and so on. No, I don't mean nakedness I also love nakedness I always have the wind the air I MEAN THE THROWING DOWN OF THINGS to go to bed with a man yes but FREEDOM IS A PLACE SOMEWHERE BETWEEN DESIRE AND I was the first to be naked believe me the first but EVERY IMPULSE CANNOT BE EVERY URGE JUST LICENSED oh yes very very naked and to look at me you might not think it why shouldn't I reveal since everyone is yes WITH ALL SORTS but never painful never hurtful never did I trespass on the rights of others freedom is the point of balance surely NIGHTS OF PASSION YES but violation I... *(She dries.)* I have not been happy... *(She closes her eyes.)* Why? Why?

(ASTROV stands up, and turns to go, as if with a decision. Spontaneously, SONYA takes him round the neck, forcing him back on his heels.)

HELENA: The worst thing in a man...
No...
The only bad thing...

Is apology… *(She turns defiantly to MARYIA.)*
Did you find that?

TELYEGHIN: *(Entering.)* It's true, Ivan Petrovich, the water is
– *(He sees SONYA is asphyxiating ASTROV.)* Maryia –

MARYIA: Shh.

TELYEGHIN: Maryia Vassilievna –

MARYIA: Shh I said –

TELYEGHIN: Vanya – Vanya – she –

VANYA: I'm not Vanya –

TELYEGHIN: Ivan, then –

(SONYA is lowering the dying ASTROV to the floor.)

SOMEONE!

(He is fixed. SONYA stands upright.)

SONYA: There will be some who will say this act – this deed
– was motivated by a spinsterish frustration. But I saw
Chekhov there. Hovering. Always, he hovers. Of course
I shall be misjudged. One lives always in the horror of
misjudgement, but so what? Chekhov was looming. We are
like boats on the pleasure pond, rather poorly steered and
sometimes we must take the boat hook and prod! Prod!
Chekhov was near and I prodded him away! *(She smiles.)*
These arms! These arms are made for prodding obviously,
and I thought they were made for love!

MARYIA: What arms! I never knew a woman with such
arms…!

SONYA: We are all given what we require, Maryia Vassilievna.
It is merely a matter of locating the requirement, isn't it?
(She looks down.) Poor Mikhail. And he did want to die!
Oh, he so wanted to die! And when death came he did not
resist me. He would have preferred Helena to –

HELENA: No – no –

SONYA: Much preferred it, yes! But frankly – *(She smiles.)*

HELENA: I haven't the arms...

SONYA: You haven't the arms, no. *(Pause, then with childish glee.)* I shall talk about Mikhail all the time now! I shall be such a bore! Mikhail this and Mikhail that! Oh, on and on until I die! I pity all of you! There will be this person Astrov and he will be a saint, a myth, a martyr! He will be a marrow, a balloon pumped up at a fair, pumped and pumped into extravagance! The inflation of the dead! That was my finest moment and it's all downhill from now!

VANYA: And now there is no doctor. Now, the community must endure all its pains. No wheedling, no whimpering, 'Doctor, doctor, prolong my melancholy life, lend me another summer!' How they pleaded, and now he hated them. But also, how ashamed he felt. Ashamed for hating them. No wonder he wished to die...

(SONYA suddenly cries.)

Yes, weep! Do weep!

SONYA: I don't know why I'm –

VANYA: You must weep! Weep, and look him in the eyes!

MARYIA: No, that is –

VANYA: Look at your deed, Sonya –

MARYIA: That is morbid and obscene –

VANYA: *(Turning on her.)* Is it morbid to stare death in the face? How tiring you are with your celebrations, your festivals and your street affairs! No, we must stand alone with Death, look at it and say – say – *(He hesitates.)*

SEREBRYAKOV: Pain
  And
  Civility

VANYA: *(Moving away from SONYA.)* I don't know, I don't know, but that's because –

SEREBRYAKOV: Pain because we do not act…

VANYA: Because we are - still at the beginning!

MARYIA: The beginning! Two deaths and that's the beginning?

VANYA: And Civility because we do not act…

SONYA: *(Recovering.)* Who knows! Perhaps you should die!

MARYIA: Me!

SONYA: You sit there and you – perch there and –

MARYIA: Me?

SEREBRYAKOV: Pain
 And
 Civility

SONYA: Yes! Why not you! Do you think age lends you immunity? If you knew how I detested your maturity and sense, your experience and your sound conclusions –

MARYIA: I was not happy! I have said how unhappy I have been, Sonya!

SONYA: MUCH DESERVED UNHAPPINESS I SAY

MARYIA: That is so –so very –

(MARINA enters.)

Marina! Mikhail is dead!

(MARINA looks at the dead man.)

MARINA: Now, that's peculiar because only this morning he said to me, 'Nanny,' – he called me nanny –

TELYEGHIN: Everybody did –

MARINA: Everybody did at one time, yes – 'Nanny, how long have we known one another?' Eleven years I said. He must have known he was about to die… *(She goes out.)*

MARYIA: He – he – *(Pause.)* What? *(She looks to VANYA.)* Was there an accident?

TELYEGHIN: *(Getting up.)* ACCI – DENT?

MARYIA: A fall, was it…? *(She drifts out.)*

TELYEGHIN: ACCI – DENT…!

(Pause.)

SONYA: Telyeghin, what is the matter with you?

TELYEGHIN: With me? The matter with me? First there is is a sea which is not there and now there is a murder which is called an – *(Pause.)* Where is my guitar? *(Pause. His shoulders heave.)* Oh, where is my guitar…?

VANYA: You trod on it. *(Pause. He looks around, red-eyed.)*

SONYA: Telyeghin…

TELYEGHIN: Yes…?

SONYA: The gag. Remember the gag.

Pause.

TELYEGHIN: I wish to say
Come what may
I have to state. *(Pause.)*
How profoundly I regret
My spontaneity… *(Pause, he sits.)*
Now, do what you will.

(SONYA laughs loudly.)

Yes…

SONYA: You have all the arrogance of the incurably feeble, Telyeghin. WHO WANTS TO DO ANYTHING TO YOU?

HELENA: Do you not think we should bury him? I am all for looking Death in the face but not for days on end and there are shovels there.

SONYA: Yes! Wonderful Helena! Yes! But not you! No, you –

HELENA: I want to dig.

SONYA: Ivan, she is not to dig, is she? I am the digger. I have the arms. Marina, help me carry Mikhail Lvovich to the beach –

HELENA: Why can't I dig?

SONYA: BECAUSE HE'S MINE. *(Pause. HELENA looks at her.)*

HELENA: Yes.
And digging would –

SONYA: Spoil your hands. *(Pause.)* It would. And I believe in your hands. I believe your hands should not be soiled. No sarcasm. No wit. They should be perfect. They should be the merest – suggestion – of your body, lying like pale flowers, yes, I do mean this. *(Pause.)* Marina!

(MARYIA, MARINA and SONYA remove the body of ASTROV.)

SEREBRYAKOV: Civility he thought hung between desire and the act, but culture –

TELYEGHIN: *(Standing.)* You've forgotten the gun –

(They ignore him.)

Ivan Petrovich – The gun... *(He points to the gun lying on the floor which has slipped from ASTROV's pocket.)*

VANYA: You have the gun, Telyeghin.

(Pause.)

TELYEGHIN: Me? Don't you want the gun?

VANYA: I've used the gun. I no longer require the gun. Whereas perhaps you do?

55

(Pause. TELYEGHIN goes gingerly to the weapon and picks it up. It weighs heavy. He looks at it. Slowly, he walks out.)

SEREBRYAKOV: Culture
Culture

(ASTROV returns as a corpse, like SEREBRYAKOV, and takes position.)

He had no theory of

HELENA: You are so beautiful, I would not care if I died. *(Pause.)* You are so perfect to me I am afraid to know you better. *(Pause.)* I am fixed between wanting you and dreading you. *(Pause, then with despair.)* I am artificial, Ivan! Are you?

VANYA: Yes.

(Pause.)

HELENA: Thank God.

VANYA: I am the creation of my own will, Helena. And possibly entirely false. And yet this falseness is –

ASTROV: Give us Chekhov
Give us
Give us
Chekhov
Who helps us to die

VANYA: QUITE UNASHAMED, HELENA *(He smiles.)* What do I care if he violated you! Did he? It's nothing to me, on the contrary, it is another aspect of your intangible perfection yes, it is a further – did he do it – element of your distinction and even – yes – a peculiar contribution to your innocence –
HOW
WHERE
NAKED OR NOT
STANDING OR
And a testimony to your

OBVIOUSLY IT FAILED
Describe it to me

HELENA: No

VANYA: Yes

HELENA: I can't

VANYA: Who knows what detail might unlock the gates of
  your appalling history to me

HELENA: HOW CAN I DESCRIBE IT

VANYA: What insignificant gesture will

HELENA: I can't I said

  (Pause.)

VANYA: Lodge in my imagination and shake my doors all
  hours of the night? *(Pause.)* All that befalls you, Helena, is
  enhancement. YOU KNOW THAT AND SO DO I.

  (Pause.)

HELENA: Am I clean?

VANYA: Yes.

HELENA: Infinitely clean?

VANYA: Yes.

  (Pause. Distant cries on the beach.)

HELENA: He abused me –

VANYA: Obviously –

HELENA: And this abuse was –

VANYA: Mundane –

HELENA: Mundane, yes, but –

VANYA: Vehement –

HELENA: Vehement, yes, and his face!

VANYA: A mask of anger –

HELENA: Anger, yes, and I said –

VANYA: Pleaded –

HELENA: I think so – pleading – yes, I suppose it was a plea but –

VANYA: Shh!

(He walks a little, sits, and putting his hands to his face, appears to think. The sea. The cries. After a long time HELENA begins to laugh. VANYA also, before standing and confronting her.)

AND PREGNANT!

HELENA Yes!

VANYA: Obviously, yes!

(They stare at one another.)

I will be merciless to you.

HELENA: And I
MERCILESS TO YOU, IVAN

(MARYIA hurries in, windswept.)

MARYIA: Come and see this boat!

(They are oblivious to her.)

This boat is

(And still.)

Don't you want to see this boat?

(VANYA turns to her.)

A man is drowning…

SONYA: *(Hurrying in.)* It tacks one way, then the other, but it can't possibly survive, do witness this, Ivan!

MARYIA: We think the man can't swim, but even if he could –

SONYA: The sea is so –

MARYIA: Even the swimmers drown…

(VANYA looks at her.)

VANYA: We must guard our lives. Having made our lives, we must be on guard for them. We must stand guard over our creations.

MARYIA: Yes…

VANYA: Let him drown, therefore.
Mother.
Can you do that?
Watch?
Just watch?

(Pause.)

MARYIA: My instinct – my whole instinct is to –

VANYA: No, that is not your instinct. (Pause.)

MARYIA: Isn't it?

VANYA: No. You no longer know the difference between your instinct and your culture. It is your culture that impels you to rescue someone who might perhaps, who knows, be your worst enemy.

(Pause.)

SONYA: Ivan is correct but *(Pause.)* I need a man. *(Pause.)* Perhaps this is a man whom I might love. A poet. Or a fisherman. NO NOT A POET WHO WANTS A POET no, it is a fisherman who as he staggers up the beach I shall embrace, I shall crush him in a consuming love! *(She looks at her arms.)* These arms have killed but they might also shield… in them a child might hide as a city hides inside a wall. I already love him!

MARYIA: *(Decisively.)* I have to save him! I have to and you are wrong!

(SONYA hurries out.)

VANYA: Wrong?

MARYIA: Wrong, yes. *(She shrugs her shoulders.)* Wrong *(She goes out.)*

HELENA: *(Watching her depart.)* Your mother will drown, won't she?

VANYA: It would be entirely appropriate, a fit ending to her life. *(He goes to the doorway, watching her.)* Goodness excited her. It's true. Serebryakov made her throb with his politics. His utopias. She trembled in her bowels.

(Cries of the WOMEN on the beach.)

She can perhaps conceive of no better death than perishing for a stranger. Who this stranger is, his complete worthlessness, perhaps, is irrelevant to her… *(He is seized by a thought. He turns.)*
I KNOW WHO IT IS!
I KNOW
I KNOW WHO IT IS! *(He rushes about.)*
The gun! Who has the gun! Look for the gun!

HELENA: Telyeghin had the –

VANYA: TELYEGHIN!

HELENA: Ivan – who is it –

VANYA: TELYEGHIN!

HELENA: WHO IS IT I SAID.

(VANYA stares at her.)

ASTROV: Man is beautiful but under what conditions the play asks under what circumstances can we let our whole hearts flow only in despair the play says and I agree.

(Pause. TELYEGHIN sits up from behind the furniture. An unpleasant smile crosses his face.)

TELYEGHIN: Hidden it. *(He laughs.)*
Hidden it and not telling!
(He covers his face in terror.)
Not telling even if you
TORTURE ME
CASTRATE ME
HANG ME FROM A TREE

MARYIA: *(Off.)* He's alive!

SONYA: Alive!

(Joyous laughter. MARYIA appears in the doorway, sodden, flushed. MARINA enters, looks.)

MARYIA: Marina! He's alive!

(She opens her arms to MARINA. MARINA slaps her brutally across the face.)

ACT TWO

All the characters are standing in a row. Their heads hang like penitents.
They are motionless. CHEKHOV, a figure in a crumpled, stained suit,
is walking up and down towelling his hair vigorously. He stops, stares
at VANYA.

CHEKHOV: Uncle
Uncle *(Pause.)*
UNCLE VANYA! *(He laughs, towels again, tosses the towel aside,*
reaches for a packet of cigarettes, extracts it from his soddened
pocket, looks at it.)
I must stop smoking.
I must stop and as if to influence me in this wisdom the sea
has spoiled the packet
THE COMPENSATIONS OF SEVERE EXPOSURE *(He tosses*
the packet to MARINA.)
Dry them out I may smoke them later *(He laughs at himself.)*

MARINA: I won't.

CHEKHOV: You're a servant aren't you? Do as you're told.

MARINA: No.

(She is rigid. CHEKHOV walks around, stops.)

CHEKHOV: Uncle
Uncle
UNCLE VANYA

TELYEGHIN: I nearly died! They nearly killed me! She
especially wanted to castrate me and tread on my eyes!

CHEKHOV: Shh…

TELYEGHIN: Sonya, little Sonya Alexandrova, who would
have believed?

CHEKHOV: Shh…

SEREBRYAKOV: We all know what a play is but what is an author?
The author also sins
The author is not very clean
Is he clean
I often wonder

ASTROV: His impeccable authority I must say I

SEREBRYAKOV: His infallibility sometimes strikes me as

CHEKHOV: The sea!
Certainly it was rough!
And certainly I was in danger of my life! The foam, as it were, reached out for me! This impatient foam required my body for its satisfaction! I enraged it by continuing to exist! *(He laughs.)* But I am inextinguishable, it seems. I am beyond the reach of temper or of climate, and like a cork still bobs in quiet bays long after ships have foundered, I endure, why, what is it gives me this –

(VANYA lets out a profound sob. His shoulders heave.)

This perpetuity? Clearly, I am necessary. In me, there lies a terrible significance. Don't think I exaggerate or indulge! I am the least indulgent of men but.

HELENA: *(To VANYA.)* Don't. Don't sob.

CHEKHOV: But it is as well to know these things about yourself. It is pitiful to shelter behind disavowals and pandering humilities, no, it is obvious even to those who do not care to heed me, even they must admit my – religiosity *(His hand goes to his pocket, stops.)* Look, reaching for my cigarettes again! That is how poor my discipline is! That is the extent of my convictions! But I have been ill. I, the doctor, have been ill...

HELENA: Voinitsky is my lover.
Ivan Voinitsky is my lover
Stop sobbing
Him and I

MARINA: Good girl!

HELENA: Naked

MARINA: Tell him!

HELENA: Half naked

MARINA: Yes!

HELENA: In the street and out of it

MARINA: I love you, you bitch!

HELENA: His hand in the very heart of me
    His hand
    In
    My
    Heart!

MARINA: Yes!
    My
    Mistress
    I
    Long to serve a
    BITCH LIKE YOU!

(She laughs. Pause. CHEKHOV walks up and down.)

CHEKHOV: Uncle,
    Uncle,
    You are in luck.

TELYEGHIN: They go on like that all the time it sickens you
    they can't keep their fingers out of one another's clothes –

CHEKHOV: Shh…

TELYEGHIN: It's true –

MARINA: Shut up –

TELYEGHIN: You know it's true –

MARINA: YOU COULDN'T KEEP YOUR OWN WIFE, WAFFLES!

(Pause.)

TELYEGHIN: So what? I loved her. Even when she abandoned me, I loved her. I still love her. THAT IS LOVE. Love, and no returns. *(He smiles, shrugs.)*

CHEKHOV: You see, I don't know which of you is the more comic.
AND I LOVE TO LAUGH
OH, TO LAUGH DELIGHTS ME
The strenuous or the spineless both of whom in the last resort appear equally absurd both of whom are smitten with self-adulation, both of whom are posturing and yet so frail I could
I almost could
EMBRACE YOU
Vanya of you I am particularly fond.

VANYA: I am not fond of you

CHEKHOV: You fill me with laughter.

VANYA: Do I?

CHEKHOV: A laughter which is without malice or contempt, a laughter such as the moon might laugh at the homeward journey of a drunken man…

VANYA: I would rather kill myself than –

CHEKHOV: Shh…

VANYA: Live one hour as –

CHEKHOV: Shh…

MARINA: DON'T SHUSH HIM YOU – YOU –

(CHEKHOV laughs at MARINA's vehemence.)

VANYA: This self-defiling man –

MARINA: YOU – *(She shakes her head in frustration.)* CREEPING PRIEST!

VANYA: Called Vanya!

CHEKHOV: I do love a mutiny!

MARINA: AND I LIKE PRIESTS, BUT NOT THE CREEPING SORT!

CHEKHOV: A mutiny is merely the affirmation of things after all, isn't it, Helena? Helena knows a mutiny is only a despairing love…

HELENA: I want to say
Without temper
If possible without the least sense of the heroic
Without even that measured ambition to speak the truth
which is only another vulgarity
To say
I am not what I was
Indeed
I was nothing and now I am at least a possibility of
something
And this
I will defend.

(MARINA claps. MARYIA follows suit, even TELYEGHIN.)

No, you see, you have – you've spoiled it – you have encrusted it with virtue… *(She shakes her head bitterly.)* You will drive the sea away…!

SONYA: *(To CHEKHOV.)* Go away, now, you have seen what hope she has, you can see the frail and precious hope she – *(Pause.)* You're smiling… *(She turns to the others.)* He's smiling…!

ASTROV: The theatre is a contract

SEREBRYAKOV: Between the living and the dead

ASTROV: The dead inform the living of their fate

SEREBRYAKOV: A requirement.

ASTROV: A necessity

ASTROV/SEREBRYAKOV: CHEKHOV
    HOW
    TOLERANT
    YOU
    ARE

SEREBRYAKOV: He makes it possible for us to forgive ourselves the crime

(Silence.)

CHEKHOV: I have a disease…

SEREBRYAKOV: Of self-murder

CHEKHOV: Listen…

SEREBRYAKOV: Self-betrayal

CHEKHOV: I have a disease…

ASTROV: And self-disgust.

VANYA: *(As if clinging to a rock.)* I AM A MURDERER.

CHEKHOV: *(Standing.)* Yes, so you are…

VANYA: Serebryakov has no face

CHEKHOV: Yes…

VANYA: No face and I

CHEKHOV: You did it, yes –

VANYA: DO YOU KNOW HOW HARD IT IS TO BE A MURDERER?

(Pause. CHEKHOV looks at him with contempt.)

CHEKHOV: Vanya, I have such a withering knowledge of your soul. Its poverty. Its pitiful dimensions. It is smaller than an aspirin which fizzes in a glass…

VANYA: I don't give in…

CHEKHOV: An innocuous fizz audible only to those who place their ears against the rim…

(Pause.)

VANYA: I don't give in…

CHEKHOV: OH, IVAN, IVAN, YOUR RESILIENCE, YOUR ADAMANTINE NAUGHTINESS! *(He laughs at his own wit.)*

VANYA: What do you think murder is, a hobby!

HELENA: Shh!

CHEKHOV: He thinks it is a hobby!

HELENA: Ivan –

VANYA: It is an act of profound psychological and philosophical significance.

(Pause. CHEKHOV smiles.)

HELENA: Ivan, he is making you infantile. Please don't go on.

VANYA: I lost my temper.

HELENA: I know. And that is his aperture. It is the open skylight to your soul. It is the hole in your perfection by which he enters in.

VANYA: Yes –

HELENA: And burgles you. And makes a shambles of your self – your hard won self –

VANYA: Yes –

HELENA: You are magnificent and you can't be spoiled. *(She turns to CHEKHOV.)* WE ARE NOT SPOILED.

MARYIA: *(Bitterly.)* Bravo, Helena! Everybody loves Helena! Helena is the epitome etcetera the pinnacle etcetera and the apotheosis of! What a wonderful girl! What a magnificently fecund female and her depths are pure red so hot and red and she never lifted her voice for the oppressed not one syllable or lost a second's sleep for another's pain. Magnificence! And yet she has a soul, she does, she has a soul you cannot diminish Helena, can you? Obviously I hate her but you cannot – *(Pause.)* I WANT TO DIE I CANNOT TOLERATE ANOTHER HOUR OF MYSELF THIS SELF SQUATTING LIKE A BEAR ON MY BRAIN...

(CHEKHOV goes to her, and unbuttons her dress at the breast. He exposes her breasts. Others watch...)

CHEKHOV: Her breasts... are not without their power... like birds in an abandoned nest... they shan't be – and that's the beauty of it – shan't ever be touched... and if they were... how swiftly they would rise and fill like – they shan't however, SHAN'T BE, SHAN'T BE...!

(MARYIA nods, weeping.)

SONYA: You are – vile...

CHEKHOV: *(Turning on her.)* Do you want to lose your beauty? Do you want to forfeit your perfect neglect – for that? *(He indicates VANYA, then MARYIA again.)* Look at her, she is in such immaculate SOLITUDE...

VANYA: Please cover my mother's breasts...

CHEKHOV: She does not want to be covered.

VANYA: Mother, will you –

MARYIA: I DO NOT WISH TO BE COVERED.

HELENA: *(To CHEKHOV.)* You are evil. Not vile. Not common vileness, evil!

MARYIA: You would say that to a god!

CHEKHOV: She calls me a god!

MARYIA: You are! You are a god!

CHEKHOV: *(Shrugging.)* How can I refuse a compliment of such – oh, look, and I reached for a cigarette! There! Even I responded to a compliment with modesty! The cigarette was intended to cloak my embarrassment! I am human, after all!

(VANYA goes towards MARYIA.)

DON'T TOUCH HER, YOU IMPOSTER! *(He laughs, then proceeds to button MARYIA.)* I sometimes bully. I sometimes throw my weight about. And Helena's right. I'm evil. I don't like the word, it is too theological for my – *(Pause.)* No. It is the word. My crimes are, after all much worse than Ivan's, Ivan who thinks murder is serious, who sports his murder as a badge, who hangs his life from a hook, IVAN WHO IS FUNDAMENTALLY INERT. *(He turns to HELENA.)* It is preposterous you love this man, a woman with such thudding veins should cling to IVAN such flooding such pulsing in her belly IVAN OF ALL PEOPLE isn't he a fumbler in women's wardrobes?

HELENA: Yes.

CHEKHOV: There are things even I do not understand AND IMPOTENT AT THAT really it is so unclean I could laugh, I do laugh, I resort to laughter when I am deepest in offence, listen I am dying I have come here to die…

(Pause.)

ASTROV: Chekhov, how he draws a line across the world.
How kneeling to the earth with chalk
He comforts our horror of distances
STOP
STOP

(A flood of music. MARINA sings.)

MARINA: The pain of ambition is the proof of my existence give me the impossible to do…!

(The music stops. She laughs in the silence, shaking her head. Pause.)

CHEKHOV: Will someone sit with me? *(Pause.)* Ivan… *(Pause.)* Preferably.

VANYA: Me? But you hate me.

CHEKHOV: Yes.

(Pause.)

VANYA: How can I refuse, I –

HELENA: Of course you can refuse.

(Pause.)

VANYA: Yes.
I can refuse.
I CAN REFUSE.
However, I –

HELENA: I DON'T ADVISE IT.

CHEKHOV: Helena, you are the best thing ever made. How wonderfully you deny the little traps of charity! To be loved by you! Oh, to be loved by you! To be your child! How hard your hawk-eye scans the land for treachery!

HELENA: Yes.
I want this man.
Undamaged.

CHEKHOV: I promise him. How's that?

(Pause. HELENA leaves swiftly. MARINA, SONYA, MARYIA follow. TELYEGHIN hangs back. ASTROV and SEREBRYAKOV laugh, suddenly, voraciously, and are silent.)

TELYEGHIN: I put the gun –

(CHEKHOV waves a hand dismissively.)

I mention it because it's possible he may – by accident –

(CHEKHOV dismisses him again.)

stumble on it and –

CHEKHOV: The gun was always an error. The gun was always false…

(TELYEGHIN bows and withdraws. Pause.)

As Vanya knows.

VANYA: I disagree –

CHEKHOV: You disagree but –

VANYA: I merely state my differing opinion –

CHEKHOV: Yes –

VANYA: On the subject of the gun –

CHEKHOV: Yes –

VANYA: *(Suddenly and defiantly.)* 7786955797!

(CHEKHOV looks at him.)

The serial number.

(Pause.)

CHEKHOV: It's odd – and this was itself the certain proof of
the extent of my disease – its fatal dimensions – that I have
lost the will to argue, and even, dear though it was to me,
to castigate. Even as I began those cruel sentences I felt
– more is required, you are not sufficiently enraged. It was
as if I knew that what I said, whilst being true, whilst being
impeccably and incontrovertibly true, was still not fit to be
articulated, as if it was an effort greater than life itself could
justify... do you know this state, Ivan...?

(Pause.)

VANYA: Yes.
No.
Well, sometimes we all –

CHEKHOV: You are trying to protect yourself against me! *(He
laughs.)* Understandably, you are anxious to be on guard
against infection, for as I have explained, I am dying of a
disease, and no man willingly exposes himself to a disease.
I am talking of a truth so absolute, so ponderous, that even

to enunciate its laws would command more energy than we possess. It would, I honestly believe, kill us with the exhaustion of articulating it, and though it is proximate enough, though it is manifest enough – like some meteoric relic protruding from the soil – it is far better left and undisturbed. I am tired. I am tired even thinking of the labour, and in any case, who hears? Who hears, Ivan?

(VANYA shrugs.)

To grapple with this truth is fatal, obviously, so why do I persist? Why should I attempt to lift this inert mass upon my fragile shoulders? It's fatal, as you say.

VANYA: Did I say…?

CHEKHOV: Fatal, and whilst there is a certain heroism in it, heroism for whom? I am not moved by the common man, I do not love everywhere. That commandment I ruptured early on. I have no faith, Ivan, which perhaps enables me to die, don't flinch from me – you flinched like a child who cannot read the intentions of a stranger.

VANYA: Did I flinch?

CHEKHOV: You flinched to be loved – you flinched to be drawn into the agony of another man, I do understand that! I do sympathize with that. I also never trusted the extended hand, you are on guard against me all the time –

VANYA: I am, yes! I admit it!

CHEKHOV: One day I hoped I would reach out and tell myself, pour myself like a liquid from a jug into the void of another, all, entire, to the last drop, how I struggled with this dream to pour myself into another man! A woman! To be drained…!

(Pause. There are sounds on the beach of voices.)

And in abandoning that dream, I found something like freedom. In discarding all that was arguably, the best in me, I found a peace of sorts. We are entirely untransferable. So hold my hand... Ivan...

(VANYA extends a hand to CHEKHOV, who holds it. CHEKHOV dies. TELYEGHIN hurries in.)

TELYEGHIN: The sea's gone!
 The sea's gone or to put it another way –

VANYA: Shut up –

TELYEGHIN: It was never there!

(MARINA, TELYEGHIN and HELENA enter, distraught.)

HELENA: The sea –

MARINA: The sea's not there!

VANYA: All right, it's no longer there!

(TELYEGHIN squeals with laughter. HELENA stares at VANYA. SONYA enters, looks about her, goes to a chair, sits.)

SONYA: You see, the rural gentry...
 In its imagination even...
 Was constrained by economic impotence...
 IT COULD NOT EVEN DREAM. *(Pause.)*

HELENA: Ivan, you are holding his hand...

SONYA: They talk of liberty, but what is this word?
 Is this word not devoid of meaning if.

HELENA: Ivan...

SONYA: If consciousness itself is crushed by the weight of social failure? It is a paste jewel surely?

HELENA: Shut up.

SONYA: A PASTE JEWEL...!

VANYA: Chekhov's dead...

MARYIA: *(Entering.)* Marina, I think we all need a cup of tea...

(Without demurring, MARINA turns to go.)

VANYA: CHEKHOV'S DEAD!

(They all look at him. Suddenly, in a gesture of profound ugliness, he lets go of CHEKHOV's hand, which falls. MARINA turns.)

MARINA: Where's the samovar?

MARYIA: The samovar?

SONYA: You see, only with social transformation can imagination be – can life be – and until then all we can do is – work for this – postponing all and –

MARINA/MARYIA: *(Laughing.)* IT'S ON THE BEACH!

(MARINA points at the damaged tea urn.)

MARYIA: *(Springing up.)* Help me pull it in, Marina!

(They go to it.)

It's full of sand…!

(MARYIA and MARINA begin beating it to loosen the sand, giggling all the while.)

HELENA: Ivan…
Ivan…

(The sound of a guitar badly played.)

WE ARE NOT THE SAME AS WE WERE.

(TELYEGHIN holds up the guitar which is undamaged.)

TELYEGHIN: Look! *(He shows it, sits, begins a tune. The guitar, the beating of the urn.)*

HELENA: I said we are not the same as we were…

(VANYA does not look at her.)

If you betray me, I will kill you. I have the right to kill you. You don't dispute that right, do you?

VANYA: Not in the least...

TELYEGHIN: *(Seeing her expose the gun.)* There it is! Where did I leave it Helena Lienochka?

HELENA: You are making me, who was so malleable, coercive! You are making me, who willed nothing, adamantine and imperative! SO BE IT. SO BE IT. *(Pause. She sways.)* And not desirable. No longer desirable. SO BE IT. I must admit I'm spoiled for some. Are you Ivan, or are you not? Oh, are you Ivan or –

(An effect of light and sound. A monstrous mirror descends, in which HELENA sees herself. She giggles.)

ACT THREE

In the darkness, HELENA's laughter, different in tone. The light shows her sitting on a chair in front of the mirror watching herself. The other characters are sprawled lifelessly around the stage like the remnants of a party. HELENA is dressed in underthings. A few notes trickle from TELYEGHIN's guitar. A silence.

HELENA: I'm thinner. *(Pause.)* I'm thinner or is it only the glass? Some glass does that some glass has the propensity to narrow or to broaden HOW GOOD IS THIS GLASS IVAN HOW you can be starved in one and bloated in another WHERE'S IT FROM I MEAN the Venetians they make lovely glass but small chance this is from Venice surely I have lost weight but so what so what I prefer it I like to be a kite a basket of thin but pliant bones on which my skin translucently stretches etcetera you are pretty thin yourself thin and white the wonderful whiteness of your flesh it is a sign of your religion your skin is the white cope of an archbishop walk in my palace stride through my aisles an energetic archbishop obviously.

(She laughs. A silence. The guitar's three notes.)

I am talking about beauty. DOES ANYBODY MIND I KNOW HOW UNCOMFORTABLE YOU GET beauty does upset you beauty does irritate your nerves it is so very UNDEMOCRATIC BEAUTY it is an unforgivable thing I HAVE IT HOWEVER SO and all things lead to my body what else is there but my body ALL THINGS LEAD TO IT including physics mathematics linguistics WHERE ELSE COULD THEY LEAD psychology hygiene and weapons training ASK THE STUDENT ON THE TRAIN WHO SEEMS CONSUMED BY NUMBERS where his efforts lead my body is the end of thought the terminus of rationality and instinct both my husband thought that but he couldn't say it it depressed him it humiliated him but not you surely I AM

THE POINT AND PURPOSE OF THE WORLD which dared to announce itself and that surely is SIN is it, is it sin?

(She turns to look at VANYA, who is standing watching her with his hands in his coat pockets.)

It's sin, I think, to state the obvious…

(VANYA makes a move towards her.)

DON'T TOUCH.

(He stops.)

This thinness of mine. I am a rack of bones from which swords might be made. Did you know the body was a resource for instruments, the ribs for needles and the shoulder blades, what are they for, axes probably I AM A LETHAL OBJECT careful you might cut your fingers and bleed from a caress. How is your sickness today?

(Pause. VANYA walks a few paces, stops, is about to speak.)

I do hate that attitude.

(Pause. VANYA looks up, querying her.)

I mean that gesture. Those few steps, the shoulders the half-turn and so on it is the preamble to some it is a minuet to some and false as if the thing you want to say could not be relied upon to speak for itself but needed decoration I despise it.

(Pause. VANYA laughs. So does she.)

VANYA: Yes…!
Yes! How closely you observe me…!

HELENA: Yes. I love you and that permits me to see both more and less than others. I love you, Ivan, and you are deteriorating, I must say so or that makes me a liar, too. Do you want me to collude in your lies?

VANYA: *(With a gesture.)* No, no, that would be –

HELENA: There it goes again!

VANYA: What?

HELENA: *(Laughing.)* That – I know what it is! IT IS THE
REMNANT OF CHARM.

(They laugh.)

Stop it. Say what you want to say and keep still.

*(A profound silence. A faint giggle from SONYA, who is making a
ball of wool from a skein held by MARYIA.)*

VANYA: I've forgotten the number.

(Pause. A strum of four notes.)

HELENA: The number…

VANYA: The number of the gun, I've forgotten it.

(He stares at her.)

WHAT DOES IT MEAN!

MARYIA: Shh…

VANYA: I have been walking up and down out there, I've
racked my brain and thrashed my memory
But
WHAT
WHAT IS IT
Perhaps I'm happy, is that it? Is this happiness? It doesn't
feel like happiness, unless happiness is fog, perhaps it's fog,
yes it must be
778
It was a pair of sevens
77 what, though?

HELENA: Ivan –

VANYA: WHO WANTS FOG, NOT ME! May I touch you? Let me
touch you…

(HELENA does not concede herself.)

I'M SORRY I CANNOT REMEMBER THE NUMBER I HAVE TRIED.

(A wind blows through the ruins of the house. HELENA covers her face with her hands.)

HELENA: Ivan, are you afraid…?

VANYA: Only of you. I am afraid of you. I ALWAYS WAS AFRAID OF YOU

MARYIA: *(Irritably.)* Shh…

VANYA: ALWAYS
ALWAYS
AFRAID OF YOU *(Pause.)*
Which was correct. Which is the way it should have been. Which is the perfect condition of pure love. OF COURSE I AM AFRAID OF YOU this fear made me a murderer this fear drove me this fear whipped me it is a servitude a magnificence an abject and triumphant thing which is *(Pause. He shrugs.)*

HELENA: Make love now.

VANYA: Rinsing the life out of me…

HELENA: Make love.

(He shakes his head.)

VANYA: 7786955797…

(They laugh.)

He hated the gun.
Oh, how he hated the gun.
It was as if he knew it was the enemy of all his melancholy compromise…

(Pause. They look at one another. TELYEGHIN moves a chess piece in a game he is playing with himself. HELENA takes the gun from her

clothes. She sits across the chair, facing VANYA. A short giggle from SONYA and MARYIA, who are winding wool, oblivious.)

HELENA: Four bullets you fired into my husband's face.

VANYA: And two –

HELENA: Remain.

(Pause. She tosses the weapon to VANYA, who catches it. He pulls a chair to him, and sits in it, opposite HELENA. Pause. They laugh, infectiously.)

HELENA: I'm afraid of you, too.

VANYA: Excellent.

(They laugh again. MARINA shuffles across the stage.)

MARINA: Tea, anyone…?

HELENA: Am I magnificent, Ivan? Am I?

VANYA: Yes.

HELENA: I knew I was. Always I knew I was. I overcame him, didn't I?

VANYA: Yes.

(HELENA laughs.)

MARINA: *(Off.)* Or vodka?

HELENA: I'm so sorry not to be your executioner, Ivan so sorry you must do it all alone…

VANYA: I'll manage it.

HELENA: Yes!

VANYA: I have a steady hand.

HELENA: I have observed that!

VANYA: You have?

HELENA: So very steady, which surprised me, which I took as a sign of your supreme self-confidence, whereas if I were to do it, if it were assigned to me, then the possibility of –

VANYA: Ugliness –

HELENA: Ugliness, yes – would be – *(She shuts her eyes.)* Will you say or just –

MARINA: *(Returning.)* Doesn't anyone like vodka any more? *(She passes through with a tray.)*

VANYA: *(Cocking the pistol.)* I think – just do.

HELENA: Yes. Without announcing.

VANYA: I'm aiming it. *(He lifts the pistol.)*

HELENA: And so much unsaid!

VANYA: Inevitably, yes.

HELENA: Inevitably but so many of the things one said perhaps ought not to have been said whereas –

VANYA: The things one should say –

HELENA: Are forever secret! Yes! How hideous that is!

VANYA: Hideous? I don't know about hideous...

HELENA: Hideous, yes!

VANYA: But if one waited, if one postponed, until all things that needed to be said were said then –

HELENA: God, yes –

VANYA: Impossible –

HELENA: Ridiculous, oh, yes –

VANYA: Helena, my arm is aching –

HELENA: Those things must be imagined, I suppose –

VANYA: Helena –

HELENA: Or taken for granted, perhaps –

VANYA: I'm talking –

HELENA: Yes –

VANYA: We did succeed –

HELENA: I'm shaking –

VANYA: Listen to me, I am talking –

HELENA: I can't –

VANYA: KEEP STILL I'M TALKING –

HELENA: I CAN'T – I CAN'T –

(He shoots. The other characters instantaneously chant in unison.)

ALL: UNC – LE
    UNC – LE
    UNC – LE
    VAN – YA

(VANYA, kicking over his chair, walks frantically up and down the stage.)

THE MURDERER IS NEVER SATISFIED

(VANYA stops. He holds the gun at arm's length and cocks it again. Wind and a thin sound. He raises the gun to his temple. He sways in a tempest of emotion. He becomes still. He points the gun at the floor and fires the shot. Pause.)

VANYA: Missed. *(Pause.)*
Damnation. *(Pause, then he laughs. He calls.)*
Nanny! I can't look at her. You must do it. I apologize, these things are more than a servant is required in normal circumstances to perform however I and no one liked Helena no one liked such power admiration she aroused and plenty of respect but – *(He chokes in sobs.)*

ALL Shh...

(VANYA wails.)

SHHH!

VANYA: Na – nny!

(MARINA enters. Some giggles or routine sounds from the others. She looks. She pokes among the fallen chairs.)

Is it better to kill another than to kill yourself. *(Pause.)* Better for whom, however? *(Pause.)* And I'm out of ammunition... *(He throws the gun down.)* Coat!

MARINA: It's cold out, Ivan Petrovich...

VANYA: COAT I SAID.

(She waddles out. Pause.)

Better for the soul of man, of course.

(MARINA comes in with a heavy overcoat.)

Nanny, I should be dead. I failed, presumably because –

MARINA: I'll hold it for you –

VANYA: I sensed – presumably I sensed –

MARINA: Falling apart, this thing –

VANYA: Some necessity attached to my continued existence, it was not pure fear, I promise you, but this entails –

MARINA: It's heavy, Ivan Petrovich...!

VANYA: This – *(He extends his arms.)* is – a contract with – partly with Helena – partly with myself – the clauses of which demand of me the highest –

MARINA: *(Brushing the shoulders.)* What a state it's in!

VANYA: The highest responsibility towards – me – my own potential obviously – but also –

MARINA: *(Shaking her head)* And the belt...!

VANYA: Also – *(He stops suddenly.)*
WHERE AM I GOING

(A catastrophic silence.)

WHERE AM I

(VANYA closes his eyes, and with an effort of will, strides out of the room. Pause. TELYEGHIN lets out a small cry of satisfaction at a chess move. SONYA murmurs to MARYIA. Time passes.)

SONYA: He'll be back…

(Insignificant moves. Time passes.)

MARYIA: He'll be back…

(They proceed with their lives. The lights diminish. VANYA does not return.)

A HOUSE OF CORRECTION

Characters

SHARDLO

VISTULA

LINDSAY

HEBBEL

GODANSK

FIRST SERVANT

SECOND SERVANT

THIRD SERVANT

PART ONE

A MESSENGER

A damaged room. A storm of leaflets falls from the sky. They cascade onto and around a standing woman. The storm ceases. A second woman enters, and contemplates the first…

VISTULA: How very extraordinary, it is your way of standing that infuriates me now. How extraordinary this hatred is, how volatile…! Yesterday your hair enraged me, I could have torn it out by the roots…
(SHARDLO is motionless…)

Millions stand exactly like that, millions, and never until now did I find it in the least offensive. Shift, will you? Sit or something? Obviously it is not the posture – oh, you are uncompromising, you ask for all you get, oh you are so very adamantine and the less you concede the worse I become, I blame you for much of this…!
(SHARDLO does not move…)

I am not bad… *(VISTULA shakes her head…)*

I am not…

I am not bad…

(She clenches her fists… She hunches her shoulders in a spasm of pain. She hurries out. SHARDLO remains still for some time, then she erupts into movement.)

SHARDLO: *(Calling.)* PICK THIS UP…!

(She strides, she fetches. SERVANTS hurry in with straw baskets and pluck up the leaflets.)

I can't
I won't
I never do *(She flings a white sheet over an iron bed…)*
And sometimes – let us dare confess it – sometimes, yes, the poetry is good, the poetry is not without its qualities, some days rhyming, some days not, all tastes are catered for and whilst it is forbidden to allow one's eyes to drift

over the words inevitably one or two stand out good words unusual words that linger in the memory. *(She fetches more linen.)*

Paralysis I noticed and cacophony beautiful words in my opinion perhaps I should deny myself the luxury of speaking them but treason can't reside in the vocabulary or can it surely it's the attitude I don't claim to understand these things *(She stops suddenly in mid-movement.)*

Now that was false *(She is still.)*

That was so false I understand perfectly well why did I affect an ignorance not one of you would attach the slightest credence to you of all people who know the strength of my intelligence why did I

(They continue, as if deaf to her.)

Now of all times
Succumb to
A pretence

(They collect. She reflects… She crushes the linen in her hands. She falters, then swiftly walks out, throwing the sheet to the floor. The SERVANTS continue undeflected, moving like crop-gatherers. A figure rises painfully out of the bed, haggard, pale, grasping the iron to haul himself upright.)

HEBBEL: Blood…!
  Blood…!

(The SERVANTS ignore his existence… The sound of an aeroplane passing low. As it does so, the SERVANTS rise from their stooping postures in unison, and look up, then bend to continue collecting…)

HEBBEL: Blood…!
  Blood…!

(Leaflets fall in dense clouds over the stage. In an attempt to sustain order, the SERVANTS collect the remnants of the first leaflet raid before attempting to gather the second… A woman enters, briskly.)

LINDSAY: Why do you keep saying blood?

(HEBBEL ignores her…)

It is not blood, it is paper…

HEBBEL: Blood…!

LINDSAY: You will get all the blood you want, I promise you.

HEBBEL: Never
Never
Never
Enough
Blood…

(Pause… LINDSAY stares at him…)

LINDSAY: To satisfy whom…?

(The old man's hand lifts off the blanket and falls again. The last leaflets fall to the floor… The SERVANTS await an instruction to repeat their operation, and gawp at LINDSAY, baskets in their hands…)

Don't be frightened, he is not an oracle. If anything, it is his own anaemia he is referring to… *(She laughs, quietly…)*

Carry on…

(They gather again. SHARDLO returns with more linen. She looks at LINDSAY…)

SHARDLO: We shall need that bed. *(Pause…)*
Shan't we…? *(Pause…)*
We shall need all the beds we can get… *(Pause…)*
I am opposed to any sort of privilege in beds. He can stay until – *(She stops. Her hand goes to her mouth. She sways a little, recovers…)*

No, it's his bed… *(She shrugs…)*
I'm…
I'm… *(She makes a gesture of futility.)*

I have developed the aptitude for crisis when the crisis has yet to materialize… *(She smiles…)*

Never mind… when it does arrive how much more prepared I'll be…!

(LINDSAY smiles wistfully... The SERVANTS gather... SHARDLO extends a hand to LINDSAY, impulsively...)

I do want to triumph... don't you...? I do want to discover the extent of my magnificence...

LINDSAY: Yes...! And certainly this peace could not continue –

SHARDLO: Impossible –

LINDSAY: It was becoming – oh, intolerable...

(They clasp hands... LINDSAY looks down at the floor...)
I cannot wait to see your... *(She shakes her head...)*

SHARDLO: Dear one...

LINDSAY: To share in your... *(She hesitates, shrugs...)*
Can't say it...

SHARDLO: Don't say it, then... wait... witness it... and describe it afterwards...

(LINDSAY kisses her swiftly...)

I think this room can take eight beds. At a minimum. Obviously, eight is far from adequate. We shall be overwhelmed. We shall be inundated and our resources discovered to be utterly inadequate. We shall move like ghosts. Our characters, our appetites, will be suspended as we stagger under the effects of sleeplessness. Hope will evaporate. Energy will be drained. And the things we shall see...! *(She bites her lip...)*

Things the sight of which might now cause us to sink to our knees under a canopy of horror we shall – *(She stops...)* I don't know yet... *(She smiles.)* No, let us have ten in here. Five on each wall and the centre, when we are swamped, can be –

(The deep drone of a passing plane. The SERVANTS stop and gaze up, having cleared a large part of the floor. The sound fades. In the returning silence, a snowfall of leaflets begins...)

Do you read these at all...?

LINDSAY: Isn't it forbidden…?

(The SERVANTS look down, as the leaflets drift…)

SHARDLO: It is forbidden, yes…

HEBBEL: Blood…!
Blood…!

LINDSAY: It isn't blood, it's paper…

SHARDLO: What it says… the poem… on the paper… might possibly be true…

(The SERVANTS look at SHARDLO…)

There is another truth, however… which is hard for poets to believe… five times I have tried to commit suicide… five times…! *(She looks at the SERVANTS…)*

They know… they lifted me from ponds or cut me down from beams in barns… embarrassing…! For me…! For them…! *(She goes to the SERVANTS. Kisses one of them on the cheek.)*

No more of that, I promise you… *(She turns to leave…)*

When that's done, find me, I shall be in the laundry or if not there in the conservatory, I thought ten beds in there, but is it warm enough, it's summer now but if the oil is rationed it will be intolerable by the first week of September or does that *(She stops…)*

Of course the crisis will reverse our order of priorities…

(She looks at LINDSAY.) Won't that be exactly how the crisis will announce itself…?

(The SERVANTS stare at her…)

In a sense therefore, to even contemplate the crisis is a contradiction, illogical, futile, since by definition it makes havoc of the very conditions under which it could be contemplated…

(They stare… VISTULA enters, holding a bucket. She looks at SHARDLO. She looks at the SERVANTS…)

VISTULA: You hear this voice…
　　You're walking down a corridor…
　　You're in the orchard…
　　Cleaning…
　　Polishing…
　　Unblocking a drain…
　　And there's this voice…
　　It travels…
　　God knows why it's not so very… *(She thrusts the bucket to the floor. It clatters…)*
　　Like some tap running in the night some plumbing in a desolated place
　　Possibly a bath
　　Yes
　　A bath left running by a man who's died
　　A bath of useless questions

　　THIS CRISIS IS JUST ANOTHER PRETEXT FOR YOU TO TALK ABOUT YOURSELF

　　(To the SERVANTS.) Pick this up now
　　Every bit
　　I'll help you
　　I'm not afraid to stoop

(SHARDLO goes out. The SERVANTS begin to clear the leaflets…)

　　Don't accuse me I can't help myself.

LINDSAY: Is that so?

VISTULA: Can't help myself and if I don't speak I'll strike her.

LINDSAY: You have struck her.

VISTULA: I have and I was sorry.

LINDSAY: She also has a soul.

VISTULA: She has a soul and I hate it.

LINDSAY: You should be ashamed.

VISTULA: I'm not.

LINDSAY: You should be.

VISTULA: I don't deny I should be.

LINDSAY: I frequently experience an irritation when I deal with you.

VISTULA: Oh.

LINDSAY: Some habit. Some inflection. Anything. But I don't advertize my irritation.

VISTULA: Advertize it if you want to.

LINDSAY: I don't want to, but the tolerance I feel towards you is –

VISTULA: Tolerance?

LINDSAY: Yes, and this tolerance is –

(With a swift movement, VISTULA slaps LINDSAY over the cheek. Both women are shocked.)

VISTULA: I'll apologize for that.

(She bites her lip… LINDSAY stares…)

Oh let me apologize for that –

(LINDSAY strides out… VISTULA sways… The SERVANTS ignore her…)

HEBBEL: Shh…

VISTULA: Mmm…

HEBBEL: Shh…

(VISTULA shrugs wearily…)

VISTULA: How hateful to be tolerated… *(She picks up the bucket.)*

HEBBEL: It's coming to an end…

VISTULA: It is, is it…?

HEBBEL: Oh, yes.

(VISTULA goes out. The SERVANTS are picking up. A pause of labour…)

Oh, yes.

(They move like gatherers of crops.)

Oh, yes.
The fact is I have wisdom but I have no intention
whatsoever of dispensing it to you.
What would you do with it, in any case…?
Alter bits and claim it was your own.
I've seen it…!
Seen it, I've suffered it…! The very phrases…!
Oh, the reputations of these plagiarists… dwarfed my
own…
Plead, by all means.
Hammer on my doors…
Like distraught women who suspect their abducted infants
are hanging from the stairs…
Bang, bang…!
Oh, bang, bang…!

(A figure has entered. He is covered in a fine dust. The SERVANTS neither recognize nor acknowledge him. He looks around…)

GODANSK: I need water…

(They are silent.)

To be precise, it is not I that needs the water. I have a
horse.

(HEBBEL gazes at him…)

The horse needs water…

(HEBBEL'S stare renders GODANSK uncomfortable…)

It's a dancing horse… *(Pause…)*
It was not bred for distances… *(Pause…)*
Very well, if there is no water, I must – *(He goes to move, stops.)*

There must be water here.

(His firm tone causes the SERVANTS to look to each other…)

There is no other building anywhere near here so you must oblige me.

(They are still, afraid…)

I am a courier

HEBBEL: On a dancing horse…!

(HEBBEL'S scoffing tone draws GODANSK's curiosity. He walks to the bed…)

GODANSK: You have identified the first of many peculiarities that attend on this particular undertaking.

HEBBEL: Are there others? I don't speak much. I keep my wisdom to myself.

GODANSK: Several.

HEBBEL: Name another.

GODANSK: The stable was full of horses any one of which could easily outdistance mine. Younger animals in good condition and familiar with the road. Mine has rarely been outside the show arena.

HEBBEL: Fascinating but I must not become excited does yours walk on hind legs? *(He scoffs…)*

Oh, dear, I am becoming animated and you will extract something from me I've no desire to impart…! No, there is no water here.

(The SERVANTS, who had ceased collecting, return to their labour. GODANSK watches them…)

What's wrong with a motorbike…?

(Pause… GODANSK turns to him again…)

GODANSK: That also struck me as odd. And odder still is the fact that in the first place I was ordered to walk.

HEBBEL: Walk…!

GODANSK: Yes. The dancing horse was a concession to me, given my long service, a reward for loyalty. *(Pause…)*

HEBBEL: No, it's a pity about the water…

(GODANSK glares at the old man, then turns on his heel.)

GODANSK: I'll find it myself and God help anyone who obstructs me…!

(He strides out… As he does so, LINDSAY surges in.)

LINDSAY: There's a horse in the yard…!

HEBBEL: It dances…

(SHARDLO hurries in from the opposite side.)

SHARDLO: Have you seen the horse?

HEBBEL: It dances…

LINDSAY: Some stranger's here.

HEBBEL: On its hind legs apparently.

LINDSAY: But who?

HEBBEL: I denied him water but he became coercive.

LINDSAY: Who did?

HEBBEL: The courier.

LINDSAY: Courier?

SHARDLO: Give him water, whoever he is. And tell him to go.

HEBBEL: This horse was considered preferable to a motorbike.

SHARDLO: *(Fretting.)* This is the problem with the road.

LINDSAY: Is the road a problem?

SHARDLO: It draws strangers.

LINDSAY: Rather few…

SHARDLO: Rather few but we have no time to waste on strangers. Not now. Not with the crisis –

(The drone of an aircraft. The SERVANTS, who have almost finished clearing the last drop, gaze upwards in unison…)

Oh, and we have so much to do…!

(The plane passes. Leaflets begin to flutter down… GODANSK enters… He looks at them…)

GODANSK: Why do you say there is no water? There are three troughs and a standpipe in the yard…

(They look blankly at him.)

IT IS AGAINST THE LAW TO HINDER OR OBSTRUCT A MESSENGER.

(Pause… The leaflets trickle down. With a sudden gesture GODANSK plucks one out of the air. He reads it…)

SHARDLO: That also is against the law.

(GODANSK ignores her remark and continues reading…)

That also is against the –

GODANSK: Shh. *(Pause. He completes the reading of the leaflet. He thrusts it at SHARDLO.)*

It's a poem…!

SHARDLO: Yes…

GODANSK: I don't like poetry.

SHARDLO: Then they have entirely wasted their efforts.

GODANSK: In my case certainly. *(He withdraws his hand, screws up the leaflet, drops it to the floor…)*

On the other hand, others may well be susceptible.

SHARDLO: That would explain the prohibition on the reading or disseminating of the leaflets.

GODANSK: Yes. *(He looks at her…)*

Much of what the government decrees is correct, even
if it does not always seem so at the time. Sometimes its
decisions appear arbitrary, even illogical. One puzzles
over the peculiar and contradictory nature of its decisions,
thinking some error must have occurred, if not at the point
of decision, then in the system of communications, an
official misreading a letter in a word, a typist momentarily
losing concentration when a man she loves appears in
view. Invariably, the errors are our own in not possessing
the subtlety of mind to match the complex mechanisms of
the ministry. At least, this has been my own experience.
Others may disagree.

HEBBEL: So there is a reason why you have no motorbike…?

GODANSK: I don't know.

HEBBEL: And being denied a motorbike, you are also denied
a horse…?

GODANSK: I have a horse.

HEBBEL: You have a horse but it prefers to dance on its hind
legs…!

GODANSK: Yes, but the obvious drawbacks of a performing
horse as a mount for a government messenger are in my
case amply compensated for.

HEBBEL: By what?

(Pause… GODANSK looks critically at HEBBEL…)
By what?
(GODANSK stares… HEBBEL shrugs…)

LINDSAY: I feel sure the Citizen Messenger must –

HEBBEL: What is he saying? On the one hand that the
decision to supply him with a dancing horse reflects the as
yet indecipherable wisdom of the government department
that concerns itself with messengers, but on the other that
he has himself discovered means by which to frustrate

precisely these complex and byzantine arrangements, for example, by placing the horse on a railway track. Is that what he is saying? I like to know what people are saying.

SHARDLO: Be quiet, you are an idiot.

HEBBEL: All my life I have sought explanations. All my life I have been denied them.

LINDSAY: Yes…! Yes…! It's true, you have suffered…! *(She throws her arms round HEBBEL.)*

GODANSK: I can only say that in selecting me to bear this particularly important message, the provision of an apparently imperfect horse was negated to a considerable extent by my well-known expertize in short-cuts, cross-country riding, the seasonal effects of rainfall in this region on the height of rivers, and so on, all significant factors in determining the choice of courier from among a group some of whom were young and inexperienced. I admit, as we plunged through bracken and galloped over estuaries, I pondered these seeming contradictions, but to no avail. All will become clear later, I have no doubt, if not to me, to others…

HEBBEL: Will it…! Will it become clear, however…?

(GODANSK shrugs…)

SHARDLO: We have delayed you by this inquisition on the nature of things, Mr –

GODANSK: Godansk –

SHARDLO: Mr Godansk, and now you will be obliged to employ even more of your special skills to compensate for time lost at this unscheduled stop –

(GODANSK bows very slightly.)

Just as we must now work even harder to assemble all that we require for –

HEBBEL: Was it unscheduled…?

(They look at him…)

Or, looked at from another point of view, even if it were unscheduled, it might nevertheless be true that in stopping he evaded an encounter with highwaymen, murderers, those who prey on messengers and devotees of dancing horses who would most certainly have detected in its prancing style the origins of this particular and irresistible animal, mud-spattered as it certainly must be, ungroomed and unribboned…!

SHARDLO: OH, DO CEASE THIS, OH, DO CEASE…!

(She closes her eyes in agony…)

The crisis will
The crisis must
The terrible cleanliness of the crisis

VISTULA: *(Entering, seeing the SERVANTS staring idly…)* Pick up…! Pick up…!

(LINDSAY holds SHARDLO in her arms. The SERVANTS begin again to clear the floor. GODANSK briskly leaves. SHARDLO frees herself from LINDSAY's embrace, and smoothes her clothes, wiping her palms on her skirt.)

SHARDLO: How horrible that man made me. I was unfamiliar to myself.

VISTULA: You say that as if. Forgive my impertinence but you are always saying that. Isn't she? (*She looks to LINDSAY.*)

SHARDLO: Am I…?

VISTULA: As if there was another you.

SHARDLO: *(To HEBBEL.)* I apologize. I called you an idiot.

VISTULA: As if this other you was – what – immaculate – and we –

SHARDLO: We must get on –

VISTULA: Dustmen, messengers, pastry cooks, etcetera, we –

SHARDLO: Please –

VISTULA: We spoil this you, we smudge and smear it with our
  presence. *(SHARDLO looks at VISTULA.)*

SHARDLO: Well, perhaps you do… spoil it… perhaps it should
  be spoiled –

  OH GOD

  OH GOD

  HE HAS LEFT HIS WALLET

  (She beckons to the SERVANTS…) Run after him…!

  *(They throw down their baskets and hurtle off. HEBBEL is heard
  to chuckle… SHARDLO turns on him.)*

  What is funny…!

  (HEBBEL is silent…)

  Is it funny that we now must go about our business in the
  certainty that at any moment some stranger will burst in
  and throw us into absolute and total disarray, distracting us
  from all the meticulous and *(She stops…)*

  And you cannot have that bed. You cannot occupy that
  bed like that.

HEBBEL: Like what? How should I occupy it…?

SHARDLO: I don't know –

HEBBEL: You would prefer me horizontal…?

SHARDLO: I don't know, I only know the bed is

  *(She stops again… Her body heaves… LINDSAY extends a comforting
  hand to her…)*

  How absurd… I am unsettled by a single interruption
  when… the crisis… when it comes… will consist of
  interruption… will be nothing but perpetual interruption…
  interruption to the extent that we will cease to recognize it
  as such… *(She smiles…)*

  Order, which we now take as the basis of our life, the very
  thing that permits so much reflection, will evaporate in

the heat of crisis, we will exist not in our heads but in our fingertips…! *(The SERVANTS return.)*

Did you find him…?

SERVANTS: Gone, Miss…

SHARDLO: Yes, no doubt he leapt into his saddle, dug in his spurs and –

VISTULA: He'll be back –

SHARDLO: Of course he will –

VISTULA: Half-way up some mountain pass he'll think –

LINDSAY: To spare him even greater loss of hours I'll –

VISTULA: *(To the SERVANTS.)* Pick up…! Pick up…!

LINDSAY: I'll hang his satchel on the gate –

HEBBEL: Peculiar –

LINDSAY: We need not see him, he can –

VISTULA: Snatch it at a gallop…!

HEBBEL: Peculiar –

SHARDLO: *(Irritably.)* What is, what is peculiar…!

(They look at HEBBEL.)

HEBBEL: I'm afraid to speak…! So often, I'm afraid to speak…!

SHARDLO: Good, you have had a lifetime of speaking –

LINDSAY: Shh –

SHARDLO: He has, he has spoken too much…

HEBBEL: Yes, far too much, and everything I said was thieved by others –

SHARDLO: God knows why –

HEBBEL: BECAUSE IT WAS A WEALTH AND ALL THAT'S WEALTH IS STOLEN. *(Pause…)*

SHARDLO: Yes…
Yes…
That's obvious…

LINDSAY: *(To HEBBEL.)* Don't be –

(HEBBEL sobs…)

SHARDLO: I'm sorry.

VISTULA: *(To the SERVANTS, who have gawped…)* Pick up…!
Pick up…!

SHARDLO: I'm sorry.

LINDSAY: *(To HEBBEL…)* Shh… Sh…

VISTULA: I think you are almost entirely without charity. I think that's admirable but also I want to kill you.

SHARDLO: I said I'm sorry.

VISTULA: Yes and not one syllable was from the heart.

SHARDLO: I have no heart. That is something we long ago established.

HEBBEL: *(Recovered in an instant.)* Peculiar because what courier worthy of the name ever removes his satchel? Is the satchel of a courier not the vital element of his anatomy? Is it not more intimate to him than his liver or his kidney? He might as well have left his eyes lying on the table… *(Pause…)*

Possibly he is not a courier at all, therefore, but someone masquerading as a courier…

LINDSAY: The enemy…?

HEBBEL: The enemy, certainly they have agents dressed as couriers, it would be the first thing they would think of, but they would not I daresay mount their impostors on circus horses, they would, unless I underestimate their genius for complication, place them on motorbikes, motorbikes of precisely the same manufacture as our own…

(Pause…VISTULA reaches for the wallet…)

SHARDLO: I don't think we should look at it.

(VISTULA's hand is poised.)

I don't think we should permit ourselves to be distracted from the task in hand by speculating as to whether this intruder was a proper courier or not. Who cares if he is genuine? And if he is an enemy, what is that to us? The crisis will almost at once obliterate any distinction between the enemy and those we call our own. That is surely an aspect of its magnificence?

(VISTULA's hand falls…)

I think enough time has been wasted on the –

LINDSAY: Anyway, it's locked.

(They look at her.)

The satchel. *(Pause… She shrugs…)*
It has a massive lock on it…

HEBBEL: WHO'S GOT THE KEY...! *(He chuckles.)*

SHARDLO: Shut up or I shall tip you out of bed and you can crawl about on all fours arguing –

VISTULA: *(To SHARDLO.)* Why are you such a –

SHARDLO: HE ENRAGES ME HE IS ENTIRELY AND EGREGIOUSLY THE THING THAT MAKES ME ACHE FOR DEATH

(She sways… VISTULA stares at her… LINDSAY breaks the tension.)

LINDSAY: I'll organize the blankets…

(She turns to go. SHARDLO turns to her…)

SHARDLO: Can't you see…

(LINDSAY stops…)

Oh can't you see… I'm so… near to… near to something which… *(She bites her lip…)*

Of course you can see…! You see too much…!

(LINDSAY spontaneously kisses her and goes out…)

VISTULA: *(To SHARDLO, cruelly.)* And the pain of others is –

HEBBEL: A GARDEN.

(VISTULA looks at HEBBEL…)

A garden through which she walks stooping to take great lungfuls of sweet odour… (*He sneers at VISTULA.*)

YOU ARE POOR AND SHE IS EXCELLENT

(He glares.)

The more so because she sees through me. *(He turns to SHARDLO.)*

I don't require the bed. Chuck me! Chuck me!

SHARDLO: *(To VISTULA…)* This vile old man's endorsement makes me shudder, believe me…

(HEBBEL chuckles.)

VISTULA: Yes, and you should shudder, it should scald your skin to feel the truth of these appalling compliments shower you…

(SHARDLO stares at VISTULA… She sways a little between temper and resignation…)

SHARDLO: All right… *(She gropes with her hands…)*
Go wherever you –

VISTULA: I AM SO –

SHARDLO: Wherever you were going –

VISTULA: SO –

SO –

(She shuts her eyes tightly, then sweeps out. SHARDLO is quite still. The SERVANTS pick up paper. SHARDLO remains thus, observed by HEBBEL, then she herself leaves. The SERVANTS, as if by tacit agreement, straighten their aching backs, rub their shoulders. This distant sound of a horse's hooves. The SERVANTS exchange glances. HEBBEL, as if by instinct, disappears into the depths of the bed from which he emerged... The SERVANTS resume their labour as the sound of the courier comes closer and stops... GODANSK enters. He looks at the backs of the SERVANTS...)

GODANSK: Cease that now.

(They turn to peer like curious cattle...)

That futile labour.

(They stare...)

Out.

(He jerks his head... They look at one another, and concede. When they have gone, GODANSK goes to his satchel... He examines the lock. He satisfies himself it has not been tampered with. He looks around him swiftly. He stoops, picks up a poem, reads it. LINDSAY enters, alerted. GODANSK screws the paper into a ball in his fist.)

Why was this not hung from the gate?

LINDSAY: *(Puzzled...)* We –

GODANSK: My satchel. Given the loss of my precious time incurred by the error I had made in forgetting my satchel, and the further loss entailed in dismounting, tethering my horse and coming through the courtyards to this place in order to retrieve it, it would seem entirely proper and responsible to have hung it from a nail or better still, driven a stake into the ground so that I might have swept it up into my arms without quitting the saddle.

LINDSAY: We considered all those things *(She stares boldly at him...)*

Arguments were advanced in favour of hanging it from the gate and driving poles into the ground. Following

your tracks in relays and even more outlandish proposals
were seriously entertained. We concluded however that
the contents of the satchel must be of such significance,
not to mention value, that to expose them to the risk
of theft by suspending them from a pole or entrusting
them to servants would be a greater recklessness than
the recklessness of obliging you to return through these
labyrinthine courtyards. You ought to be grateful. There
was some expense of intellectual energy and even temper
entailed in this. We quarrelled. Oaths were uttered. Can I
fetch you something? I like your face. It is however, coated
in dust. I'll wash it. I'll kiss your mouth. Women must be
forever. You left your satchel and I was the reason. Feel me
beneath my skirt. Feel me. My name is Lindsay but I know
the detrimental quality of names. Give me another, I'll take
it as my own. I have a room on the second staircase –

(VISTULA enters…)

He left his satchel…! But you know…!

VISTULA: The servants have stopped working…

GODANSK: I told them so.

VISTULA: You are a courier.

GODANSK: Yes, but the sight of their futile efforts obliged me
to overstep my authority. It happens frequently.

VISTULA: That is an unfortunate characteristic, if I may say so.

GODANSK: I am certain it will lead to my death.

LINDSAY: He is staying for a little – I say little – why not a
great deal of – refreshment…

GODANSK: *(With a slight bow.)* You are too generous –

LINDSAY: Not at all –

GODANSK: I must however, refrain from losing further time –

LINDSAY: But that's absurd…!

GODANSK: Possibly, but –

LINDSAY: No, that is really, really absurd, to say you must
  not lose more time when you have already forfeited God
  knows how long by your own incompetence and now are
  quite prepared to offend the laws of hospitality by – oh, go
  if you want to, go, go, I've no interest in preparing meals,
  it's not my vocation, ask her, it's not, is it…? *(She looks at
  VISTULA… Then swiftly back to GODANSK.)*

  Do you like bread? My father was a wood cutter, but he
  did not eat bread. *(Pause…)*

  I mention that because… *(She shrugs.)*

  The outdoor life… air and forests… you'd think –

  (He is still, his eyes on VISTULA…)

  Bread or not…?

  *(The sound of an aircraft fills the air. They are quite still as it
  passes, fades…)*

GODANSK: Possibly the sole advantage in having been
  provided with a circus animal is its relative immunity to
  taking fright. The shrieks of children, the discharge of guns,
  brass instruments and so on, have no perceptible effect on
  her, but low-flying planes might cause her to rear and jerk
  the halter from the ring, or given the antiquity of this place,
  pluck the ring out of the wall…

  (He turns to go. The first poems cascade from the sky…)

LINDSAY: Are you coming back…?

  (He looks at her…)

  I ask because… I know I shall be more than a little piqued
  if having gone to the expense of time and energy in
  making you a sandwich you simply – *(She stops…)*

  I say a sandwich, but possibly like my father, you don't like
  bread…? *(Pause…)*

  Leave your satchel, won't you…?

(He goes out, the satchel over his shoulder… The two women are still in the falling leaflets…)

VISTULA: He despises you…

LINDSAY: I don't think so…

VISTULA: Yes, he despises you and the more you –

LINDSAY: I don't think he does –

VISTULA: The more you –

LINDSAY: I don't think he despises me at all –

VISTULA: What does he care for your father's antipathy for bread?

LINDSAY: I never had a father –

VISTULA: What –

LINDSAY: Silly –

VISTULA: What –

LINDSAY: I want a little happiness –

VISTULA: You just –

LINDSAY: Before the crisis comes from him from anyone –

VISTULA: YOU JUST SAID YOU –

LINDSAY: DON'T SLAP ME.

DON'T.

YOU MUST STOP SLAPPING PEOPLE.

(VISTULA's hand is raised but the blow does not fall…)

I lie all the time. I have always lied. I feel certain that the crisis will cure me of lying but will it make me happy?

VISTULA: No.

LINDSAY: Exactly. I am making him a sandwich.

(She goes out smartly. VISTULA stands in the falling leaflets… GODANSK returns… He looks at VISTULA…)

GODANSK: This profusion of leaflets, or more precisely, this concentration of leaflets, which may or may not be profuse when considered from the point of view of an overall strategy of leafleting – the availability of pilots and of paper, of suitably patriotic poems, etcetera – but which certainly appears profuse when viewed from this single place, is no more than the consequence of your isolation…

(VISTULA examines GODANSK… The leaflets cease…)

Your isolation and your position relative to the road, both of which became evident to me as I travelled here, away, and back again…

(They do not remove their eyes from one another…)

The road being a ribbon of white chalk not only visible but compelling, hypnotic to a navigator's eye and this building notwithstanding its decay being a welcome and gratifying subject of human occupation in a landscape which is frankly monotonous, the domain of cattle and predatory birds…

(Pause…)

One must also acknowledge that universal element in the human character which prefers a safe journey to an heroic death and see these storms of paper as a reflection of the pilot's natural inclination to discharge his burden over an unprotected target rather than expose himself and his crew, some of whom will certainly be married and others mothers' sons, to the aerial defences of a town… *(Pause…)*

VISTULA: Yes. *(Pause…)*

Yes. That was my conclusion also.

(GODANSK smiles, strokes his chin… Pause…)

She is taking such a long time with that sandwich –

GODANSK: Oh, please don't hurry her on my account –

VISTULA: Don't hurry her?

GODANSK: She might slip, the knife might slice her finger –

VISTULA: That's very thoughtful of you but surely –

GODANSK: Thoughtful? No, I was concerned to forestall an accident –

VISTULA: YOU'RE IN A HURRY, AREN'T YOU? *(Pause…)*

What with this – *(She shrugs…)*
Inappropriate horse and… *(She lifts her hands…)*
Important orders, I… *(Pause… She shuts her eyes…)*
People lie and… lie… and… *(Pause…)*
The way they… speak… and stand even is… *(Her eyes open again…)*

This has to be picked up… this paper… because to be so – supine – in the face of things is – it's not the orders of the magistrates, it's a moral and – *(She moves swiftly to call the SERVANTS.)*

PICK UP…!

PICK UP…!

(She goes out… GODANSK does not move… HEBBEL begins to stir in the bed… He appears, having hauled himself onto the pillows…)

HEBBEL: Killer…

GODANSK: Who…?

HEBBEL: Her…

GODANSK: Which one…?

HEBBEL: Killer…

(GODANSK turns to HEBBEL at last…)

GODANSK: What is this place…? It resembles a convent and like many convents it seems at first glance to be fortified. The moat, for example, whilst stagnant now, suggests some military function, but its width is insufficient to discourage access to the walls, and the walls themselves, whilst inordinately thick, lack height. A determined thief could make his way into the heart of it, given he was not discouraged by the puzzling nature of the courtyards, none of which is connected to another except in a wholly arbitrary way...

(He waits for HEBBEL to reply... HEBBEL merely looks at GODANSK...)

Notwithstanding this, it might well be a convent, since I have observed not a few convents are located in buildings the original function of which had little or nothing to do with the service of God... *(He waits in vain...)*

On the other hand, where is the bell...? *(Pause...)*

The crucifix...? *(Pause... He resolutely pursues the argument.)*

Unless some persecution has obliged the women to conceal their practises, it is hard to avoid the conclusion that despite appearances, this place is not a convent at all, but rather –

(SHARDLO enters with a sandwich on a plate...)

SHARDLO: You required a sandwich...?

(GODANSK smiles.)

This is a sandwich.

(He bows his head slightly...)

Don't please, take too long to eat the sandwich.

GODANSK: Don't take to long to eat it...?

SHARDLO: I want to wash the plate.

(Pause... GODANSK nods...)

You are in any case, unlikely to want to eat it slowly, given the even greater urgency that now –

(She stops, as the SERVANTS, with their baskets, appear and begin working on the litter...)

Having gone without the satchel, and been obliged to retrace your steps you must be frantically impatient to make up lost time... *(She extends the plate to GODANSK.)*

It stands to reason.

(He takes it…)

GODANSK: Certainly, it would seem so given your own
estimation of the situation. *(He bites into the sandwich, chews
it thoroughly, swallows…)*

And I don't criticize. One who is relatively stationary
enjoys a perspective of such a different order from that lent
to another by his incessant mobility. It is frequently the
case with the best couriers that on cresting an escarpment
one's gaze detects a vastly shorter route – perhaps through
woodland even a few hours earlier impenetrable to the eye
– which if taken, might have halved his journey time… *(He
bites again, chews unhurriedly, swallows…)*

Just such a case occurred on leaving here. Even in retracing
my steps several times I might cover that same stretch and
still have time to spare… *(He bites, chews, swallows…)*

But you require the plate… *(He bites again…)*

HEBBEL: Why didn't she wrap it in a cloth? *(Pause…)*
Or paper…?

(Pause… They ignore his interventions…)

A courier is used to eating in the saddle…
Singing in the saddle...

(GODANSK finishes the final part of the sandwich.)

Dying in the saddle, probably… *(Pause…)*
Yet she provides a plate… *(Pause…)*
It's inconsistent…

*(GODANSK goes smartly to SHARDLO with the plate. She
hesitates. She accepts it. GODANSK turns on his heel to leave, goes
three paces, stops…)*

GODANSK: This message…

(The SERVANTS cease… Their heads turn… Pause…)

I don't know what it says…

*(They stare… A pause… SHARDLO lets fall the plate, which
shatters…The SERVANTS turn, shocked…)*

SHARDLO: Don't just stare… fetch a dustpan quick… quick…!

(They all turn to leave.)

Not all of you…!

(They hesitate… One goes still looking back apprehensively… GODANSK has not moved… Pause…)

How should you know…? You are the courier…

(GODANSK looks bewildered… Then he leaves abruptly. SHARDLO is still, then recovers her animation…)

The crisis… its peculiar effects…! And that is the merest indication of the profound and subterranean changes it will inflict on all of us…! A courier, whose honour and efficiency are beyond reproach, finds himself troubled by his ignorance of the contents of his saddle-bag when that ignorance is precisely what qualifies him for his task…!

(She shrugs, laughs…)

Everything that seems confirmed, self-evident and beyond evaluation suddenly is – *(She controls her pleasure…)*

Not *suddenly*…

It will have *seemed* sudden, when viewed in retrospect… in actual fact, it will imitate a cataclysm of the natural world whose origins are subtle and scarcely observed… the first few flurries of an avalanche… the rising of a river, and the uncommon anxiety of swans… manifestations of overwhelming alteration which only the most perceptive minds – those predisposed to welcome it – can sense before it topples and crushes them beneath its debris…

(Pause…)

If it does crush…! Some will be crushed, but others, they will – *(Pause…)*

Obviously emerge… *(Pause…)*

HEBBEL: Me… I…

(SHARDLO looks at HEBBEL.)

Shan't emerge…

SHARDLO: Not you, no…

116

HEBBEL: HAVE I EVER HAVE I EVEN ONCE

SHARDLO: *(Fatigued.)* I don't know…

HEBBEL: Never
  Never
  Emerged…

SHARDLO: *(With a gesture.)* I haven't the time or patience to –

HEBBEL: And what prevented that emergence…?

SHARDLO: Others…?

HEBBEL: OTHERS YES…

  (She stares at him, half-pitying, half-bemused…)

SHARDLO: Yes…
  Yes, and how… insignificant… that suddenly appears…

HEBBEL: Yes, oh, yes…

SHARDLO: *(Tearing her gaze from him.)* I must –

HEBBEL: Insignificance itself –

  (She is departing…)

  YOU GAVE HIM A PLATE…

  (She stops. She slowly turns back to him.)

  I am not stupid. How much better it would have been
  if I were stupid. I longed for it. You heard me, I craved
  stupidity. The stupid are not plagiarized.

  (SHARDLO shuts her eyes in her impatience…)

SHARDLO: You were never, never to my knowledge,
  plagiarized…

HEBBEL: Ha…!

SHARDLO: *(Patiently…)* As for the plate to which you are
  according such inordinate significance –

HEBBEL: Me…? I'm not…!

SHARDLO: THE SANDWICH WAS HANDED TO ME ON A
   PLATE

HEBBEL: Obviously –

SHARDLO: I DID NOT PLACE IT ON THE PLATE, I COLLECTED
   IT ON THE PLATE AND DELIVERED IT TO –

HEBBEL: So…?

SHARDLO: SO

   SO

   OH, ALL THIS IS *(She shuts her eyes…)*

   GOING UNDER THE AVALANCHE…!

   *(She strides out… The SERVANTS pick up paper. LINDSAY
   enters… She drifts… Staring at the two SERVANTS… She hugs
   herself, for comfort…)*

LINDSAY: How splendid to live a life on horseback…

   (They ignore her…)

   Of course it is easy to exaggerate the pleasure of an
   outdoor life… for one thing, in this particular region we are
   blessed with too much rain… but even rain… if you were
   clad in oilskins… its faint patter on your hood… might
   be…

   *(The SERVANT enters with a dustpan and broom and sweeps up
   the remains of the plate…)*

   Music of a sort… I'm certain as he gallops over flooded
   meadows, the hooves of his white mare flinging –

THIRD SERVANT: *(Unbending again.)* He's in the fifteenth
   courtyard, Miss…

   (LINDSAY stares at the SERVANT…)

LINDSAY: He's…?

THIRD SERVANT: *(Beating the broom on the side of the pan.)* Lost.
   (She goes out again… LINDSAY goes to follow her.)

LINDSAY: Lost…? *(She frowns.)*
Lost…?

HEBBEL: I'm not particularly perceptive…
(VISTULA enters. LINDSAY turns to her.)

LINDSAY: He's lost, apparently…

HEBBEL: It was never the accuracy of my perceptions that I valued in myself…

LINDSAY: *(Shrugging.)* Wandering in the courtyards…

HEBBEL: But all the same…

LINDSAY: *(To HEBBEL.)* Shh…!

VISTULA: How peculiar… when on previous occasions he was able to negotiate the entrance he should now be sacrificing vital minutes by –

LINDSAY: I'll go to the tower –

HEBBEL: GO TO THE TOWER YES –

LINDSAY: *(Turning on him.)* Be quiet, I said –
(HEBBEL chuckles…)
And from the tower –

HEBBEL: SIGNAL HIM –

LINDSAY: *(Furiously.)* PRECISELY MY INTENTION
(She leaves the room, as the SERVANT returns…)

HEBBEL: AND WAVE… IF HE IS UNOBSERVANT… WAVE…
Your skirt…
Your heart…
Your underwear… *(He laughs, mildly…)*

VISTULA: You enrage everybody…

HEBBEL: Yes…

VISTULA: By announcing what is obvious…

HEBBEL: Yes…

VISTULA: When what is obvious –

HEBBEL: Is the very thing nobody wants to hear…! *(He grins…)*

VISTULA: Yes… on the other hand… this tin whistle… this tuneless flute… of your incessant –

HEBBEL: Oh, terrible, I know –

VISTULA: It is, yes –

HEBBEL: I know, I know –

VISTULA: Grates on every –

HEBBEL: Sets your teeth on edge, I know… *(He looks at her…)*

VISTULA: Yes… *(She shrugs.)*
You know…
(She is about to leave when GODANSK enters.)

GODANSK: This is ridiculous…!
(She stops. He lifts his shoulders, as if bewildered.)
Since we parted I have been stumbling from one courtyard to another…!
(She turns. The SERVANTS look up…)
The error was entirely mine. For some reason, on my departing here I turned left three times in succession when I knew perfectly well the opposite was the direction I required. As I wandered from place to place I tried to understand the reason for this apparently wilful miscalculation. I could only deduce that having drilled myself so thoroughly to turn right, the very recollection of the fact I had required such discipline in the first place compelled me to opt for the less familiar word –

HEBBEL: This happens –

GODANSK: This does happen, and certainly it can only be the effect of excessive repetition. I had memorized the word when I should have done better to memorize the wall, the paving, the situation of a sprouting weed, though it must be said even here the absolute similarity of things might well have rendered such a mnemonic less effective than you might expect. But this was only the beginning of my troubles… Recognizing the gravity of my error, I resorted to the expedient of whistling my horse –

HEBBEL: A courier would…!

GODANSK: A courier would not fail to summon his horse, if only to enable him to spare his legs by riding through the courtyards, and this I did, I whistled her and certainly she heard, she heard and she obeyed, her loyalty was unimpeachable, but what neither of us understood, or even having understood, would have possessed the knowledge to effectively mitigate against, was the wholly deceptive nature of an echo in enclosed spaces when the walls are of a certain height relative to the angle of the roofs. Thus, she always sought me in a place, which if I had visited at all, I had certainly left minutes or perhaps only seconds before she arrived there. I suffered the profound frustration of hearing her hooves clattering on cobbles which for all I knew, lined the very courtyard next to that in which I stood, yet running in this direction only rendered us further apart…! *(He looks at VISTULA, shaking his head…)*

Predictably, such a nightmare could only be resolved by accident. Coming past here for what may well have been the fifth or seventh time, I saw the broken pieces of the plate on which I think the sandwich had been served to me, or possibly another plate from the same service but all the same sufficient to persuade me I –

VISTULA: Where exactly were the pieces of the plate…?
(Pause…)

GODANSK: Not far beyond the door, they –

VISTULA: I do find servants odd.
(Pause. The SERVANTS hang their heads…)

Odd

And

What is it surely not simple idleness not sullen anger
sabotage or anything so malevolent as that it comes from
some obscure instinct and it isn't mutiny it's *(Pause…)*

I wish I knew what it was… *(Pause…)*

And sometimes they are scrupulous…! *(She bites her lip.)*

It could be the weather… I am affected by the weather
why shouldn't they be today for example it's oppressive
and these little flies…

HEBBEL: And still he lingers…! *(He scoffs…)*

I hate to say what can only spoil the comfortable and
collusive nature of this silence but

Or do I

No

Try honesty

The unplumbed horrors of authentic honesty

I don't hate it at all I like it

I announce the peculiar lethargy of a courier

There

HATE AWAY LADIES…!

(LINDSAY enters, sees GODANSK…)

LINDSAY: He hasn't gone…!

HEBBEL: *(Replete with sarcasm…)* Gone? No, he's still here…

LINDSAY: I'm breathless… *(She hangs her head, breathing deeply.)*

HEBBEL: Far from gone, his footsteps are, as it were, encased
in lead, no longer the swift servant of his master Mercury,
he has the lumbering instincts of an antediluvian reptile for
whom mud, not cloud, is his natural environment –

VISTULA: All right, lie down, now…

HEBBEL: I will, I will lie down…

(VISTULA goes to assist him…)

LINDSAY: I ran up the stairs, I'd forgotten how many flights there are...

HEBBEL: I am lying down...!

LINDSAY: And the view was magnificent, I had forgotten how extensive the view is on a perfect day, but I was not there for the view... I was there to guide you through the courtyards...

GODANSK: Certainly I was in dire need of it...

LINDSAY: You were...? I looked, but I saw nothing, neither you nor your horse...

GODANSK: At the very moment you flung open the window –

LINDSAY: There isn't a window, it's a –

GODANSK: No window...?

LINDSAY: It's open to the elements –

GODANSK: At the very moment you leaned over the parapet, I discovered a vital clue to my whereabouts –

LINDSAY: Good –

GODANSK: A servant's negligence was my salvation –

LINDSAY: Good –

GODANSK: Or else I might have wandered until your cries alerted me –

LINDSAY: If they did alert you... I must admit as I leaned out it occurred to me that my voice, which is not strong, would have been borne away on the wind...

GODANSK: That's something the architect of this place never thought of...! If indeed, it ever occurred to him that the tower might be employed to guide lost messengers through the labyrinth of courtyards...! *(He laughs...)*
Your father is correct however, in his –

LINDSAY: He is not my father… *(Pause…)*

GODANSK: How strange… I could have sworn…

VISTULA: Nor mine, either…

GODANSK: Not yours, either…?

(He walks a little way, profoundly puzzled… The SERVANTS look at him out of the corners of their eyes.)

VISTULA: *(Detecting this.)* Pick up…! Pick up…!

(The drone of an approaching airplane. The SERVANTS ignore VISTULA and gaze into the sky… It passes low… fades… SHARDLO enters… A pause… Leaflets trickle from the sky…)

GODANSK: *(Turning.)* Whose father is he, then…?

(No one replies. The poems fall. GODANSK bends, plucks one off the floor. They stare at him…)

SHARDLO: If you intend to read that, I must warn you I shall inform the relevant authorities.

(He looks at her…)

Alternatively, you can put it in your pocket and at your own risk, examine it elsewhere.

(He is quite still.)

Certainly you may not read it here.

(He screws it into a ball and drops it on the floor.)

WE HAVE SO MUCH TO DO AND YOU ARE A DISTRACTION

(He is still…)

What's more, despite your official status, your continued presence constitutes a trespass –

GODANSK: Is that so?

SHARDLO: Certainly, under the law of 1909.

GODANSK: And that applies to government officials?

SHARDLO: They are included in a sub-section.

GODANSK: Sub-section 8?

SHARDLO: Exactly.

GODANSK: Sub-section 8 has always been the subject of controversy.

SHARDLO: It may well have been.

GODANSK: Some clarification was in preparation when the crisis developed, but so many details had accumulated from reports submitted by couriers, some of whom had been abused and others physically maltreated, pursued by dogs, and even in one case, mauled by a bear that had been educated to identify him by the colour of his tunic, that it required a whole contingent of lawyers to prepare even draft legislation, but these lawyers are now scattered among the many emergency committees that have sprung up to provide for the exigencies of the crisis, causing me to conclude that however pressing the need for unambiguous codification of the law on trespass, we shall for the present need to show considerable restraint in our interpretation of the existing and unsatisfactory paragraphs…

(Pause. They stare at him…)

Not your father, but what else could explain his…

(The leaflets have ceased…)

VISTULA: Pick up…! Pick up…!

(The SERVANTS continue their task.)

SHARDLO: I am not sure you are a courier.

LINDSAY: *(Dismayed…)* Oh, but he –

SHARDLO: He has a courier's bag –

LINDSAY: Not only that –

SHARDLO: And on the bag, a badge –

LINDSAY: I wasn't referring to the badge –

SHARDLO: He could have stolen the bag –

LINDSAY: It's not the bag that –

SHARDLO: Killed a bona fide courier and –

LINDSAY: ALL COURIERS USE MOTORBIKES.

(Pause…SHARDLO is patient. She places the tips of her fingers together…)

SHARDLO: Forgive me, but are you suggesting that the fact of this particular impostor failing to procure a motorbike but appearing on a horse instead, is precisely the evidence that satisfies you as to his authenticity? *(Pause.)*

LINDSAY: Yes

SHARDLO: It's illogical.

LINDSAY: Yes. *(Pause.)*

Yes, it is illogical, I think I intended to say that

HOW SILLY IT DOESN'T MATTER TO ME WHETHER HE STAYS HERE OR NOT My point was this, that had he killed a genuine courier about whose identity there is no question, he could not have been satisfied merely to steal his satchel but, intending to mislead others, would have carried his act to perfection by appearing mounted on his victim's motorbike, that is my contention –

SHARDLO: It's dishonest –

LINDSAY: What is –

SHARDLO: What you're saying –

LINDSAY: Is it –

SHARDLO: Yes, horribly dishonest –

LINDSAY: Is it, why –

SHARDLO: YOU KNOW PERFECTLY WELL –

LINDSAY: Do I? I thought I was putting a case for something which needed clarification –

SHARDLO: *(Turning wearily from her gaze.)* Oh…

VISTULA: *(To LINDSAY.)* She's right, you're lying.

(LINDSAY looks to VISTULA, horrified.)

And that is why she is so offends me. Look at her, quivering, throbbing, incandescent with the satisfaction of exposing your flirtation with a stranger, who, quite possibly, receives –

LINDSAY: Not a flirtation –

VISTULA: A dozen such proposals in a single ride –

LINDSAY: Not a flirtation, I said –

VISTULA: Very well –

LINDSAY: Not a flirtation at all, if you call it a flirtation again I shall do something –

VISTULA: What…?

LINDSAY: I don't know –

VISTULA: I do all the violence round here – *(She laughs, against herself.)*

LINDSAY: Yes, you do –

VISTULA: I am the monster –

LINDSAY: The word flirtation fills me with disgust I hate the word and you employ it precisely to humiliate my instinct which –

VISTULA: I apologize –

LINDSAY: Which I do not deny repudiate or suffer any shame for I do not know if I love this man I simply want him to kiss me I have thought of nothing else since he came here. There. Perhaps you feel the same.

VISTULA: Certainly not.

LINDSAY: Very well, you don't.
 (To SHARDLO.) I was moving beds from the dormitory to the conservatory, shall I continue or –

GODANSK: It gives me no pleasure to be the cause of this dissension that has sprung up between you, I assure you, but whilst it might seem obvious that my swift departure would bring it to a close, things cannot be that simple…

SHARDLO: Why not?

 (He declines to reply…)

 You are in dereliction of your duty, which, if you are a courier, will almost certainly result in your trial and execution, since the death penalty has been restored for the duration of the crisis and reluctant couriers will need to be made examples of, rightly in my opinion, if only to remind the population of the gravity of their situation and the new energies and disciplines that are required if they are to overcome their passive and dilatory – *(She stops…)*

 On the other hand, if you are not a courier but a criminal, it is all the more necessary we eject you now and –

 (She addresses the SERVANTS.) STOP PICKING UP PAPERS NOW

 (They look at one another.)

 Yes

 Return to that another time

 (They straighten up.)

 Escort this man to the gate
 He has a horse I understand
 The horse also
 And shut the gate behind him
 Bolt it
 Bar it
 Unpleasant but we must accustom ourselves to things which in our other life we might have flinched from
 Yes

128

That is how we recognise the crisis
Then come back and carry on

(The SERVANTS shift uneasily, exchanging glances with one another…)

Now, please…

(They put down their baskets and prepare to move towards GODANSK…)

GODANSK: I feel sure you are making a mistake…

SHARDLO: How? In obliging you to carry out your orders…?

GODANSK: Quite possibly.

SHARDLO: How can that constitute a mistake?

GODANSK: I don't know.

SHARDLO: You don't know why you should not carry out your orders?

GODANSK: I cannot say with any certainty why I should not carry out my orders. On the other hand many things suggest that these orders are perhaps not the most suitable orders, or that, even given their suitability, they are being frustrated by circumstances outside of my own control.

SHARDLO: *(With a glance at LINDSAY.)* Her, for example?

GODANSK: It's possible that the love she feels for me, sudden and unexpected as it was, is yet another manifestation of that innate obstruction of my mission that began so long ago with the substitution of a circus horse for my motorbike…

(Pause… The SERVANTS look confused…)

LINDSAY: Yes…!

(She looks to VISTULA… Bites her lip… SHARDLO ignores this. She sways a little.)

SHARDLO: What you are saying is inconsistent.

(GODANSK looks at her…)

Every aspect of things that has hindered your journey has
arrived in the form of an accident, at least as far as you are
concerned. The substitution of a horse for a motorbike,
the fact of the horse's unsuitability for cross-country riding,
the fact that on leaving here you forgot your saddlebag
and your subsequent confusion in the maze of courtyards,
all occurred apparently in contradiction to your will. Your
reluctance to continue with your journey is an altogether
new factor however, not circumstantial in the least, and
motivated possibly by cowardice or desire for a woman
who has had the misfortune to pity you –

LINDSAY: I don't pity him –

SHARDLO: *(To the SERVANTS.)* Please, now, escort him to the
gate.

LINDSAY: Not pity.

SHARDLO: Call it what you like.

LINDSAY: Not pity

SHARDLO: No…

*(The SERVANTS edge towards GODANSK, who bows very slightly
to SHARDLO, and turns on his heel. He walks out smartly. The
SERVANTS follow. The women are still, speechless… At last, they
move, but aimlessly, and stop again…)*

I felt then… *(Pause…)*
In the middle of that argument I felt…

(Pause…)

Oh, that bottomless exhaustion of the soul that's like some
vast bay in which the sea has died… is motionless… the
corpse of the sea beneath my ribs.

VISTULA: *(Extending a hand to her.)* But the words came…

SHARDLO: Yes, they did… *(She shakes her head…)*
Oh, and the crisis rushes on…! Really…! I exchange these

arid syllables with some pensive stranger, but for the last time, surely…!

VISTULA: Surely, yes…!

SHARDLO: He drew me, staggering, back towards my
suicide… *(She shudders…)*
If he comes back, it's you that must – *(She stops…)*
Comes back…? Why should he come back…? *(She laughs, crushes VISTULA's hand in hers.)*

HEBBEL: Of course he will…

(They are still…)

He will…

(Their stillness, their silence is a threat…)

WHY SHOULD I NOT TELL

WHY

WHEN NOTHING ELSE AT ALL

NOTHING

CAN JUSTIFY MY CONTINUING TO SIT THE BLOOD
REVOLVING AND THE KIDNEYS FLUSHING LIQUIDS
IN THEIR DARK AND THICKENING CANALS GASES
EXCRETIONS SQUEALS IN THE BOWEL

I leak the truth…

(Pause… They look at him…)

From *one* orifice… *(He smiles…)*
Malodorous commodity…

(He chuckles… They stare bitterly…)

It's the horse, you see… *(Pause…)*
Its musical inclinations…

(He laughs… They stare…)

As long as I was loved, the truth was something I could
happily forego… is it not the enemy of love, in any case…
but unloved I find it has the fascination of an outlawed
faith… I mutter it… I see the countenances of you all

131

obscured by a cloud… you squirm… you look the other way… Christ announced in Mecca… Luther in Rome…

(Pause… The SERVANTS return… They stand uneasily.)

SHARDLO: *(Turning to them.)* Has he gone…?

SERVANTS: Yes, Miss.

SHARDLO: You saw him?

SERVANTS: Yes, Miss.

SHARDLO: Riding?

SERVANTS: Galloping, Miss.

SHARDLO: Galloping… *(She smiles…)*
You see we recalled him to his duty…! He did not look back?

SERVANTS: Never…

SHARDLO: There you are…! The crisis has this effect on individuals, even those of criminal or idle dispositions, that they are rinsed, cleansed, wrung out of their melancholy introspection and – in a straight line, undeviating, was he?

SERVANTS: Straight for the frontier, Miss…

SHARDLO: I should have liked to see him, the cloud of dust raised by his horse's hooves…

(LINDSAY bites her lip… SHARDLO goes to her, holds her in her arms… The SERVANTS return to their work.)

This is only the beginning of so many pains, pains which will like forest leaves, thickly smother one another in the torrent of their fall… *(Pause… Her expression changes…)*

The frontier…? *(She releases LINDSAY.)*
The frontier…which…?

(The SERVANTS are engrossed in their labour…)

You said the frontier…

SERVANTS: *(Aroused, straightening their backs.)* Miss…?

SHARDLO: Which frontier…?

SERVANTS: *(Pointing.)* It's that way, Miss…

SHARDLO: Of course it is, but… *(Pause… She ponders…)*
He might well be… *(She knits her brows…)*
Why did you say the frontier…?

VISTULA: It lies in that direction –

SHARDLO: *(Crossly.)* I know perfectly well the direction of the
frontier, I wonder why they specified the frontier as his
destination, perhaps he indicated this –

SERVANTS: He said nothing, Miss –

SHARDLO: He said nothing –

SERVANTS: Not one word –

SHARDLO: Not one word did he say and yet they assert
without the slightest hesitation that he was making for
the frontier, these who, for all their loyalty and capacity
for unstinting labour are not known for their speculative
capacities –

VISTULA: You are becoming fretful –

SHARDLO: Am I –

VISTULA: Fretful and ugly, yes –

SHARDLO: There are a hundred places to which a courier
might be despatched between here and the frontier –

VISTULA: Places of no significance –

SHARDLO: Insignificant places, but who are we to judge
their significance in a crisis, quite possibly the crisis
has bestowed significance on farms and hamlets whose
previous obscurity –

LINDSAY: Shh –

SHARDLO: I AM QUITE PREPARED TO BE UGLY.

(A sullen pause… At last SHARDLO shrugs…)

They don't know why they said the frontier… obviously, it was an intuition…

(She is uneasy… She lifts her hand, and lets it fall. VISTULA looks at the curious SERVANTS.)

VISTULA: Pick up…! Pick up…!

(The SERVANTS obey. VISTULA swiftly leaves…)

LINDSAY: I want to see you… I want to witness you… in full possession of yourself… I always have…

(Pause… SHARDLO looks at LINDSAY…)

SHARDLO: Have you…? I'm touched…

LINDSAY: Are you…

SHARDLO: Yes… *(She shrugs…)*
No…
What is it to me that you –

LINDSAY: But not at some appalling cost… to me… *(Pause.)*

SHARDLO: Too bad. *(She lifts her shoulders…)*
It's too bad…!
(LINDSAY stifles a reply. She leaves, bitterly…)
AM I SUPPOSED TO CEASE BECOMING ME FOR YOUR
She's gone
Am I supposed to fade and falter in some airless half-life in order that
She's gone
Like some plant which instead of reaching for the sun for fear its leaves might overshadow others willingly wilts droops turns yellow in obscurity
Anyway she's gone
I HAVE STOOD FIVE TIMES AT THE DOOR OF SUICIDE
No
It's a terrible injustice
Five times

Twice in the moat
Three times in the orchard
Brought gasping from some smothering death
THEY PREFER TO PITY ME THAN THAT I SHOULD STEP
INTO MY OWN CHARACTER

Too bad
Really, just too bad
She's gone I needn't *(Her hand waves in the air. She holds her cheeks in a sudden seizure…)*
You can go, this –
This –
Picking up paper –
Just go –
Go –

(The SERVANTS hesitate… They exchange looks and then go to leave.)

This frontier. *(She becomes upright, still, masterful.)*
It explains everything…

(The SERVANTS hesitate, then go out with their baskets, uneasily… HEBBEL, low in his pillows, observes SHARDLO…)

No, it's hard to resist the feeling that not only my personality but also the objective circumstances of the world militate to bring about my death... *(Pause…)*

And when I say death I do not mean it literally I do not mean silence lifelessness extinction and so on I mean the very low habit of the morning… and the very low habit of the night… *(Pause…)*

The courier is delivering the message which will terminate the crisis… *(Pause…)*

It couldn't be otherwise…!

(She half-laughs, she bites her lip… HEBBEL's long, thin arm reaches out for her, hangs in the air. She sees it without accepting it…)

You know…
How terrible that you know everything…

*(She takes the hand in hers… She presses it to her breast…
Her hands fall… His hand remains… His fingers work at the
buttons of her dress, exposing her breasts. A pause, of wonder
and contemplation… The COURIER enters the room… Neither
SHARDLO nor HEBBEL react, but are still… The COURIER
flings down his satchel… He leans against a wall… A long pause
elapses…)*

GODANSK: We encountered gipsies… *(Pause…)*
These gipsies played violins… *(Pause…)*
To be precise, one viola and three violins… *(Pause…)*

And whereas at one moment we were cantering, the next,
the mare had ceased in her velocity and like a puppet
drawn up on silent strings, was finely balanced on hind
hooves. My astonishment was matched only by my
frustration when she began to dance, to sway from side
to side and drawing back her lips, to whinny an equine
accompaniment… *(Pause…)*

For a while this was humiliating… I, a courier on urgent
business and carrying a possibly significant dispatch
which – so we were constantly reminded at the Academy
of Messengers – might alter the course of History, I was
mounted on a dancing horse so captivated by the music of
a band of pedlars she would not heed even the most savage
application of the spurs…! *(He shakes his head.)*

So I came back.

*(His smile disappears… His stare is fixed on SHARDLO. He defies
her to speak. Their gaze holds, second after second…)*

SHARDLO: *(At last.)* Yes…well, you had no choice…

*(GODANSK leans off the wall… He goes to SHARDLO and taking
her behind, draws her away from HEBBEL's feeble hand. She emits
a single gasp as he sinks with her to the floor… HEBBEL's hand
remains loosely in the air…)*

HEBBEL: *(Without anger or bitterness.)* And this road… this
road to which the pedlars were fixed like greyhounds to
a track… though less urgently… this road could not be

bypassed… four gipsies with their innocuous instruments had more power to disrupt the course of History than forts bristling with rocket-launchers and machine guns…! *(A brief pause…)*

The field which stretched on either side… the meadows… firm and flat… the courier deemed unsuitable, a certain sign of the inevitable deterioration of imagination, I have identified this phenomenon in other walks of life, and in this instance it is perfectly exemplified, THE COURIER'S FIXATION WITH THE ROAD… *(A brief pause…)*

You had no choice and who knows these gipsies were perhaps not gipsies at all, or if indeed they were authentic gipsies, nevertheless authentic gipsies recruited by the agents of a government precisely to distract your mare, and who, had you thrashed her into a state of continuing obedience, might have flung aside their musical disguise and shot you, yes, their quaint clothing possibly bulged with weapons…! *(He chuckles.)*

Certainly one must conclude that all things without exception have conspired to delay the delivery of the courier's despatch…even the flesh of these no-longer young young women…

(A pause…SHARDLO hauls herself from the floor… She wipes her hands on her skirt… She spits at the still-prone GODANSK, who makes no response… She then laughs, half-hysterical… Then she spits on him again… And laughs again… She shakes her head, trying to clear her thoughts…)

SHARDLO: These… vile acts… erupting in the middle of… *(She gestures vaguely…)*

These… perversities of human relations are… *(She shrugs…)*
Obviously… *(She draws her hands down her skirt again.)*
Manifestations of the crisis…
Repellent…
Degenerate…
Necessary…I feel sure…

(With an effort of will she goes to leave the room. She is unsteady however, and almost collides with a wall. She regains her composure. She walks out. In the silence that follows, GODANSK climbs to his feet. An aircraft is heard approaching, low. It passes, the sound fades…)

HEBBEL: The crisis will certainly dispose of me… and that I daresay, is its purpose…

(He laughs. Leaflets tumble from the sky…)

Am I not entitled to view it from my own perspective? Why shouldn't I? Haven't I suffered? I am entitled to conclude that the entire cataclysm that hangs over the world has no other purpose than the disposal of a man who has outlived his time, a man who arguably was never equipped to survive his infancy but who through the untiring ministrations of a possibly deranged parent was enabled to cling to life, to describe life according to his own distorted vision, and to earn the love of certain women. But the game's up. They want the bed. For whom? Some disembowelled wretch who cannot possibly in his final agony comprehend the meaning of his ordeal but believes it to be the consequence of the grinding engines of diplomacy. On the contrary, it is no more than an element of a complex plan for my obliteration.

(GODANSK idly retrieves a leaflet…)

I look forward to it. Long after I am disposed of, in a world replete with values no more sympathetic to me than those which now wash over the world like urine on the floor of a pitching ferry, some disordered mind will alight upon my poetry – some fragment of which has lodged behind a criminal's library shelf – and declare it –

GODANSK: *(Extending the leaflet limply.)* This is yours.

(Pause… HEBBEL is speechless…)

This is… *(He screws it into a ball and throws it down with studied indifference...)*

The problem surrounding my return is complicated. On the one hand, by submitting to the musical fallibility of my mare I was only fulfilling what must have been known, if not intended, by the ministry, namely, that I should be constantly delayed by the sound of instruments, but by not exerting myself to discover an alternative route, I perhaps went further than anyone might have predicted, for an expert courier, which I was, would not allow himself to be frustrated by a gang of gipsies. On the other hand, I must confess to the magnetic effect this building and its occupants has had on me, almost certainly robbing me of that particular energy in enterprise that characterized me only a short time ago. But even that may have been calculated at the highest level. How am I to know? The fact of the matter is that the woman who was here just now not only expected me but was glad of my return, notwithstanding my brutality towards her. I cannot deny I am profoundly troubled by this, not to say –

HEBBEL: *(Still gazing at the floor.)* What do you mean, *mine*…?

(The SERVANTS appear with baskets…)

SERVANTS: Shall we or shan't we…?

(GODANSK looks at them.)

One Miss says pick up, the other says not to.

(VISTULA enters. They flinch and start to gather the leaflets into their baskets.)

VISTULA: The gates were barred…

GODANSK: Closed, certainly…

VISTULA: Barred and bolted…

GODANSK: I leaned from the saddle, pushed, and they swung open.

VISTULA: They were not barred, then…

HOWARD BARKER

GODANSK: Certainly not to me…but others, leaning against
them in an identical way, might have found them
unyielding…

VISTULA: What others?

GODANSK: Are there no others?

VISTULA: I shall study servants. I shall keep a notebook in
which I faithfully record which orders they adhere to
and which they choose to ignore. I shall discover the
characteristics of the latter and attempt to classify them.
Armed with this knowledge I shall know in advance of
issuing instructions the likelihood of them ever being
carried out IF WE DO NOT BAR THE GATES PEOPLE COME
IN

(The SERVANTS shrink…)

THE GATES ARE FREEDOM THE GATES PERMIT US
TO DISCRIMINATE BETWEEN THE WELCOME AND
THE UNWELCOME THEY ARE THE FULCRUM OF
HOSPITALITY

(The SERVANTS are bent double with shame.)

Yes I must keep records or heaven knows my complacency
will engulf me, wandering about in the absurd conviction
my instructions have been heeded I do so hate to be made
foolish other things solitude pain or failure I can tolerate
but to be made a fool of I really I *(She writhes, she goes to the
SERVANTS…)*

I shan't hit you… I shan't hit you…

*(She embraces one… His face is nevertheless a picture of
anxiety…)*

GODANSK: Even had the gates been barred I must tell you
I think they would not have been effective. Given the
narrowness of the moat and the generally poor condition
of the walls, my return was probably inevitable, even were
the servants as efficient as brutality or loyalty could make
them. But the question which presents itself is not to do
with my arrival but rather the conditions under which I

shall be able to achieve my third departure, if I am able to achieve it at all, given the apparent fascination this place holds for me.

HEBBEL: Besides, the mare is dead...

(GODANSK casts a swift glance at HEBBEL...)

GODANSK: Dead...?

HEBBEL: The dancing horse, sensing how ill-equipped she was for the new conditions that will hold sway during and following the crisis, lost the will to live... and anyway, you galloped her... this heat...

GODANSK: I forgot to water her...!

HEBBEL: Well, you say *forgot*... the watering of horses is surely an instinct in a courier...?

GODANSK: *(Hurrying to the door.)* She – I – *(He looks back.)*
These courtyards are – *(He is still...)*
You're right, I am perhaps no longer a courier. And despite the fact I carried out my tasks effectively for fifteen years this failure was certainly dormant within me, a sickness that the arrival of the necessary circumstances would unleash, like some plague bacillus dormant in the rotting timbers of a barn which an unprecedented heatwave could –
(Pause...)
Of course I might proceed on foot... *(Pause...)*

HEBBEL: It isn't such a very heavy satchel...

GODANSK: On the contrary, it's...

(LINDSAY and SHARDLO enter, hand in hand. SHARDLO is dressed in a new, clean garment...)

LINDSAY: *(Sadly.)* Your mare's – *(She lifts her hand...)*
She –
All at once –
A felled tree –

Oh, a never-to-be-forgotten sound –
On to the cobbles of the yard –
And lay –
We ran and took her head –
We lifted it –
This mighty head in which the eyes were wide with a
bewilderment and –

GODANSK: What is in the satchel, anyway?

(Pause… They examine him… Furrowed with anxiety.)

A document, perhaps…

Certainly I have always taken it for granted that the thing
I transported was, if not a document, an object whose
associations were so powerful that it was, so to speak, a
substitute for a document, a thing which might articulate
more by its very appearance, its revelation, than whole
sheafs of correspondence crafted by the finest poets and
the most subtle diplomats working in tandem. This was
the case on one occasion, when I carried nothing but an
empty lipstick case, a thing of no intrinsic value or artistic
interest whatsoever, but which when presented by me to
a certain individual, caused her to display such agitation
that I feared for my own life, and looking back to that
period, I have no doubt that a number of military disasters,
the decimation of promising cadets, and the obliteration
of certain villages, could be traced to that transaction,
though I have no evidence to substantiate my claim. In this
instance however, I suspect the bag is empty.

*(They stare… They fathom… SHARDLO laughs, a short half-
mocking laugh…)*

SHARDLO: Certainly, that would relieve you of any urgency to
reach your destination… *(She bites her lip…)*

HEBBEL: Why?

SHARDLO: Because if there is nothing to deliver –

HEBBEL: Precisely that nothingness is what he was required to
carry –

(GODANSK laughs.)

Yes…!

My unfailing vision…!

Yes…!

My repellent fingering of truth…!

NOTHING IS ELOQUENT AS OUR MASTERS KNEW…

VISTULA: *(To HEBBEL.)* I think you should shut up…

HEBBEL: Yes…

VISTULA: For your own sake…

HEBBEL: Yes, I should –

VISTULA: Your life is in the balance –

HEBBEL: Is it?

VISTULA: I think so, yes –

GODANSK: Of course, it's possible I am mistaken, that this particular item is written on paper of so little substance as to be almost transparent, light and fragile as the wings of butterflies, but in fifteen years a courier becomes acutely sensitive to the minor changes in the weight of satchels and what's more the expression on the face of the official who handed me the bag was distinctly sinister, pained, clouded, as if he sensed he was participating in a deception the outcome of which might prove fatal to me but which I was nevertheless already party to. This expression had never to my knowledge, been attached to him before. *(Pause...)*

SHARDLO: Open the bag.

GODANSK: It's locked.

SHARDLO: Unlock it, then.

GODANSK: The couriers do not have keys. The key is –

HEBBEL: OVER THE FRONTIER...!

(Pause... GODANSK turns to HEBBEL....)

GODANSK: Yes…

> *(Pause… HEBBEL looks to SHARDLO…)*

That is exactly where it is. And the individual who holds it is almost certainly expecting me…

> *(Pause… They exchange glances with one another…)*

VISTULA: *(Observing that the SERVANTS are gawping.)* Pick up…! Pick up…!

> *(They bend at once. LINDSAY steps forward to GODANSK.)*

LINDSAY: I think you have ceased to be a courier. I think whilst you feel yourself to be an honest servant of the state, loyal and diligent, the state has not been honourable to you –

GODANSK: Honourable…?

LINDSAY: Yes. I think you have been ill-used. Furnishing you with a circus horse, when it is perfectly obvious the poor animal had not been bred to ride, and then to put precisely nothing in your satchel when you are risking life and limb transporting it is a mockery of your profession.

GODANSK: Perhaps… I never thought of that…

LINDSAY: No, you are so dedicated to your vocation such ideas would not occur to you, but your loyalty is being abused and –

GODANSK: *(To HEBBEL.)* If this is not a convent, what is it?

> *(Pause. LINDSAY bites her lip. VISTULA clenches her fist… HEBBEL is silent. GODANSK glares round the room.)*

Three women and a bed-ridden architect –

HEBBEL: Architect…?

GODANSK: *(Turning on LINDSAY.)* No, it is you who is dishonourable –

HEBBEL: Architect…?

GODANSK: The entire character of this place, the eccentricity of its plan, causing me to lose my horse and probably intended to swallow me up in its incomprehensible design in order that I might starve to death or suffocate in some abandoned drain, the persistent coming and going of women so patently obsessed with fornication, nakedness and erotic oblivion, and this recalcitrant and unbiddable family of fictitious servants, all confirms my sense I have been abducted, seduced from my proper function and made the victim of a conspiracy, notwithstanding I have chosen three times to incarcerate myself in your –

(He stops… His eyes travel around the room…)

What is that sound…?

LINDSAY: Sound…?

GODANSK: Sound, yes what is it…?

(They strain… They hear nothing… GODANSK looks from one to the other…)

I am profoundly lonely, and detecting my loneliness you thought me vulnerable, whereas –

WHAT IS IT A SORT OF RING A CLOCK IS IT –

(They gawp…)

A BELL A LITTLE BELL BUT FRANTIC –

(He prods one of the SERVANTS…)

Look for it…

(The SERVANT looks to VISTULA for instruction.)

Look for it, I said…!

(The SERVANT frowns…)

VISTULA: There are two hundred rooms here –

GODANSK: Go into every one –

(The SERVANT is pitiful.)

And the cupboards, open them –

LINDSAY: It will take all day –

GODANSK: Longer, possibly, he must be thorough, take a candle, light it, and stand it at the head of every stair, then I shall see you are methodical –

IT'S STOPPED… *(Pause. He listens, turning his head…)*

Yes… *(He smiles…)*

It's stopped… *(He looks at HEBBEL.)*

I must tell you, the depths of depravity that you have plumbed, the arcane and tortuous contrivances your malice has inspired in you to lure and to trap the unsuspecting –

HEBBEL: I am not an architect –

GODANSK: NO MORE AN ARCHITECT THAN I AM A COURIER… *(He stares fiercely at the women…)*

SHARDLO: Oh, God, you are the crisis… *(She lets her hand travel to her face…)*

The crisis is you… *(She looks to LINDSAY, to VISTULA…a short laugh comes from her…)*

My innocence…!
My intellectual lethargy…!
My dismal and somnolent imagination…!

I COULD RIP MY FACE WITH MY NAILS

It's shame
It is
It is embarrassment

The humiliation of a mundane mind which entertained such – *(She laughs, shaking her head…)*

As if authentic crisis would stoop to represent itself in colours such as I described… *(Pause…)*

I have read too much. This reading inflamed my mind. Perhaps if I had never read I should not have recognized the melancholy nature of my life. I blame him. *(She indicates HEBBEL.)*

Yes, he is the cause, and having read so much is it surprising that, encouraging, if not the crisis, the rumour of the crisis, I should picture it as crisis is conventionally presented? The beds? The blood? The terrible shortages of bandages…? I LONGED TO TEAR MY DRESS INTO SHREDS FOR SOME POOR CHILD'S WOUNDS… *(Pause…)*

The ordeal will not be familiar. The blow will come from the unexpected place. And the experience will be for all its savagery, cheap… *(Pause…)*

I daresay

VISTULA: I very nearly pitied you… so nearly pitied you I felt the warm tears rising in the bottom of my eyes, and then…! *(She shakes her head…)*

You lurch from one conviction to another…

SHARDLO: Leave me alone…

VISTULA: For one brief moment I thought, she is beautiful, she doubts –

SHARDLO: Please –

VISTULA: And then the doubt went out, like a light –

SHARDLO: Please –

VISTULA: Smothered by another galloping intransigence –

SHARDLO: THIS MAN HAS VIOLATED ME…

(Pause. LINDSAY looks with horror at SHARDLO…)

Yes

And I am believe me tired of drawing your attention to –

(VISTULA scoffs.)

Yes

It was five suicide attempts and now –

(VISTULA shakes her head.)

Yes

Another triumph of evasion I employ it all to suffocate your criticism –

GODANSK: THERE IT GOES AGAIN…!

(He listens… He strains his hearing…)

Not a bell… *(Pause...)*
Water…

LINDSAY: Violated you…?

GODANSK: Shh…! *(He is still… He looks to HEBBEL.)*

Water… cascading down the shaft of some… bottomless well… *(He looks at LINDSAY.)*

The bag is locked but since the bag will never be delivered, since I am already in defiance of the law, it can hardly compound my offence to burst the lock or cut the leather –

LINDSAY: Violated her…?

GODANSK: That will also be entered against me. Fetch a tool, a knife or wrench –

LINDSAY: BUT I LOVED YOU.

(GODANSK stares at her. LINDSAY suddenly puts her hand to her mouth, gnawing her knuckle…)

GODANSK: You did but I was a different person then. At that stage I was not fully apprized of my peculiar obsession with this place. I believed I was a courier. My destiny appeared to be bound up with the exigencies of the ministry. But now…! I shall never leave this place again, and your love might come back stronger from its little offence… who knows?

(VISTULA pulls a knife from her belt. For a moment, GODANSK falters…)

Is that… *(He smiles with relief…)*

For a moment I thought…I was about to remind you of the penalties for obstructing the imperial despatch, yes, that is the official terminology for murdering a messenger…! *(He removes the satchel…)*

Shall I cut it or shall you…? *(Pause…)*
The seal's intact…we only need to –

HEBBEL: KILL HIM… KILL HIM…!

(GODANSK looks with contempt…)

KILL HIM I SAID…!

(No one moves… GODANSK is wary… VISTULA holds the knife…)

SHARDLO: Kill him…? But he's the crisis…

(The anticipation lingers until VISTULA snatches the satchel from GODANSK and kneeling with it, prods the brass lock with her knife, clumsily attempting to burst the lever…)

HEBBEL: It would seem obvious to everyone who thought about it that the bag is empty, but this very obviousness, the shrillness of the logic, makes me for one suspicious. I would go so far as to say the bag itself is an element in a deception –

VISTULA: *(Nicking herself in her haste.)* Ow…!

LINDSAY: What have you –

VISTULA: It's all right, it's all right, I –

HEBBEL: But whose deception? Not the courier's, I think, for whilst we are correct to regard the courier, now no longer a courier, as an ambiguous and possibly delinquent personality –

VISTULA: *(Beating the bag to the floor.)* I CAN'T DO IT…!

LINDSAY: I will –

VISTULA: No, I can do it –

LINDSAY: Your thumb's bleeding…!

VISTULA: I KNOW IT IS –

HEBBEL: The greater and more tantalizing prospect which now presents itself is that this courier is himself no more than a whim –

VISTULA: *(Injuring herself again.)* Ow…!

LINDSAY: Oh, do let someone else –

VISTULA: I WILL DO IT GO AWAY...!

HEBBEL: A spasm in the universal and irresistible eruption of malevolence which now engulfs the world and which like some ravenous monster emerging from the waves can be satisfied by one thing only – sacrifice –

SHARDLO: Whose?

VISTULA: I WILL DO IT I WILL I WILL...!

SHARDLO: Whose sacrifice?

(HEBBEL turns to SHARDLO...)

HEBBEL: Mine...

(SHARDLO smiles, gasps...)

SHARDLO: Oh, the vanity of this man... I thought I was vain... but you...!

VISTULA: *(Scrambling to her feet, enraged.)* All right, you do it! *(She thrusts the knife at LINDSAY.)*

SHARDLO: He thinks the accumulated rage of the entire universe, the friction of the planets, the temper of animals, the boiling of youth, and wailing of widows –

HEBBEL: Yes –

SHARDLO: All can be subdued –

HEBBEL: Yes –

SHARDLO: Storms of violence and howling packs of unrepentant criminality –

HEBBEL: Yes –

SHARDLO: AND BY WHAT? HIS OWN EXTERMINATION...! YOU SHOULD NEVER HAVE BEEN GIVEN POETRY.

(Pause. She shrugs at her own rage.)

Funny, this indiscriminate dissemination of extraordinary qualities –

LINDSAY: I think we ought to cut it –

SHARDLO: He gets the poetry, and you –

LINDSAY: Slit the leather –

SHARDLO: What did you get…?

(She stares at GODANSK. He shrugs his shoulders.)

LINDSAY: I'll slit it then –

(SHARDLO slaps GODANSK over the cheek. He does not retaliate…)

I AM CUTTING THE BAG…! *(She sobs against her will…)*

SHARDLO: *(Not taking her eyes off GODANSK.)* Cut it, then…

LINDSAY: *(Sniffing as she works.)* It's so – I can't make any impression – *(She hacks at it with less and less resolution.)*

Perhaps it isn't meant to be – *(She falls onto her hands…)*

WHY DO YOU STARE AT HIM ALL THE TIME…?

(Pause… At last SHARDLO removes her eyes from GODANSK…)

SHARDLO: Because he is a liar…
And liars I study with the intensity of connoisseurs transfixed by works of art…
Perhaps I have never ceased to be amazed by it…
The audacity of it…!
Perhaps I like liars…
And harbour secret longing to lie myself…
But on a massive scale…
Little lies I don't think I would have the patience for…
(Pause…)

GODANSK: A liar, me…?

SHARDLO: Yes.

GODANSK: Everything I have recounted approximates as near as possible to the events as they occurred. Sometimes the order of my thoughts may well have become distorted, scrambled by the effort to recollect what was after all, frequently a violent cascade of impressions not always susceptible to methodical description, but on the other hand, no sooner had I recovered my normal condition of calm objectivity but I rehearsed the situation I had recently experienced, knowing that I should at some point have to deliver a report. All this is normal practice for a courier whose accuracy must be relied upon if officials are to arrive at proper judgements yes I am a liar I love to lie the lie is everything to me the facts however are as stated...

(Pause... Then SHARDLO goes to the satchel and picking it up, rips away the seal and releases the catch. She lays back the flap and inserts her hand.)

SHARDLO: Not empty... *(She does not withdraw her hand...)*

HEBBEL: I SAID —

VISTULA: Yes —

HEBBEL: NOT EMPTY I SAID —

VISTULA: We heard you —

HEBBEL: I SAID
    I SAID
    OH GOD
    MY
    TERRIBLE
    MY

VISTULA: Shh...

HEBBEL: Don't look at it.

VISTULA: Shh...

HEBBEL: NEITHER LOCKED NOR EMPTY
    I'm unforgivable
    I'm all the world detests

VISTULA: *(Losing patience at last.)* Oh, shut up...!

HEBBEL: *(Grasping her, pulling her close to him.)* Is it not extraordinary? Confess it is extraordinary...!

VISTULA: IT'S GROTESQUE... *(Pause.)*

HEBBEL: Yes, it is...! It is grotesque... *(Pause...)*

It is grotesque and must be punished... *(Pause...)*

Look if you wish...

(Pause, then SHARDLO swiftly withdraws her hand. It contains a small and faded photograph. She does not examine it, but lets it hang at her side...)

SHARDLO: I'm hesitating...

And this hesitation can only be a consequence of anxiety... Why should I be anxious...? *(She looks at HEBBEL...)* When what is in the bag was never – however great its significance for the future of the world – never intended for me...?

Most likely it will be meaningless, a – *(She swiftly, wilfully, casts a glance at it before turning it aside again...)* It is...

Meaningless... *(She snatches another glance...)* It's... *(She shrugs... She shakes her head...)* A schoolboy...

GODANSK: It never occurred to me that the satchel was not locked... *(He smiles wistfully.)*

Always we underestimate the flexibility of the officials, as if routine alone would guarantee the unfailing repetition of an action, but no, still they are able to discriminate –

LINDSAY: A schoolboy...?

GODANSK: I must have made a thousand journeys for the ministry and every time the bag was locked, I'm certain of it, and locked for the very good reason that the contents were of particular significance, state secrets and so on, and now, on this solitary occasion, which also happens to be my last mission, albeit I was unaware of this on setting out, the item I am the bearer of is of so little import that –

LINDSAY: We don't know that. *(Pause…)*

Whether this document, which happens to be a photograph, is of significance or not, depends on its many meanings. For all we know, this schoolboy's face might be sufficient on its own to cause a revolution, and the fact your bag was never locked might be a reflection of the terrible anxiety that this official suffered even in handling it, you said yourself he had a strange look on his face, no, the only useful subject for interrogation must be this – what is this child's identity? *(She laughs nervously. She bites her lip…)*

Surely…? *(Pause…)*

You see, I think like you…! Isn't that a certain sign of love?

(Pause… SHARDLO, without examining it again, extends the photograph to LINDSAY. She collects it. She looks at it…)

LINDSAY: *(To GODANSK.)* It's you…

(In the ensuing silence, HEBBEL's deep and guilty laugh comes from the bed…)

HEBBEL: I knew…

I knew…

VISTULA: Of course you knew…

SHARDLO: The messenger has nothing to deliver but himself…

(Pause… GODANSK takes the photograph from LINDSAY and examines it…)

And this spectacular redundancy is the triumph of the crisis…

LINDSAY: *(Perplexed.)* The official looked sad…!

SHARDLO: Obviously he looked sad…! He knew never in his life would he dispatch a messenger again… the crisis will see to that… this sad expression was undoubtedly the melancholy of a man who knows the world has ended… in its existing form… *(She looks at GODANSK…)*

A similar expression no doubt could have been seen inscribed on your face when this building with its spires and turrets came into view… a sense of profound helplessness, such that even to lift a finger to avert it, to effect the slightest correction of the circus horse's rein and thereby pass it at a distance, seemed… *(Pause…)*

Infantile…

(Pause… The throb of aircraft engines fills the air. The SERVANTS, exchanging swift glances, fling down their baskets and rush out… The rest remain motionless, anticipating the fall of leaflets. The engines fade… Nothing falls…)

GODANSK: They have ceased to value poetry… at least as a means of coercion… from this moment on, poetry is restored to its original function…

HEBBEL: It has no function…

GODANSK: So you say and yet it was your verses that were being scattered across the land…

HEBBEL: Mine…?

GODANSK: Yes, and without regard to copyright. The most powerful and yet most primitive sentiments of a distinguished mind drifting in profusion over a landscape inhabited largely by cattle not one of whom –

HEBBEL: *(Intuitively disturbed.)* I am an architect –

GODANSK: Was observed to do more than flick its tail in irritation –

HEBBEL: An architect, you said so yourself –

GODANSK: As if a swarm of flies had descended from the heavens to add to their bestial burdens

YOU ARE A POET AND THESE ARE YOUR DAUGHTERS

Yes
The courier discerns
The courier detects

Intuitive the courier
You have suffered long enough the indifference the abuse
the plagiarism and now the wholesale dissemination of
your work taken out of context and on paper of such dire
quality I cannot see you squirm a moment longer let us
pray the crisis will destroy a world which could not tolerate
your dazzling superiority –

HEBBEL: I AM AN ARCHITECT –

GODANSK: *(Going to the bed.)* Up now, your terrible ordeal is
over –

*(He flings back the blankets and seizes HEBBEL in his arms. The
women stare fixedly…)*

HEBBEL: The courier's a murderer…!

*(GODANSK hoists HEBBEL over his shoulder and starts to go out with
him. At the entrance, he stops. The horrified face of HEBBEL, mouth
open but now speechless, appeals to them over GODANSK's shoulder.
His lips move. After some seconds, GODANSK turns, concealing the
old man…)*

GODANSK: No words, which for a poet, must be death…
*(He walks out with the old man on his back. The women avoid
each other's eyes… A pause… The distant and sudden eruption
of HEBBEL's cries… The women remain still, then by tacit
agreement, they go to the bed and strip it, folding the blankets and
sheets between them in a businesslike manner. The cries fade with
distance. The women work…)*

PART TWO

A WELL

*The bed is stripped down to the mattress, the blankets folded on top.
The women stand posed about the bed. They are silent. GODANSK
returns…*

GODANSK: I found the well…

(They look at him.)

The well I first thought was a clock…

(They look blankly.)

You did not know there was a well…?

(They stare…)

Peculiar because at first this place was like a maze to me but now it is as familiar as a kitchen must be to a cook… I can put my hand to anything. I found the servants cowering and told them to dig a grave for the no-longer dancing horse. In this heat corruption is accelerated and we must consider – *(He stops… He moves his mouth thoughtfully… He walks a few paces, and turns back to them…)*

Forgive me. *(Pause…)*

I have lived a life of virtual solitude and this whilst not obliterating the natural delicacy of my feelings has to some extent robbed me of the facility of expressing them… *(Pause…)*

Naturally, you will look on me with some distaste for having performed a task which –

SHARDLO: Yes.

(GODANSK slightly inclines his head…)

On the other hand, it was the very thing that he predicted.

GODANSK: Quite.

SHARDLO: And not only predicted it. He craved it.

GODANSK: Yes.

SHARDLO: His horror of death, whilst painful to observe, was nothing more than the apprehension which attends on every moment of decision –

GODANSK: Quite so –

SHARDLO: And if the decision was not, strictly speaking, his own, we all know how frequently he invoked his death as something intimately bound up with the crisis –

GODANSK: I heard him myself –

SHARDLO: I am not without feelings –

GODANSK: On the contrary –

SHARDLO: On the contrary, yes, if anything I am encumbered with an excess of feeling –

GODANSK: Perhaps –

SHARDLO: We all are, we all have this tendency to extremes in our emotions which he separately detected and almost certainly exploited, but in the new conditions of the crisis this feeling of affection rapidly acquired the character of history, I think I speak for all of us when I say the passions we had known for him were not recognizable any more, were impossible to recall, and if by some strenuous effort of imagination one could evoke the actions which desire had driven us to perform, a powerful embarrassment caused it to be swiftly repressed again.

VISTULA: *(To GODANSK.)* If you had not disposed of him, she would have.

SHARDLO: Yes, I don't flinch to confess it.

VISTULA: She flinches at nothing at all, but why should she, she is magnificent, and the man who both created and subsequently maimed her character, paddling at this moment in a pitch black well from which he can never emerge, has already shrunk to occupy an infinitely obscure corner of her memory, a well itself, down which no bucket of recollection will ever plunge, I daresay –

SHARDLO: Possibly not –

LINDSAY: *(To GODANSK.)* Surely you – before you dropped him – slit his throat or something –

GODANSK: I'm not sure that I did –

LINDSAY: Not sure you –

GODANSK: I didn't, no, I tipped him in –

LINDSAY: Alive…?

GODANSK: Alive, yes, I distinctly heard him cry as he –

LINDSAY: HEARD HIM CRY –

GODANSK: Yes –

LINDSAY: Where…! Where…!

> *(She goes to attack GODANSK, who seizes her wrists to protect himself.)*
> WHERE…!

SHARDLO: It doesn't matter where –

LINDSAY: I'll call to him…!

SHARDLO: Call what…?

LINDSAY: WHERE IS THE WELL… *(She glares at GODANSK… She struggles…)*
> THE WELL… *(She struggles. She stops.)*
> WHERE IS IT…?
> *(GODANSK does not reply… Pause…)*

SHARDLO: I think, looking at it from every point of view, to have you calling over the rim some shame or consolation will only serve to prolong his struggle, lend him hope, or even stimulate him to yet another effort of valetudinary poetry, whereas abandoned and alone, his spirit, like some guttering candle, will be extinguished all the quicker.

VISTULA: That's perfectly true, but how can she forgive herself for suppressing an impulse which, however it might actually contribute to another's pain, is nevertheless spontaneous, human and –

SHARDLO: I don't know.

> *(She looks boldly at VISTULA. LINDSAY, slack, is freed by GODANSK. She thoughtfully massages her wrists…)*

LINDSAY: If I have to forgive myself for that, must I not also have to forgive myself for failing to intervene when the courier, barely disguising his intentions, carried off the old man in the first place? The fact that I love the courier and will continue to love him no matter what terrible acts he perpetrates can't relieve me of –

GODANSK: Shh… *(He listens acutely…)*

LINDSAY: Forgiveness is an aspect of the crisis which –

GODANSK: Shh… *(Pause…)*

I should have cut his throat… *(Pause…)*

Another time I – *(Pause…)*

Purely for my own peace of mind, given the state of my hearing, I ought to have – *(He listens…)*

Or beat his head against a wall – *(Pause… He is suddenly animated.)*

One must live with the consequences of one's actions, or more precisely, with the consequences of the actions one failed to perform –

SHARDLO: We are in your debt but the crisis alters everything, even the relationship of creditors to debtors. If you set off now, you can find some lodging before it's dark. *(Pause…)*

GODANSK: Set off…? *(Pause…)*

SHARDLO: Yes.

GODANSK: But I am not a courier.

SHARDLO: You are not a courier but –

GODANSK: Absolutely not a courier and I have met my bride.

SHARDLO: Carry her with you.

(Pause… GODANSK stares at SHARDLO…)

I am not going to be destroyed by you. The man who five times brought me to the edge of destruction is drowning in

a well. This well he trod over for fifty years not knowing of
its existence.

LINDSAY: *(To GODANSK.)* We'll go. *(She extends a hand…)*
We'll go and –
(Pause… GODANSK looks at her. A darkness fills her gaze…)
I'm not the bride… *(Pause…)*
I love you but the bride's not me…? *(Her hand falls…)*
When you were here the time before… the time… of your
first or second visit I can't remember which I made you a
sandwich –

GODANSK: Second –

LINDSAY: Second visit, was it, and having made this sandwich
I could not deliver it –

VISTULA: She wanted to –

LINDSAY: I wanted to but great as this wanting was I wanted
even more for you to suffer the fact that I had failed to
return with it, I wanted my absence to wound you and in
wounding you to inform you of a need that perhaps had
not been fully recognized –

GODANSK: It was not recognized at all –

LINDSAY: Not then –

GODANSK: Nor at any other time –

LINDSAY: No, I had entirely misjudged things –

SHARDLO: It was I who delivered the sandwich –

LINDSAY: She delivered the sandwich and as a consequence
– it's all so obvious in retrospect – she became the object of
your fascination –

GODANSK: Not at all –

LINDSAY: No?

GODANSK: The violence of my actions towards her later on was conditioned by so many things I hesitate to place them in any order –

LINDSAY: Try –

GODANSK: I will try –

LINDSAY: I have said I love you and this love will not be bruised by truth I assure you, rather the truth will strengthen it –

GODANSK: Is that so?

LINDSAY: I affirm it absolutely –

GODANSK: Notwithstanding the fact I never for one moment have regarded you as either my lover or my bride?

LINDSAY: Even so –

GODANSK: Very well, I can state with certainty that my behaviour was compelled not by any powerful feeling I harboured for her, either as a consequence of her delivering the sandwich or of my recollecting her at any moment during my last attempt to leave, but purely from observing her body fondled by the old man now swimming in the well, a touch of such profound possession, so intimate and yet so unresisted, I was seized by a rage of envy, a passion for usurpation swept over me whose origins lay in my first glimpses of this place. It was a touch which for all its beauty condemned the senile poet to his death. *(Pause...)*

SHARDLO: It is impossible to like you... but you have perhaps dispensed with liking, or with being liked. So have I. And far from being humiliated by your announcement that I was, in my indignity, merely an instrument of your malevolence, I feel cleansed by it –

VISTULA: Shh –

SHARDLO: Why shh, nothing was more loathsome to me than the idea of this inept and misappropriated courier –

VISTULA: Shh –

SHARDLO: Should have entertained feelings of insatiable desire for my naked flesh –

VISTULA: You are too shrill –

SHARDLO: I am not shrill in the least I am expressing my satisfaction with his account of my ordeal, I might have been a chair, I might have been a cabinet, on which he could wreak some petty havoc with a knife, I assure you I feel wholly and completely disassociated from a sordid transaction which threatened to –

(She stops. A silence imposes itself... Pause...)
I heard him...

LINDSAY: Yes –

SHARDLO: Calling –

LINDSAY: Crying –

SHARDLO: My name –

LINDSAY: Yours, yes –

SHARDLO: Terrible, I –

LINDSAY: Yours because –

SHARDLO: Mine, why –

LINDSAY: Because you –

SHARDLO: *(To GODANSK.)* Has the well a cover?

GODANSK: A cover?

SHARDLO: A lid, a cover, yes –

GODANSK: I don't recollect a cover, but I was agitated and quite possibly failed to observe the existence of an object which, whilst not altogether familiar to me, would certainly, in other circumstances, have represented itself to me as –

(The SERVANTS enter, pale with fear…)

SHARDLO: It's all right, we know –

(They point, with faltering finger, to the depths of the house…)

We know
We know
All about it
Is the pit dug for the horse
A deep pit
Horses are so huge
So very huge
And what you've dug is certainly inadequate
The rains
The frost
A little soil erosion
Up come the hooves
No
Deeper please

VISTULA: Deeper

SHARDLO: Yes

VISTULA: Deeper, please

SHARDLO: *(Turning abruptly to GODANSK.)* It's self-evident to me that whoever constructed the well would not have failed to supply a lid for it –

GODANSK: It is a very ancient well –

SHARDLO: So what – *(The SERVANTS have not left. She turns on them.)*

DIG…!

DIG…!

(They edge out…)

GODANSK: Far older than the house –

SHARDLO: Quite possibly –

GODANSK: I am not an archaeologist but the most cursory glance convinced me that the well is Roman –

SHARDLO: Is that so? And did the Romans not place covers on their wells?

GODANSK: I am not an expert in –

SHARDLO: They preferred perhaps to fall headlong into them?

GODANSK: I couldn't say, I am only attempting to suggest that the lid provided by the Roman well-diggers has certainly at some stage in the passage of time either decayed or more likely, been appropriated for firewood –

SHARDLO: If the lid was wooden –

GODANSK: *(Coldly.)* If it was wooden, yes…
   (Pause… They glare at one another…)
   Whereas, if it were iron – *(Pause…)*

SHARDLO: I must go to the well –

VISTULA: I don't think you should go to the well –

SHARDLO: I MUST DO, MUSTN'T I… *(She appeals to the women…)*
   It was my name he called…
   (They frown…)
   When I get to the well –

GODANSK: It is a hundred metres deep… *(Pause…)*

SHARDLO: Arriving at the well I –

GODANSK: I discerned the depth more by accident than design. In stepping back from having tipped the poet in I clumsily dislodged a section of the coping stone, which fell away and plunged after him. I counted the seconds, being careful to distinguish the first splash from that which followed afterwards. I calculated the rate of acceleration as –

SHARDLO: Why me though…? *(Pause…)*

Certainly, in his extremity, he might have many reasons for privileging my name above all others – *(She flinches.)*
THERE IT IS AGAIN… *(Pause…)*

Certainly it cannot be assumed this choice is a mark of favour, the expression of a deeper love, on the contrary, it might merely be a testament to my greater efficiency… his estimation that I am more equipped to extract him from the well than either you… or you… *(She bites her lip, looking at the other women all the time…)*

LINDSAY: I'll come with you… *(Pause…)*

Standing either side of the well-hole we could lean out, clasp hands and thereby look down directly to the depths whereas alone you could only perch precariously on the rim
YOU DO NOT WISH TO JOIN HIM DO YOU
Say
Say if you do
I don't
Myself I
Speaking as truthfully as possible I must say whereas I now regret failing to prevent
To speak
To anything
Now he is gone I

SHARDLO: I shan't leap in… *(Pause…)*

Or, more precisely, I shall not leap in drawing you after me…

(LINDSAY smiles. She extends a hand to SHARDLO who accepts it. They go out. VISTULA remains, still, her gaze on GODANSK… A pause elapses…)

VISTULA: I'm not certain if I wish to be your bride. *(Pause…)*
What is a bride in any case? I've never been one. *(Pause…)*

Presumably it's ecstasy. *(Pause…)*
I've had ecstasy. *(Pause…)*
Never in a white dress but I've had it
YES
LET'S

(Pause… He does not move his gaze from her…)

And afterwards, the grim, slow grind of our degeneration –
Yes –
I –
Why not –
Yes –
Yes –

(The SERVANTS enter, uneasily.)

What is it now the hole can hardly have got deeper can it
in five minutes you are peculiar it is as if having declared
the hole completed no amount of argument or logic can
persuade you to return to it I'll look and if it's shallow I will
– *(She stops, turning to go. She looks at GODANSK.)*

Yes *(Pause.)*
The word's –
I like the word…

(She goes out. The SERVANTS hang in a group, moving like weed in a current…)

GODANSK: Say then…!

(They lift their eyes to him…)

Say what this place –

(VISTULA enters briskly…)

VISTULA: Ridiculous…! The hole is… *(She lifts her hands…)*
You saw the horse…
How can you dig a hole which is so completely unrelated
to the proportions of a horse…?
I – *(She is speechless with disbelief…)*
Go and measure the horse.

(They begin to move off…)

Wait.

(They stop…)

When you have measured the horse, mark out the width
and length of it, with chalk, using the excavation that
already exists

DO NOT BEGIN ANOTHER HOLE

The depth of the existing hole is more than adequate
It must however be extended
Hugely extended
In all directions

(They start to move…)

Wait.

(They stop.)

There is something in your attitude that is so grudging and
reluctant that I

WHY WHEN THE NECESSITY OF BURYING THE HORSE IS
SO OBVIOUS TO ALL

Do you want to be ill
Do you like diseases
Stench
Flies
Maggots
When the hole is finished attach ropes to the horse's
hooves and pull it to the hole

HURRY PLEASE

(They go off, swiftly…)

I am not a bad person
I would not hesitate if I were a bad person to say so
I know what badness is
I've seen it
Oh, the real thing
Kiss me
Kiss me but in such a way I

*(SHARDLO enters. GODANSK and VISTULA look at her. She looks
boldly at them.)*

SHARDLO: This well is peculiar. *(Pause…)*

I know nothing whatsoever about wells but looking at
it from a general point of view it would seem to me that
falling fifty metres down a well-shaft, suffering the glancing
blows that would inevitably be inflicted during the descent,
and plunging into ice-cold water which might, if shallow,
not even serve to soften the impact, could only impair an
old man's grasp on life. *(Pause…)*

Not so… *(Pause… She perches on the side of the bed, her hands
loosely clasped…)*

He is if anything, restored to vigour…

(LINDSAY enters, pale with horror…)

LINDSAY: He shouted at me…

SHARDLO: I heard… *(She shakes her head…)*
This is a crisis, obviously, but not the one I wanted,
the crisis I required was altogether more – universal,
horrifying, and sublime, whereas this is, if anything –
No it is –
It is horrifying –

GODANSK: The water is restorative. *(They turn to look at him…)*

What other explanation is there…? The Romans built it
as a spa. This well, and possibly others, is situated over a
stream, a spring, whose contents are so rich in minerals
that even a brief immersion is sufficient to –

SHARDLO: *(Standing with decision.)* The well must be filled in.

(LINDSAY looks to GODANSK, to VISTULA.)

Tell the servants –

VISTULA: They are digging a hole –

SHARDLO: The hole must wait –

VISTULA: The horse is putrefying –

SHARDLO: I recognize the odour of corruption just as well as
you – Why does he shout my name…? Why me…? Why

not you also…? He is persecuting me… he hates me… *(To LINDSAY.)* Call the servants…

VISTULA: THE SERVANTS ARE FULLY OCCUPIED

(Pause…)

SHARDLO: Now, wait a minute –

VISTULA: I AM THE BRIDE *(Swiftly, to LINDSAY.)*
    Forgive me but I am
    I am
    I am
    And this
    Ask him
    This carries with it certain
    Surely
    Certain privileges
    Such as

LINDSAY: But you don't love the courier –

VISTULA: Don't I –

LINDSAY: No, you don't –

VISTULA: YOU MAKE TOO MUCH OF LOVE…! *(Pause…)*
    Forgive me but we are familiar with your claims on this
    man –

LINDSAY: How can you marry without love…! *(Pause…)*

VISTULA: I know nothing of marriage. I only know I am the
    bride. *(She turns to SHARDLO.)*

    Take the servants. Possibly the rubble which has been
    excavated for the horse's grave could be employed to fill
    the well. I have never set eyes on a wheelbarrow, but he
    had no antipathy to wheelbarrows that I recall, and if there
    are no wheelbarrows, let them transport it all in buckets –

GODANSK: Or failing buckets, bowls –

VISTULA: Bowls, yes, or cups for all I care…!

>KISS ME
>
>I am submitting myself to an ordeal…
>
>*(SHARDLO hesitates, wavers, leaves…)*
>
>An ordeal she envies, it appears…
>
>*(Pause. She wipes her hands on her skirt. SHARDLO enters again, seething…She goes to VISTULA.)*

SHARDLO: Kiss you…? *(Her eyes close.…)*

>You are smothering your responsibilities in the fiction of a life which cannot possibly occur, the spurious propositions of an uninvited stranger who has insinuated himself into the melancholy grave of your ambition and like some thrusting weed has cracked you open, split your walls and tilted you until
>
>I AM NOT THE WELL
>
>You also are the well
>The well is all of us
>Let us all kiss but with the joy that makes a kiss ignite the soul a blaze a conflagration please
>
>MY NAME
>MY NAME AGAIN
>
>*(She raises a fist, clenched, and lets it fall…)*
>
>His kisses were like that
>Did you think so
>Only in kissing did his horror recede
>Some childlike rage
>Some precious and unguarded extravagance
>Oh
>We never exchanged the details of these intimacies
>Never in so many years discussed the subject of our servitude
>Until he's dead perhaps that isn't possible… *(She goes out…)*

GODANSK: How hard it is not to be a messenger… *(He walks idly across the room, stops, turns back to VISTULA…)*

Already I feel the terrible lethargy that comes not from
inactivity but from ceasing to occupy a vital function in
the organization of affairs, if it is organization, it is perhaps
not organization at all only the counterfeit of it, but all the
same YOU DID NOT INDICATE THE OLD MAN WAS YOUR
LOVER *(He turns to LINDSAY.)*

And yours also it appears
I should have known

My instincts were keener once a glance was adequate to
know the entire world of a household
Its contracts
Frauds
Defaulters

Perhaps I was already failing perhaps had I succeeded in
delivering the final message and even in returning with
an answer I should have been retired nothing escapes the
officials I have seen retired messengers they grapple always
with the agony that at some point in their careers their
unsuitability was revealed but where the ministry is silent
on this point they cannot sleep they stare at the horizon
even retrace the journeys of their final years sometimes
are found dead in their mildewed uniforms it is only hours
since I ceased to be a messenger and already –

VISTULA: I will give you messages –

(He casts a withering glance at her… She is bold…)

Why not
Why not my messages
My messages might be more
Yes
Even more
IMBUED WITH SIGNIFICANCE THAN

(He turns away.)

Yes…!

*(SHARDLO hurries through the room, her hands uplifted as if
she had touched something loathsome. LINDSAY, shocked at her*

appearance, hurries after her. Immediately, both surge back into the room.)

SHARDLO: HE LIKES THE WELL *(She paces furiously up and down.)*
NOT ONLY THE WELL *(She continues pacing, and stops…)*
ALL THAT FALLS DOWN THE WELL

VISTULA: Sit down –

SHARDLO: Sit down yourself –

VISTULA: I'll fetch a bowl –

SHARDLO: Yes –

VISTULA: A towel –

SHARDLO: Yes –

VISTULA: Soap and so on –

SHARDLO: Soap, yes –

(The SERVANTS appear as VISTULA is about to hurry for a basin and water…)

SERVANTS: WE CAN'T DO THIS

VISTULA: Just wait…!

SERVANTS: WE CAN'T
WE CAN'T
WE CAN'T DO THIS

(They wail, their hands hanging at their sides… VISTULA hurries out… SHARDLO lies on the mattress… GODANSK observes the spectacle with a certain detachment…)

LINDSAY: Why not? What prevents you doing it?

SERVANTS: HE'S IN THERE, MISS…!

LINDSAY: He's in there, yes, and the horse is in a similar position –

SERVANTS: BUT HE'S NOT DEAD –

LINDSAY: Don't argue…! Always you argue…! Always you are reluctant…! What have you ever done that you were not driven to…?

(They hang their heads…)

The horse is dead, and he is so nearly dead that… *(Pause… She bites her lip…)*

There is a difference but… in perfect justice one must say that whereas the horse was an innocent and inoffensive creature…he was so critical of life… so argumentative and recalcitrant… to bury him is not comparable to the burial of any other individual who might happen to have fallen down a – *(She falters.)*

He required it and so do we.

(VISTULA returns and proceeds to wash SHARDLO's hands. GODANSK is pondering the photograph…)

GODANSK: It's obvious that in the bottom of a well a man might be the subject of terrible perceptions that had evaded him in every other circumstance of his life. This flood of perfect knowledge would certainly compensate him for the many terrifying aspects of his situation and with certain men of intellectual character, render the place preferable to the mundane influences of daylight, nourishment, human company, etcetera, that he was accustomed to in the world above. I think – to choose only one among many devastating truths that must have certainly presented themselves to him – he can only be luxuriating in the dazzling discovery that in choosing from a world of women three to adore and be adored by, he was simultaneously selecting the agents of his own extinction. What distinguished them and at the same time delighted him, however it was unappreciated at time, was their common capacity for murder… *(He shrugs…)*

No wonder he is unaffected by cascading bricks. Possibly he experiences the bricks as massage… *(Pause…)*

LINDSAY: *(To the SERVANTS.)* Continue, please.

(They decline to move...)

Filling the well...

(They are stubborn, whilst avoiding her eyes...)

OR YOU WILL JOIN THEM IN THERE...

(They exchange terrified glances. SHARDLO climbs off the bed.)

(To SHARDLO.) They must do as they are told –

SHARDLO: Yes –

LINDSAY: Mustn't they –

SHARDLO: Yes –

LINDSAY: *(To the SERVANTS.)* Go out and fill the well....! *(She turns back at once to SHARDLO...)*

I am not happy –

SHARDLO: No one is –

LINDSAY: How can I be? How can I be happy?

SHARDLO: I don't know, perhaps by ceasing to desire it –

(LINDSAY swiftly, unreflectingly, smacks SHARDLO... In horror, she bites her fingers... VISTULA, shaking her head, faintly laughs...)

It's all right...

It is –

(LINDSAY makes an uncomplicated gesture of regret...)

I do enrage... I always have... enraged... the universe...

VISTULA: The universe...

SHARDLO: Clouds... fields of wheat... yes... boats at their moorings... fret... jostle... when I appear...

(She turns to the SERVANTS.) He cannot be recovered from the well, he is profoundly altered and so are we. The world is furthermore, no longer what it was. All this makes it impossible to even contemplate the restoration of the conditions that originally prevailed. On the contrary, we must move with the current of events. That is what she

meant by saying you would join him in the well. If you do not embrace the future you will be consigned to the damp dark of the past. That is what she meant and I agree. Now let us finish what we have begun.

(They shift… Squirm…)

You transport the bricks and I will drop them in.

(They twitch…. Their feet lift and fall again…)

I can and so can you…

(SHARDLO leads. They follow… The remaining women stare, open-mouthed… The hiatus is ended by GODANSK, who goes to the mattress and lies on it…)

GODANSK: I must confess a certain chill suffuses me when in spite of my reluctance I am at intervals drawn, as if by a morbid fascination, to contemplate the remainder of my life. A peculiar blindness descends on me, such as I have on rare occasions known in blizzards or in fogs. I cannot discern what lies ahead. This does not in itself prevent my making progress, only this progress is predicated on an act of faith, namely, the existence of the road. Quite possibly the road has finished, or worse, leads into a gravel pit… quicksands… or over a cliff… *(Pause…)*

The one who is my bride… *(Pause…)*

Surely she should remove my boots…?

(Pause… VISTULA goes to obey his order. But LINDSAY fixes her by the shoulder… Pause… GODANSK is perfectly still, as if asleep… SHARDLO returns, alone… They look to her…)

SHARDLO: His cries have ceased… *(Pause…)*
Or… *(She shrugs.)*

If they have not, I have ceased to hear them. And since they were addressed exclusively to me, that is all that needs concern us… *(She turns suddenly to them…)*

OH, DO ADMIRE ME MY

(She cannot find a word… Pause…)

Capacity to love…

(They are puzzled…)

Things… *(Pause…)*

No, of course you can't… *(Pause…)*

You can't… *(Pause…)*

You dare not… *(She laughs, stopping at once. Without turning, she senses the reappearance of the servants in the door…)*

KEEP FILLING…!

KEEP FILLING THE WELL…!

(They seem unmoved by her exhortations… They shift… A faint air of embarrassment surrounds them… SHARDLO turns to them.)

It must be filled…to the top…and then, paved over… *(She laughs, short…)*

Quick…!

(They do not move, but instead point to the bed where GODANSK lies…)

Yes…?

(They point with more emphasis… SHARDLO turns to look in the direction they indicate…)

The courier is not a servant. He does not dig or fill. Surely three of you can – *(She stops, and goes towards the bed. She looks at the body of GODANSK, then back to the SERVANTS…)*

Oh, you – *(She gasps in wonder. She turns to VISTULA…)*

Are they not the most –

And I think I –

I flatter myself –

THEY DO NOT WANT TO DIG ANOTHER HOLE…!

(She bites her lip… Disbelief suffuses her… LINDSAY, looking in horror from SHARDLO to the SERVANTS, rushes to the bed and stares at the still form of GODANSK…)

I think –

What do you think –

I think beside the horse –

Whilst I did not sense in him any great affection for the horse, there is a certain obvious –

And to cast him in the well would I think be –
Could you bear that –

AND THE SATCHEL, OBVIOUSLY…!

(She goes briskly to the satchel and plucks it off the floor. LINDSAY remains staring at the body of GODANSK. SHARDLO stops, the satchel hanging from its strap…)

LINDSAY: Why not the well…?

(SHARDLO shrugs…)

I'm not the bride but –

(The SERVANTS look from one of the women to another, attempting to follow the debate. LINDSAY suddenly snatches the photograph from GODANSK's grasp where it has been clasped…)

Not the bride but entitled to my own opinion and –
(To VISTULA.) I'M NOT PARTING WITH THIS SO DO NOT TRY TO MAKE ME –

I think the well
I do
I *(She holds it out…)*
What a serious face…!

(She kisses it, deeply… VISTULA suddenly marches to the body and tugs off the boots. She places the boots side by side…)

SHARDLO: *(To the SERVANTS.)* In the absence of any unanimity on the subject of the interment of the courier –

VISTULA: I don't care –

SHARDLO: My own preference for the grave of the dancing horse being almost certainly affected by a lingering sense of order which –

VISTULA: I don't care at all –

SHARDLO: With the increasing intensity of the crisis will seem positively sentimental –

VISTULA: Chuck it in the moat for all I care –

SHARDLO: You must in this instance put aside the natural instincts of a servant and allow the choice to be dictated purely by your own convenience. Can you manage that? Which of the two is nearer, the well-shaft or the horse-pit?

(The SERVANTS mumble…)

Which…?

SERVANTS: The well-shaft…?

SHARDLO: There you are, then…

(They go to march to the bed. SHARDLO intercepts them and draws them into her arms, entwining herself about them. Their discomfort grows as she crushes them in her embrace, and they form strange, drifting, murmuring body until at last SHARDLO tears loose. She staggers, and stops…)

The odour…! The odour of them…!

(They look over their shoulders at her…)

Labour…!

Lassitude…! *(She smells her own flesh, her palms, her wrists…)* Same smell…

(She laughs… The SERVANTS, in a methodical way, go to the bed and prepare to lift the body of the messenger. They do not complete the action however, but remain holding his limbs in a fixed position… Their eyes meet the eyes of VISTULA. LINDSAY's gaze, lifting from the photograph, meet's SHARDLO's… Pause… They are still …)

We are all –

How extraordinary –

And I have no particular affectation for unanimity –

SEIZED BY A SINGLE THOUGHT… *(She bites her lip…)*

A thought which arrived without an invitation but which all the same, once recognized, seems to possess an irrefutable authority…

(Pause… Their eyes shift, from one another…)

HOW HARD IT IS TO SPEAK… *(She sobs, laughs…)*

You think –

I think myself –

I SHOULD BE FLUNG INTO THE SHAFT. *(She smacks her hand to her mouth. In the ensuing silence she walks a few wild paces and stops… She repeats this, stops again…)*

He knew…

Oh, how he knew…

The well could not be satisfied…

(She is galvanized by her own logic…)

The courier knew many things but all the time, for all that he exerted to the full his powers of logic and experience, he succeeded only in acquiring the barest understanding of this house and its inexorable character, how could he be expected to when even we – *(Pause…)*

The well is not Roman. If it had Roman elements that merely reflects the limitless capacity for deception employed by its architect. Nor was it designed for drinking – *(She looks to the SERVANTS…)*

Carry him…!

Carry him if you want to…!

I AM DESTINED TO DIE IN THE WELL AND SO ARE YOU…

That is its only function…

(The SERVANTS, in their anxiety, let fall the limbs of the dead courier. They are panicked by her verdict and back away from the bed… SHARDLO is overcome by pity for them…)

It can't be helped…!

Come…!

Come…!

(She opens her arms to them… They back away… SHARDLO drops her arms in irritation…)

Oh, you are so silly…! To squeal…! To fret…! When it is so obvious the courier arrived only to reveal the well to us…

(She is radiant. VISTULA and LINDSAY spontaneously burst into tears…)

OH BUT IT IS GOOD TO KNOW…!

And knowing… to be resolute enought to –

LINDSAY: I AM NOT GOING IN THE WELL**…!**

SHARDLO: *(Complacently.)* That may be how it appears to you –

LINDSAY: I REFUSE…!

SHARDLO: Yes… and yet the man you love is about to do
    precisely that –

LINDSAY: I'D RATHER LEAP OFF THE TOWER…!

SHARDLO: Well, you could always try, but –

*(She stops… She closes her eyes in a spasm of pain… She extends
her hand to LINDSAY… who hesitates… SHARDLO rocks on her
toes…)*

The way we –
Always we –
Coerce –
And are coerced –
Violence –
Pity –
Laughter –
AND THE WEAK ARE THE WORST…! *(She looks clearly at
LINDSAY…)*
Take my hand –
You must forgive me for being – in this instance –
Wholly correct –

LINDSAY: It's not correct –

SHARDLO: You do not wish it to be correct, but
    notwithstanding your preference it remains –

LINDSAY: It is not correct it is your own –

SHARDLO: Yes –

LINDSAY: Your own –
    Your very own –

SHARDLO: Yes –

LINDSAY: INSPIRATION –

SHARDLO: Quite –

LINDSAY: And I –

(SHARDLO pulls LINDSAY towards her and kisses her hand…)

SHARDLO: Yes…! Yes…! That is what it is…! And you must
go –
(She turns to VISTULA.) The pair of you –
With hats and coats and little bags –

LINDSAY: Why –

SHARDLO: Through the rockets and the firestorms you must
leap onto the running boards of flaming trains –

LINDSAY: What –

SHARDLO: In no matter what direction because –

LINDSAY: Why –

SHARDLO: I SHALL CERTAINLY DESTROY YOU. *(She looks into
LINDSAY…)*
Hurry… *(Pause…)*

VISTULA: She says that because
ONLY BECAUSE
She is certain we could only fail
That we would return with our coats dragging in the dust,
apologetic and ashamed…
(SHARDLO makes no reply…)
That is the extent of what appeared for one fleeting
moment to be –

SHARDLO: Yes –

VISTULA: Her generosity…
(SHARDLO lowers her head… Pause…)

SHARDLO: Certainly… *(She shrugs, her hand lifts, falls…)*
Certainly, that's – *(She shrugs again…)*
The case… with me…

(She turns to leave the room. The SERVANTS, galvanized by a mutual instinct, grab her clumsily. She is spun round, and falls among them. LINDSAY and VISTULA are shocked into paralysis for some seconds. VISTULA, recovering first, barks orders to her…)

VISTULA: Coats…!

Hats…!

Bags…!

(LINDSAY is beyond hearing…staring at the spectacle of the knot of struggling figures…)

COATS…!

HATS….!

BAGS…!

(She is still fixed to the spot…)

BAGS…!

BAGS…!

(LINDSAY obeys the last injunction. The two women tear from the room… Meanwhile the struggle between SHARDLO and the SERVANTS, close, suffocating, and nearly soundless, continues like a subdued dance… After some seconds, the sound of aircraft is heard in the distance. This time their approach has no effect on the SERVANTS, who are too engrossed in the attempt to stifle SHARDLO to react. As the planes pass low, their guns rattle. The grotesque dance is stopped by this new and ominous sound echoing through the courtyards. The group is still. Hands fall to sides. Heads hang. The sound of the planes recedes. At last SHARDLO emerges from the group, her clothing torn, dishevelled… She rubs her neck, comforting the bruising… She massages her wrists…slowly, contemplatively…She seems to speak, but her ordeal obstructs articulation… She swallows… She opens her lips again…)

I'm not dead… *(Pause…)*

I'm not dead…

(The SERVANTS burst into a flood of weeping, wailing, inconsolable …)

Shh…! *(They heave, shudder…)*

LISTEN, I'M NOT DEAD...!

I

I for whom

Suicide was intended

For whom

Rage was designed

Am

Shh...!

NOT DEAD AND THEY –

(The SERVANTS are hushed by her appearance... They watch her furtively as she frowns in her struggle to achieve lucidity...)

Climb the tower... all three of you... and look... *(Pause...)*
In one of the thirteen courtyards you will see the bodies of your mistresses... *(Pause...)*
Together...
Or possibly, apart... *(Pause...)*
When you have ascertained this, return to ME WITH THE PRECISE LOCATION ETCHED UPON YOUR MINDS...

(They nod and leave... SHARDLO stares in the direction of their departure. Her loosely hanging hand is taken by the courier, otherwise unmoving on the bed... She is perfectly still... She is suspended between disbelief and bathos...)

Oh... *(Pause...)*
Oh... *(Pause...)*
Oh...

(He sits upright, an abrupt movement...)

Now, listen, I –

(He draws her with a powerful movement of his arm backwards to the mattress, holding her so firmly that in spite of her efforts she is fixed to the spot. She concedes to his superior power, and ceases the attempt to regain her feet. A light, frivolous laugh comes from her. Again her legs writhe as she tries to sit up, but the courier's hand remains around her neck. She stops. A pause. She laughs again, longer. His expression is unchanged... She is silent...)

GODANSK: As I lay on the bed I could not divest myself of the thought that the bed, whilst inanimate, had somehow proposed itself to me as the solution to the pain of my redundancy. So perfect was my stillness as I contemplated a life of horizontal inactivity you not unreasonably concluded I had expired… *(Pause…)*

I am however, certain that whilst the entire purpose of my coming was to expose the hitherto secret existence of the well, and subsequently to fling the poet down its shaft, all this occurred solely in order to make the bed available to you…

(Pause… SHARDLO kicks violently in an attempt to sit upright, but GODANSK's firm grasp leaves her helpless. She is still…)

I would go so far as to say that the apparently arbitrary choice of a circus horse, and even the peculiar smile on the face of the official at the ministry, could be related to the dominant imperative of your occupancy of this –

SHARDLO: IT IS YOU THAT KEEPS ME ON THE BED –

GODANSK: Obviously, it's me –

SHARDLO: Let me up…!

GODANSK: Everything is me –

SHARDLO: *(Writhing.)* Let me –

GODANSK: The development of the crisis, possibly even the origins of the crisis, hard as it is to decipher at this stage, belong inexorably to me –

SHARDLO: *(Calling to the servants.)* GET THIS MAN OFF…!

GODANSK: They've gone –

SHARDLO: HELP ME…!

GODANSK: They are running pell-mell for the horizon –

SHARDLO: Oh…

GODANSK: Shh…

SHARDLO: Oh…

(She sobs. Her struggles subside... At last, GODANSK removes his oppressive hand... SHARDLO does not move. He stands... He moves away from the bed... He drifts out... For a long time she is still... So long that the sky darkens. With nightfall, the sound of distant gunfire, heavy, thudding... The light of gunflashes illuminates the bed...)

LET ME

'The Timid Whom Fear Makes Ruthless…'
Pasolini, 'La Realtà'

Characters

COPOLLA

A Roman Aristocrat, 70

EUCLID

His Son, a Lawyer, 30

APHRODITE

A Slave, 70

AGRICOLA

A Postman, 40

A CHILD

Of the Barbarians, 11

I

A Roman house in the provinces.

COPOLLA: I'm not putting up with it

  (Pause.)

Such is the situation here I am afraid to put my head
outside the door I draw the bolts I slip the chains my
fingers trembling like a palsied pensioner I open it an
inch or so I look I gasp I slam it shut again the trouble is
nobody wants to know

  (Pause.)

You create your life you shape your life refining it a
little more each day until it sings until it murmurs with
contentment like a little stream when suddenly from
nowhere

  (Pause.)

And I so loved the mornings I washed I shaved greeting
the sun and grateful for the rain a cupboard of clean linen
and an apple from the orchard a strict life possibly but
beautiful beautiful if severe when suddenly from nowhere

I'M NOT PUTTING UP WITH IT

EUCLID: *(Entering.)* THERE'S ANOTHER ONE

COPOLLA: I know

EUCLID: You've seen it?

COPOLLA: Yes

  No

  Not yet

  Not yet I haven't no

EUCLID: AND IT'S NAKED

COPOLLA: Naked yes I'm so

EUCLID: NAKED AND

COPOLLA: So sorry

EUCLID: THIS IS HORRIBLE ITS HAND IS

(Pause.)

COPOLLA: Knocking at the door?

EUCLID: Yes

COPOLLA: It's string

(Pause.)

They string the arm up from the knocker so

(Pause.)

At first glance you'd think

(He is nearly humorous..)

That corpse is trying to get in

(Pause.)

Which it is of course it is trying to get in it has been sent ahead so to speak it is along with all the others

(Pause.)

A messenger

(Pause.)

I am so isolated here which once I experienced as privilege the birdsong the sheep uninterrupted views etcetera but what's a source of satisfaction one day is a thrashing on another I am exposed to every sort of mischief and the trouble is nobody wants to know the police

(He laughs mildly.)

The police are too fatigued to travel

(Pause.)

You must go it really was so kind of you to take these days out of your

EUCLID: *(Kindly.)* Shh

COPOLLA: Your life of frantic and indispensable activity and you're a city boy I could not help noticing that when the wolves bark the corners of your mouth turn down with dismay

EUCLID: Yes well I

COPOLLA: *(Cheerfully.)* I was the same a partridge flying from a bush would make me leap whole inches off the ground

EUCLID: Father

COPOLLA: *(Dismissing his son.)* Thank you thank you thank you and forgive this spoiled hospitality leave by the back door I think don't you nothing hanging on the back door usually

EUCLID: Father

COPOLLA: And don't fret for me I keep my sword sharp

EUCLID: Yes I know you do

(COPOLLA ushers his son along.)

COPOLLA: Speaking of which it occurred to me to hack them through the wrists untying cadavers is so sordid when they drop fluids and tissue splash all over you

EUCLID: Oh God

COPOLLA: And they are watching obviously from underneath the trees they see us me and the poor old woman grappling with this

EUCLID: Oh God

COPOLLA: This flopping and exploding packet of corruption and decay

EUCLID: Please you are

COPOLLA: And they are in fits of laughter we are vomiting they are hooting

EUCLID: Father please

COPOLLA: *(Persisting.)* So this time I think hack it hack it through the wrists and after a few days a bunch of hands will dangle from the knocker like a string of onions and this will say

EUCLID: YOU ARE DELIBERATELY OFFENDING ME

COPOLLA: He also has a sense of humour the Roman he also wrings wit from his despair

EUCLID: FATHER

COPOLLA: *(With a choking sob.)* I CANNOT BEAR THIS ANY LONGER

(He snorts. His son embraces him.)

Some of these corpses were my friends not friends not friends exactly familiar I mean they were familiar to me they drag them out the cemetery hair teeth and bits of last week it was a woman I had slept with

(He snorts.)

Only once I never knew her name

(He recovers.)

EUCLID: You are coming with me to the city

COPOLLA: No

EUCLID: Yes we are boarding up the house and all the furniture can be stored until the day when the authorities

COPOLLA: No

EUCLID: Restore the situation in the outlying districts

COPOLLA: NEVER WILL BE SUCH A DAY

EUCLID: Silly

COPOLLA: NEVER AND NEVER CALL ME SILLY

(Pause.)

EUCLID: I apologize

COPOLLA: If you wish to help me stay and we will kill them

(Pause. EUCLID is shaken.)

EUCLID: I

(He falters.)

KILL THEM?

I

(With sudden resolve.)

Obviously I can't stay I am in the middle of such a critical preparing all these documents and little Claudia has scarlet fever it was difficult to get away my wife and you know she not possible this vital court case we

2

APHRODITE: He's gone then?

COPOLLA: Yes his daughter has scarlet fever and a court case of profound significance is pending the outcome of which will dictate the direction of his whole career I was lucky to see him even for a day

APHRODITE: Such a clever man your son

COPOLLA: He is clever

APHRODITE: With clever young men like your son in charge I always say

COPOLLA: Very clever

APHRODITE: Things can only get better

COPOLLA: Things can only get better or what's the use of cleverness Aphrodite you do not have to stay you are seventy years old and I am the same we need no longer talk of loyalty no family had a better servant consider your own interests we will neither of us know another decent hour I'm crying I'm crying at my own litany please don't leave I do not mean a word of what I say on the contrary I insist you stay everything I uttered was designed to make you contradict me contradict me Aphrodite please now I sound like the slave while you regard me with a mistress's disdain how hard it is not to be a slave how very hard contradict me then

(APHRODITE is silent, COPOLLA complacent.)

I interpret your silence as

APHRODITE: *(Supressing a wail.)* I will be beheaded

(A shock…)

I will be

(Pause.)

Beheaded

(Pause. COPOLLA moves to her.)

COPOLLA: Sit down

APHRODITE: No

COPOLLA: Please sit and we

APHRODITE: The sheets and

COPOLLA: Never mind the sheets

APHRODITE: The sheets and pillowcases need to be

COPOLLA: Forget the pillowcases please the sheets the towels the pillowcases

(APHRODITE sobs.)

And tell me who

(She wails.)

WHO IS BEHEADING YOU WHO

(She is obedient. She inhales…)

APHRODITE: As I was coming in today two of their children stopped me they blocked my way where do you think you're going they said you old you old something something rude you old

(She sniffs…)

Bitch it was where do you think you're going you old bitch the same place I always go to I said the same place I have been going to for forty years it isn't forty is it it's more like forty-five what for they said to cook his dinner I said to clean his shoes from now on they said let him cook his own dinner let him polish his own shoes I don't think he knows how to I said forgive me I know you do but I was trying to be funny make today your last day they said and if we see you in this road again your head is coming off your shoulders silly I said then I saw their brothers in the trees why are they always in the trees they don't stand in sunlight do they always under trees and they took a long sword out from underneath their clothes and did this did this

(She sighs.)

Joking probably I

(Pause.)

Joking I expect

(Pause. With an intake of breath she goes to resume her duties, but stops.)

Really the police ought to protect us shouldn't they they should protect ordinary people who the army or the police?

(Pause.)

COPOLLA: Strip the beds now

APHRODITE: And you live here on your own I do think

COPOLLA: Yes

(Pause.)

Now do the laundry while I get whoever it may be from off the door at least I know

(He half-laughs.)

Strange where one finds one's consolations in extremity

APHRODITE: Shh

COPOLLA: I know I shall not find myself looking in the empty sockets of my wife

APHRODITE: Oh shh

COPOLLA: She's ashes Thalia

APHRODITE: I'll strip the beds

COPOLLA: Ashes isn't she?

APHRODITE: Ashes yes

COPOLLA: *(A new horror.)* BUT WHAT ABOUT THE URN?

(A fractional reflection.)

Fetch the urn please Aphrodite

APHRODITE: Now?

COPOLLA: Yes this minute get my darling's ashes and never mind the beds the beds can wait quick please IS THE URN THERE IS THE URN IN ITS USUAL PLACE?

APHRODITE: *(Distantly.)* Yes

COPOLLA: Good good the urn is in its usual place silly how one silly how I

(APHRODITE returns.)

Give it to me put it in my hands my darling she

(He chokes. He recovers…)

I never travelled much did I I think you could say of me he was Roman in every way but not at all Roman in curiosity the seven years I served in the army I served here whereas my classmates ended up in Syria

APHRODITE: You were too delicate for Syria

COPOLLA: Much too delicate

APHRODITE: The heat

COPOLLA: I would have suffocated as for Germany

APHRODITE: All swamps

COPOLLA: Swamps yes the mosquitoes would have done for me but Thalia oh what a brave girl was my Thalia she thrived on adversity plagues blizzards frontier wars her spirits rose like the sun I bored her probably

APHRODITE: Never

COPOLLA: Ha

APHRODITE: Never bored her never

COPOLLA: And now all that I so assiduously avoided comes to me if you dread shipwrecks you shouldn't go to sea that's good that's very good but what if the tide comes flooding

through the garden I wish I was ashes in the urn and
Thalia was holding me I DO I WISH I WAS ASHES

3

APHRODITE: See you tomorrow

COPOLLA: See me tomorrow

APHRODITE: *(Withdrawing.)* I'll bring the honey

COPOLLA: The honey yes the honey please

APHRODITE: Tomorrow then

COPOLLA: Tomorrow yes tomorrow obviously

*(COPOLLA's line is cut off as APHRODITE pours back and clasps
COPOLLA.)*

WHY KISS ME WHY ARE YOU

(A wail from APHRODITE.)

WHY ARE YOU KISSING ME?

(A scuffle. The door slams. COPOLLA is alone.)

I'm dead

(Pause.)

I'm dead and she knows it HONEY MY ARSE she won't
be dithering down the lane again hot bread in one hand
onions in the other HONEY MY ARSE why lie why fatigue
yourself with lying when you are lent the opportunity to
speak a formal and a dignified farewell but no she prefers
to God knows why because she is a slave presumably she
actually prefers concocting lies of pitiful inefficacy HONEY
MY ARSE I don't mind lying in desperate circumstances or
even when the circumstances are not desperate lying yes a
lie can be a work of art but

(He rages.)

YOU BITCH OF FORTY YEARS' DURATION YOU HAVE
ABANDONED ME

(Pause. The silence sings around him…)

So what

So I am abandoned

So there is me and only me me old me solitary absolute
and utter me I prefer it yes I do the extinction the
eradication of every wretched and melancholy illusion
friendship allegiance piety the whole basket of discredited
solidarities AS FOR THE POLICE

(He half-laughs in the silence…)

Nice laugh

I had a nice laugh she said Thalia not only Thalia others
too

Once I knew how nice it was I practised it

(He laughs loudly.)

I'll hang myself on the front door

Yes

A noose of wire a toppled stool the perspiration on my
bursting forehead sponged by the moon it takes fifteen
minutes strangulation what a mask of horror and my urine
I presume will trickle down the steps to greet them I'll
shave I'll put on clean

(An abrupt pause.)

The comic gesture

(He is without irony.)

It's decay

It's the rot of pride mother father they won't say the
Roman in the big house got humour from his own corpse
better they hack me living in a thousand bits their filthy
children running with my eyes on twigs vastly better vastly
father forgive your idle son who sank his adolescent arse
in your upholstery and jeered at Caesar if Caesar walked
by I would hail Caesar I would scream Caesar from the
wreckage of my lungs and die exquisitely in some gushing
haemorrhage

(He slams the door bolts one after another.)

HANG HIMSELF A ROMAN NO HANGING'S FOR DOGS

(He hurries about the room. He slams shutters.)

It's not too late it's never too late to excavate some dignity
even from the most corrupted soul at the point of death
particularly it's as if the yawning chasm of oblivion lent
you some final

(He clatters the catches.)

Some final

(Something fractures and drops pinging to the tiled floor.)

Oh Christ these catches are rusted through this should
have been checked routinely checked the slaves are
useless what a useless parasite was Aphrodite forty years of
idleness of course a bad slave is the mirror to her mistress I
blame Thalia I do I do blame Thalia you can't keep house
and still do all the things she

THE SHUTTERS ARE USELESS THEN NOT ONLY THIS
ONE WITH THE BROKEN CATCH ALL THE SHUTTERS ARE
EFFECTIVELY ABOLISHED I'LL NAIL IT UP

(A fractional pause.)

I'll nail it up

(A breath.)

Of course this represents a significant defeat for me to turn my home into a IF I HAVE A HAMMER IF THERE ARE NAILS

(He breathes to pacify himself…)

I must not conclude because I now require a hammer so desperately I will discover one the evidence of the rusty shutter suggests to me I may be frustrated someone having used the hammer may not have replaced it it may be lying in the long grass and this idle individual might be me oh yes I don't exclude myself from this indictment of neglect EXPECT TO SUFFER that must be my motto from now on

(He is hurrying downstairs into a basement room.)

The worse things get the more likely it will be that nothing whatsoever

IT'S THERE IT'S HANGING ON ITS HOOK THE HAMMER

(He laughs.)

Darling darling hammer AND A BAG OF NAILS you see my pessimism is unjustified an indulgence possibly the mundane facts are these that things are sometimes

(The sound of nails.)

Good nails very good nails sometimes out of order but equally sometimes perfectly THESE ARE VERY GOOD NAILS perfectly to hand

(Pause.)

These very good nails I take to be a sign not only of hope if I may allow myself a little hope but also of

(He meditates.)

The excellence of my culture its arts its industry THE ROMAN NAIL Christ got three I saw one once bent bent where it had been yanked free it bleeds at Easter the other two God knows where they are I was offered a fragment

of the cross once a substantial fragment a Scythian with a
dogcart he

(He stops.)

I'm going on

(Pause.)

I'm going on as one does when one is solitary that can only
get worse and whereas it might calm my nerves it

(Pause.)

It might obscure the subtle indications of a forced entrance
how fatuous if I were so deep in conversation with myself
my voice drowned out the

(Pause.)

Footfalls of an intruder my killer possibly and they go
barefoot barefoot in winter whereas we

(He stops.)

We

We

We don't

(Pause.)

The least of our differences

4

Nails being driven home.

COPOLLA: Noise I hate it possibly because it advertises what
you would prefer to be

(More hammer blows…)

A secret I should have muffled the hammer I should have wrapped a duster round the hammer head the only drawback

(A final few blows.)

To muffling the hammer being this that it renders it a clumsy instrument and knowing me I'd

(One last blow.)

Mishit

(The hammer laid down.)

I'd mishit and the injury would given my age given my frailty

(He stops.)

I'M NOT FRAIL HA WHY DO I SAY FRAIL FRAIL ME I'VE NEVER SEEN A DOCTOR NO DOCTOR HAS EVER WAITED ON COPOLLA IT'S LEGENDARY

No

That was an affectation designed to earn me sympathy sympathy from whom there's no one here but me stop that now stop that flirting with senility from this moment on age is coincidence as for noise

(He scoops up the unused nails…)

Noise has two faces the sound and the interpretation of the sound take the gasping of a crowd an unseen crowd inside a stadium is it a missed goal or a criminal beheaded is it grief or ecstasy they can hear me hammering obviously but how have they chosen to

(A swift deduction.)

THEY THINK MY NERVE HAS FAILED THEY THINK HE'S ACTING LIKE A MADMAN UNDER SIEGE

(And another.)

I'll open them again yes fling them open with a crash puzzling behaviour but what's wrong with that it's strategy the enemy must never be allowed to gain an intellectual ascendancy it's

(A pulse of horror.)

WHO'S THERE

WHO'S THERE

THIS IS MY HOME I'M ARMED I HAVE FRIENDS MANY FRIENDS THEY'RE EVERYWHERE MY FRIENDS WHO'S THERE

(A pause of pure anxiety.)

AGRICOLA: Post

COPOLLA: POST IT'S DUSK

AGRICOLA: It wasn't when I left

COPOLLA: STAY WHERE YOU ARE WHAT POST SHOW ME

(A move.)

SHOW ME FROM THERE

(Pause.)

That's a letter where's your badge

AGRICOLA: In my pocket

COPOLLA: IN YOUR POCKET IN YOUR POCKET WHAT GOOD'S THAT I MIGHT HAVE I COULD SO EASILY HAVE BADGES ARE FOR WEARING IN A PROMINENT PLACE THE LEFT SHOULDER FOR EXAMPLE TO IDENTIFY AN OFFICIAL OF THE STATE

(A breath.)

An insignificant official you're all wet give me the letter why are you wet THE LETTER'S WET AS WELL

AGRICOLA: I crossed the lake

COPOLLA: IT'S ILLEGIBLE

AGRICOLA: I can tell you what it says

COPOLLA: CAN YOU CAN YOU INDEED

(He alters.)

Sit down sit down and take off your clothes I am grateful to you profoundly grateful I have been so

(The postman shows his badge.)

Thank you that is the badge of the Imperial Post Office

AGRICOLA: It's cold that lake

COPOLLA: It's fed by streams the streams start in the mountains

AGRICOLA: I heard the fish

COPOLLA: It's full of fish

AGRICOLA: Carp

COPOLLA: Carp and bream the lake was excavated by my grandfather it is fifty metres wide there was a bridge a stone bridge the bridge deteriorated and was not repaired I don't know why I should have repaired the bridge why didn't I?

AGRICOLA: I waded

COPOLLA: It isn't deep

(He tears the envelope open…)

AGRICOLA: And they were singing

COPOLLA: It's from the Department of Justice

AGRICOLA: Sad singing I thought now or never

COPOLLA: A short letter

AGRICOLA: Or maybe not sad what we call sad they might call happy

COPOLLA: Very short

AGRICOLA: Anyway I slipped in Christ it's cold I thought

COPOLLA: *(Perusing.)* My name's mis-spelt

AGRICOLA: I held my breath

COPOLLA: *(Straining.)* As for the rest

AGRICOLA: And walked

COPOLLA: It's

It's

It's completely illegible

(Pause.)

Well since you say you've read it perhaps you'd be so kind as to

AGRICOLA: I haven't read it

COPOLLA: You haven't read it but you claim to know its contents?

AGRICOLA: I do know the contents

COPOLLA: How if

AGRICOLA: Because it's the same as all the rest

(Pause.)

COPOLLA: The rest?

(He fathoms…)

THE REST HOW MANY THEN HOW MANY OTHERS HAVE

(Agricola sneezes.)

You're shivering

(And again.)

Forgive me I am allowing my impatience to smother my hospitality I'll fetch a towel

(He hurries away. He is distant.)

You live alone you lose all sense of common courtesy

(A third sneeze.)

And I see so few

(Cupboard doors smack…)

So very few people

CORPSES MOSTLY I DON'T EXAGGERATE

(He returns.)

People whose funerals I attended it's

AGRICOLA: *(Taking the towel.)* Thank you

COPOLLA: Peculiar

(AGRICOLA towels his head vigorously. COPOLLA attends, scarcely able to conceal his impatience.)

So

(AGRICOLA sneezes yet again.)

They're identical these letters

(AGRICOLA blows his nose on the towel.)

 I'm not alone in

AGRICOLA: You've got to go

(A knife turns in COPOLLA. AGRICOLA clears his throat…)

 The text reads if you want the full text the Department of Justice Region Five North Rhone regrets to inform you that it is no longer able

(He sneezes…)

Oh…

(He clears his throat.)

Were was I?

COPOLLA: No longer able…

AGRICOLA: No longer able to extend protection civil or military to citizens living in estates and villages lying outside the line described as A to B on the accompanying map I lost the map a map was meant to be attached to every letter but they ran out of maps I got one but it was nicked off me anyway that lake would have buggered it frankly you are strongly advised that's them talking not me strongly advised to make arrangements immediately to move to one of the following centres where preparations have been made to welcome you then there is a list and one is underlined the underlined one is the most proximate to you but you are not obliged to go there you may choose another one it goes on the Department can assume no responsibility for personal loss or injury resulting from failure to act upon this advice signed I think his name is Diopodius but none of us could read it in the office I am ashamed to have to give you this that's not them that's me

COPOLLA: Yes

AGRICOLA: And A to B keeps shifting

COPOLLA: *(Strangely placid.)* Necessarily

(COPOLLA is contemplative.)

I do think it is wonderful wonderful and strange that you a Roman messenger will march a freezing lake in darkness upholding thereby the great tradition of your profession and please believe me I am not mocking you in order to deliver me a statement so pitiful it is the last humiliation of all that lent dignity to that tradition in the first place no wonder you do not care to wear the badge

AGRICOLA: It's dangerous

COPOLLA: Obviously

AGRICOLA: They beat a postman half to death they broke his knees

COPOLLA: No more walking for him now I think you should be going but not via the lake there is a track running between high weeds and by crawling you need not be

(He stops.)

Crawling

(An intake of breath.)

I a Roman tell a Roman crawl through weeds

AGRICOLA: *(Blithely.)* Romans have crawled

COPOLLA: *(Matching him with a short laugh.)* Frequently but not through their own gardens I believe

(A fractional triumph.)

You crawl however and I will hammer the hammer will distract them those who are not singing or desecrating graves and in five minutes you will be free there is a culvert over a ditch stay in that ditch it's dry and leads to houses you will recognize the houses probably

(They walk to the door.)

It's strange the army wins battles many battles if the news is to be believed but these battles have become wholly symbolic in character they alter nothing nothing stops the oozing of the tribes as for the thing called A to B

AGRICOLA: That line and me

COPOLLA: You and that line a job in perpetuity I daresay

(They stop at the back door.)

I am not leaving here

AGRICOLA: *(Not unkindly.)* They all say that

COPOLLA: Do they?

AGRICOLA: The women especially they stamp their feet they break things kids cowering in the corner I've had precious china chucked at me the husbands it's funny with the husbands they seem to sink you think he's sinking whereas she

COPOLLA: No wives here only me

(He unlatches the back door but fails to open it. He is puzzled.)

It's bolted

AGRICOLA: Wisely bolted

COPOLLA: Certainly so how was it you

(A fractional pause.)

The Messenger of Misery did he come through

(He tries the window.)

No

The window's locked you how did you

AGRICOLA: The door was open

COPOLLA: Open was it so who bolted it someone bolted it after you

(He dismisses the confusion from his mind by an act of will.)

I DID I DID

I do things I forget I've done them it's partly age partly partly age but also I think one must include the situation goodbye now goodbye and

(With a sudden shock of violence COPOLLA thrusts AGRICOLA against the door.)

WHOSE SIDE ARE YOU ON

WHOSE SIDE ARE YOU ON

(AGRICOLA chokes.)

I HAVE LIVED HERE SIXTY YEARS YOU UTTER

(And chokes…)

UTTER

(He drags back the doorbolts and thrusts the postman into the night.)

GET OUT AND MAY THE DARK DESTROY YOUR BRAIN

(COPOLLA sobs in his rage. He slowly bolts the door. He draws deep breath…)

It's not his fault it's not his fault

IT IS

IT IS

I didn't bolt the door

IT IS HIS FAULT

Did I I know I did not bolt the door I passed the door to fetch the towel I did not bolt it possibly I kicked it shut with one foot as I passed GIVE HIM A TOWEL THE TRAITOR WHY the relics of a hospitality I presume HE BRINGS ME EVIL NEWS AND I GIVE HIM A TOWEL that's wrong that's an abuse of my humanity HE'S HAND IN GLOVE WITH THEM they want to break his knees he says quite possibly they do but only because they are in blissful ignorance if they knew the significance of what he carried they would kiss his postman's arse

(He is still…)

'I cannot use that towel it is too clean for a filthy and degraded wretch such as I am…'

(Pause.)

He might have said that

He might have created from his humiliation an heroic apology

Oh yes

Oh yes postmen can utter

Postmen also have their pools of sensibility turbid but

I KNOW I DID NOT BOLT THAT DOOR

5

A child's giggling laugh. It ceases. It comes again.

COPOLLA: Put down the jar

Put it down the jar put it on the table please

The jar is not an ordinary jar

If you want a jar I will find you one

(The mischievous giggle.)

I know a little girl like you you are a girl aren't you she is mischievous she giggles sometimes her daddy smacks her are you a girl the jar is

(A fractional pause.)

PUT IT DOWN

(A long pause. The faint sounds of a barely-inhabited house…)

You see my wife is in the jar

(Giggling.)

That's funny to you…!

I suppose it is I suppose if you are whoever you are coming from wherever you do and your fathers and your brothers routinely dig up graves and strew the parts around then you would

(Giggling.)

YES IT WOULD TICKLE YOU

(And more.)

You do not understand a word of what I'm saying not a word do you you

*(The urn is dropped. It smashes on the floor. An intense pain engulfs
COPOLLA.)*

Oh

Oh

You ugly stunted and misbegotten scrap of human
perversity

Oh

You

Barbaric

Bit of

I'm

Killing

You

(A sudden move.)

DON'T RUN YOU BIT

(The move stops.)

YOU DREADFUL BIT

Anyway the door is bolted isn't it you bolted it yourself
God knows why why did you bolt the door it's criminal is
it some criminal trick it failed then it failed

(COPOLLA seethes…)

You are stupid every one of you clumsy ugly and stupid
and like all stupid people also cruel but cruel in such a
poor way if you want to see real cruelty I will show it
to you do you want to see real cruelty beautiful cruelty
cruelty refined that also is a culture

LET A ROMAN SHOW HOW DARK AND LOUD IT IS THE
ROMAN MIND LET HIM

(COPOLLA gasps at his own violence…)

The way you look at me

The way you a filthy child of the migrations studies a
Roman

I think you bolted the door how strange this is oh how
strange because you did not think of yourself as a thief but
in your dim way as the proprietor yes I see it in your eyes

PREMATURE

PREMATURE THE PROPRIETOR STILL EXISTS

*(COPOLLA's vehemence at last collapses the child. She wails. Gratified,
he lets it continue for some time, echoing in the house…)*

Stop now

Stop

Stop you bit of

(She wails…)

No

Cry on

CRY AND LET THE WHOLE TRIBE KNOW YOUR MISERY

(He flings back one of the shutters and calls into the night.)

SHE'S IN HERE

SHE'S IN HERE SHE OR HE AND THE WRONG SIDE OF
THE LINE

*(He laughs, semi-hysterical, and slams the shutter… the child falls
quiet…)*

There's a line called A to B Rome is one side of it and your
lot's on the other official oh I don't invent things from this
moment on you are designated C C is your name what is
your name your name is C

(He threatens.)

C

C

(A pause. The house moves…)

I don't like you I did not kill you though I was entitled to I stayed my hand but I don't like you

6

A handbroom sweeps the tiles.

COPOLLA: Good

Good

Now tip the ashes on the tray on the tray just tip them

Good

And tap the dustpan with the broom

Tap

Tap

Just tap the

(A metallic tap.)

Good

My wife is on the tray my wife who was formerly in the jar is now on the tray Thalia who was thin and beautiful and liked to travel and meet strangers is now on the tray as for me I like neither travel nor strangers in many ways we were not compatible I stayed here and she went away possibly I preferred it when she was away at this moment I am not prepared to say she died beside a road the stars were out apparently and the ruts in the road stood stiff with frost it was bitterly cold I was in bed here with a log fire burning in bed and not alone I am prepared to admit that now that is how it goes when one of you likes travel and the other likes to stay at home on the tray my Thalia my wife on the tray I wasn't sorry

(A beat.)

You're shocked you're shocked to hear me say what I have never said before her death created in me DON'T LOOK AWAY a surge of pleasure blood rushed to my brain they thought he's grief-stricken he's blasted he'll never be the same

IT WAS EUPHORIA

(A beat.)

WHY DO YOU LOOK AWAY

(Pause.)

Maybe a bad thought communicates itself in any language maybe the unwashed child of the barbarian is censorious her girlish dreams of matrimony spoil when ugly old men utter the unutterable you smashed the urn not me

(A faint tapping on the shutter. COPOLLA is silenced. After a few seconds the tapping is repeated.)

Someone wants you

(And again, more softly still…)

How furtively he taps the shutter this desperate parent I am almost

(And again…)

Charmed

(And yet again.)

A besotted lover could not stroke the fevered forehead of his lover more tenderly

(The child shifts.)

DON'T MOVE I'LL CUT YOU IN TWO PIECES

(Pause. The taut breathing of man and child in the silence. Now the tapping is sharp, irritable.)

Finite is his patience the barbaric summons must be answered

AFTER YOU

(He grabs the child, who squirms.)

And if they toss a spear their precious child will catch it

(He drags her over the floor.)

Yes

Yes

I sense you are apprehensive

ME TOO

(COPOLLA flings back the bolts of the shutters and throws them open. Silence, but for wind and a high, crying bird…)

The postman smiles

(Pause.)

I wonder what he found funny or do all severed heads grin possibly the facial muscles in a mortal spasm drag the mouth to one side and as smiles go the postman's is ghastly but

(The child squirms and is fixed by COPOLLA.)

YOU'RE SHARING THIS WITH ME

THIS

THIS

STRICTLY ROMAN OBJECTIVITY

(He gasps.)

Yes

Yes

And on further consideration say if you disagree his whole expression is characterized by ambiguity the eyes turned up like that suggest contempt as if the world caused him to shudder with distaste but on the other hand

KEEP STILL AND STUDY

(He drags the child back.)

The mouth has something pitiful about it it is as if he were warning me to

(The child lets out a cry.)

I ALSO FEEL SICK BUT SICKNESS IS A DOORWAY

COME THROUGH IT WITH ME

(The child cries out, as if a name.)

That's them your brothers lurking under the trees and your mother surely YES SAYS THE POSTMAN'S HEAD THE ENTIRE FAMILY

HE KNOWS

HE KNOWS

SAY GOODBYE THEN SAY

(He hauls the child back and slams the shutters then bolts them. His horror spills out…)

POOR

POOR

POSTMAN

OH

POSTMAN FORGIVE ME

(COPOLLA snorts his tears. Pause. He inhales deeply…)

Peculiar the barbarian mentality they think to show me
the spiked head of a decent man will cause me to what
panic presumably to throw open the doors and then what
crawl down the steps mumbling my apology apology for
what no it's not a clever strategy I wonder if they love you
yes I wonder if they do because most men would reply to
that provocation by flinging bits of you out of the window
childish hand and childish foot certainly they love you in
a strange way if they love you you're a sacrifice perhaps
yes that is what you are they're sacrificing you that's
compatible with love…

7

A view.

COPOLLA: What you see before you is the terrace I say the
terrace strictly speaking it is the upper terrace you can see
the lower terrace has been swallowed by the ferns terracing
enables us to walk easily within the perimeters of the
property to sit to converse and so on my mother walked
there frequently terracing is civilized as the sun sets on the
statues we

(Pause.)

Oh I'm

(Pause.)

I cry easily perhaps that is also civilized I think tribes do
not cry from nostalgia do they they are nomadic you tell
me if they cry no I think one has to say there is crying
and crying we have our own crying it comes from loving
one place century after century then there is the fishpond

seven actually but six got silted and I rarely eat fish I
did not spend my money wisely some would say but if
I had maintained this landscape perfectly I should have
been yet more bitter at your trespass I think when your
horde swarms over my corpse I at least will not resent the
energy expended on renovating the water-gardens what do
gardens mean to you not a lot I

(The child laughs excitedly.)

Yes

Your cousins are assembling for some mischief in the

GET DOWN

(He hurts the child. She squeals.)

GET DOWN AND SHUT YOUR

Oh what I would not give now for a one javelin from here
I

(Pause.)

If it were not for my shoulder

(Pause.)

My rheumatic shoulder I

(Pause. He studies.)

They are dragging hay great bales of hay

(He is instantly intuitive.)

If they put torches to that hay

IF

IF I SAY

Obviously they are going to ignite the hay the wind is
blowing hard in this direction it's a perfect day to smoke
me out of doors

(He grabs the child.)

THIS CONCLUDES YOUR EDUCATION FOR TODAY

(He slams the shutters.)

You look afraid a little less defiant a little more afraid and that's sensible because

(He stops. He sniffs.)

Yes

Yes

The sacrifice is rarely willing is she her parents have betrayed her and she knows

(He sniffs.)

I'm tying you to the doorframe and when the wind blows a little less they'll glimpse you through the smoke shout shout no or yes to their barbarity

(The child squirms.)

Yes

(They grapple.)

UP YOU GO

APHRODITE: *(Below.)* Mr Copolla

COPOLLA: *(To the child.)* DON'T QUARREL WITH ME I WILL

APHRODITE: Mr Copolla

COPOLLA: BREAK YOUR BONES

APHRODITE: Smoke Mr Copolla

COPOLLA: *(Tying the child.)* Smoke yes but it won't be me who's choking on it

> *(He turns and leaving the child tied hurries down the wooden stairs. He flings back the bolts.)*

APHRODITE: Smoke

COPOLLA: Get inside

APHRODITE: *(An irritated cough.)* Brought your honey

COPOLLA: Honey

How kind of you how very kind

(The child cries above.)

HOW DID YOU GET HERE

APHRODITE: That's a child

COPOLLA: It is a child yes a crying child did you walk down the road the postman's head is

APHRODITE: Postman?

COPOLLA: POSTMAN YES HIS HEAD IS ON A POLE

APHRODITE: What's the matter with that child?

COPOLLA: *(Seething.)* Ignore the child the child is my affair I asked you how came here did you come down the road?

APHRODITE: Of course I did

COPOLLA: DON'T SAY OF COURSE I DID LIKE THAT AS IF THE ROAD WAS NORMAL THE ROAD IS FAR FROM NORMAL

APHRODITE: Normal today

COPOLLA: Normal is it if it's normal it's because

(He coughs…)

Because briefly

(And again.)

Very briefly they have abandoned menacing the road in order to swarm over the fields they are in the fields

(He coughs again.)

Because they

(Pause.)

My eyes are watering

(He wipes his eyes.)

Because they are burning hay Aphrodite my own hay

(The child wails from above.)

APHRODITE: Who is that child Mr Copolla?

COPOLLA: I don't know I call her C probably she has a name if she has I daresay I could not pronounce it

APHRODITE *(Alarmed.)* The child's in pain

COPOLLA: Yes

The smoke

The smoke created by the burning of my hay is getting in her eyes her throat and

(A fractional reflection.)

APHRODITE: I'll fetch her

COPOLLA: STAY WHERE YOU ARE YOU ARE A SLAVE

(Some distant cries, not from the child…)

APHRODITE: I

I can't

I can't stand here and

COPOLLA: You can

(They are cruelly opposed…)

APHRODITE: I CAN'T I CAN'T

COPOLLA: You can stand there you must stand there and

(He clears his throat. The child cries.)

if you try to move away I will behead you with this sword

(The threat goes in…)

APHRODITE: Mr Copolla…

COPOLLA: Forty-five years' service notwithstanding pots of honey sweet memories of old days so what I am a Roman this is my house and you are my slave

(Pause. APHRODITE wants to remonstrate…)

APHRODITE: Thalia she would

COPOLLA: THALIA IS ASH AND ON A TRAY

(A fractional pause.)

Am I mistaken or is the smoke less dense do look Aphrodite

(Suddenly.) I AM SO SORRY I HATE TO THREATEN YOU THANK YOU FOR THE HONEY APHRODITE

It is

It is clearing away

APHRODITE: *(Peering through an aperture.)* They're quarrelling

COPOLLA: Quarrelling are they good let them quarrel until they burst their veins let me see

(He peers now.)

Yes the signs of dissension are unmistakable

(He gloats.)

They are shoving one another and those who are not shoving are sullen

(He comes away.)

Give the child the honey

(APHRODITE goes to climb the stairs.)

And Aphrodite

(She stops.)

Never think to betray me

APHRODITE: Betray you Mr Copolla did you say betray?

COPOLLA: I did

(He is adamant.)

I did say betray

(Pause. They are at odds…)

APHRODITE: I am sorry if my master chooses to interpret my pity for a weeping child as treachery I have had children as you know and

COPOLLA: The child's my enemy my enemy and yours also so what if birth disposes you to pity even those whose blue-eyed charm conceals a malignant malice SHE THREW MY THALIA AGAINST THE WALL she didn't she didn't she didn't throw her SHE DROPPED THALIA DELIBERATELY so now you know and what's birth anyway it's a spasm it's a function rats do it so do worms and you what did you give birth to a brood of criminals and prostitutes I'M SORRY APHRODITE YOU MUST GO you are making me so

APHRODITE: *(Pitying him now.)* Mr Copolla

COPOLLA: Feed the child the honey and then go

(Pause. APHRODITE starts to climb the stairs. She stops.)

APHRODITE: Camilla's not a prostitute

COPOLLA: She isn't no she is nothing like a prostitute and if she were so what

(APHRODITE moves again.)

I am not leaving here

(And stops.)

To stay can also be a journey

APHRODITE: A journey to where Mr Copolla?

COPOLLA: To why I am

To what we were

To all that was pity Thalia her travelling was pure cowardice trapped in some feverish swamp she convinced herself she was ennobled by her curiosity what she had no curiosity about was Thalia herself it is an abyss the self you must equip yourself with long ropes very long hurry now Aphrodite the wriggling child will slip her knots

(The servant climbs the stairs.)

AND THEN GO

How you got here is a miracle and it will take another miracle to get you home again

8

A distant howl, as APHRODITE is tortured

COPOLLA: *(Throwing back the shutters again.)* Two miracles no one is entitled to

APHRODITE: *(Sobbing.)* Mr Cop – olla save me …

COPOLLA: The postman he took my advice go through the long grass I said advice which effectively delivered him to his killers I squirmed if you remember do you remember me crying I did briefly so with Aphrodite I kept my mouth shut I did not want the onerous responsibility of

APHRODITE: *(Bawling.)* MR COP – OLLA

COPOLLA: Of murdering my slave albeit unintentionally and she knows the district God knows every track and henhouse in the vicinity but still

(The child laughs…)

You find this

(And again.)

This disgusting spectacle amuses you

(He sighs deeply. APHRODITE wails…)

APHRODITE: Don't you like me Mr Copolla oh Mr Copolla like me

COPOLLA: *(Calling.)* OBVIOUSLY I LIKE YOU

APHRODITE: Then set the child free

(A nauseating cry as she is tortured … the child is amused.)

COPOLLA: That's the wrong way round surely that's the situation back to front we have established have we not that even to visit me

(She is hurt again.)

Even to visit me was to set your life at hazard did you not describe to me in graphic detail how they threatened to behead you why should they now when they have slaughtered the poor postman and are throbbing with animosity towards

(And again.)

towards you me and every Roman dead or alive suddenly display a diplomatic nicety never ever known in them before no no this is pure misapprehension the facts are these

APHRODITE: *(Her worst voice.)* MR COP – OLLA

(The child laughs. COPOLLA delivers a sickening smack to her jaw. She cries out.)

COPOLLA: YOU ASKED FOR THAT

YOU BEGGED FOR THAT

YOU ARE A REPULSIVE THING OF BACKWARDNESS AND SAVAGERY

Get up

Get up

Get off the floor

(He drags her to her feet.)

No the contrary is the case the contrary

(COPOLLA is breathless, but calls.)

I'LL BLIND THIS CHILD DO YOU HEAR ME

(He draws back her head. She utters a sharp cry.)

WITH THIS SWORD POINT TWO JABS

EASY

EASY

(A silence prevails but for birdsong in the fields.)

Walk away then

To your small and somewhat squalid hut

Walk Aphrodite

To your crippled husband lift him out of bed set him on the mule and quit because you also are on the wrong side of the line A B

Go on

Go on

I've got the child and they don't want me to blind her obviously it's an equation

WALK APHRODITE

(The silence again…)

She's walking

Ha

She's walking

(A beat. Suddenly COPOLLA emits a howl of horror and disgust…)

Oh my dear my dear oh my dear oh my dear

(He fills his lungs.)

Oh my dear and my dear and my dear

(And fills them again. The child sobs now.)

THAT'S SO ILLOGICAL

(He staggers, treading on the child in his agony.)

I must blind you then I must blind you now I must blind I must blind

(He draws her close.)

OH YES

OH YES

OR NOTHING I HAVE SAID IS CREDIBLE

(He chokes on anguish.)

You must agree if I fail to blind you they will think me squeamish cowardly or squeamish and they are looking look at them looking they wait to see if I

(A Beat.)

So obviously I must do it

A ROMAN DOES NOT HESITATE HE ACTS HE

You could say that defines the Roman the speed with
which he

THE ANGER AND THE ACT ONE FOLLOWS THE OTHER
SPONTANEOUSLY

(Pause. The birds…)

But arguably by not acting I pose for them the same
problem they pose for me the problem of illogicality
I predicted something and they disappointed me they
disappointed expectations of a kind possibly entirely
inappropriate and my dear Aphrodite paid the penalty just
so they are expecting me to act now in a fury but what if
I do not act if I do not act I make myself a mystery what's
more if I refrain from blinding you now it remains for
me to blind you later had I blinded you presumably they
would have swarmed through the window killing me and
killing you a wolfpack of pure madness no this is better

THE ROMAN ALSO CALCULATES

(Pause. He recovers…)

Oh God they are hacking off her head

Look

Look what your people do and I must look I must she was
my loyal and

She was my loyal and

(He falters.)

I WILL LOOK

(He is swept by nausea.)

I WILL LOOK AND SO WILL YOU LOOK I SAID

(He forces the child to watch.)

Yes

Yes

She was

She was and is no longer what she was she no longer is she
if you can call it she the thing there on the grass the thing
once known to me and others as Aphrodite

(He screams.)

CUT IT CUT IT PROPERLY CUT IT THROUGH YOU

(He is silent a moment.)

Now is

Now has no more to do with me or with the world her
voice her odour are things consigned to memory it takes
two minutes less than two

(He screams again.)

WHY WON'T HE CUT IT PROPERLY

No

No

What does it matter she isn't in her head it's not her head
the head's empty we must get used to the sordidity of
human actions and cease to say it's self-indulgence surely
that such-and-such a thing offends that such-and-such a
thing nauseates me

TOO BAD

TOO LATE

TOO EVERYTHING

Now what's he doing I can't see he's

(A pause, a breath.)

Are you watching this he seems to be

(A breath.)

He is

He is stripping her clothes off her poor Aphrodite

OF COURSE IT ISN'T HER

That is so

NOT HER AT ALL

So entirely unnecessary an old woman who never showed her knees

(He howls.)

OH

OH

(He slams the shutters in a surge of disgust and rage.)

I WILL KILL YOU I WILL KILL AND KILL YOU ASK MY HEART IF I MEAN WHAT I SAY YES IT SAYS AND SLOWLY SAYS MY BRAIN SO YOUR SCREAM HANGS OUT A RIBBON FOR THE WIND TO BLOW A YELLOW RIBBON CLINGING TO YOUR MOTHER LET HER GO INSANE FROM THE FLAPPING RIBBON OF YOUR PAIN GET DOWN

(The child is shoved to the floor…)

And I am not insane I most certainly am not whereas alone here with the passing summers of the old regime pruning the roses and propped on pillows sleepless under a sarcastic moon some quivering idiocy would have crept on me I think we can assume it's peace it's the finger of perpetual peace pressing on some vein…

9

A grinding wheel turned. A blade set on it.

COPOLLA: We sharpen the edge but the Roman sword is
not for slashing we prefer to stab to stab with it at close
quarters keep turning

(The wheel is turned faster.)

Therefore it is the point that matters the point which must
be razor sharp none of these things much interested me
when I soldiered but

STOP

STOP I SAID

(He halts the wheel. A silence…)

I thought I heard your brothers creeping near

(He listens.)

And they are near obviously always near

(He strains.)

Excellent that they should hear me making preparations
for your death but not so excellent if they

(And listens.)

Exploit the noise made by the preparations to

(He listens again.)

A man's house is like his body it has a pulse it coughs it
farts and all the joists have rheumatism I have lived here
sixty years sixty with seven in the army in there I had my
cot do you want to see the cot was

(A Beat.)

I have the cot still oh yes a settled culture has something you could never understand a continuity what did you lie in something woven out of reeds the cot it creaked a little my sisters had it after me

(He suddenly menaces the child.)

Do you believe do you seriously believe I will ever limp or creep or stagger out of here let them transport me in a dozen bits and fling me in the pond mockery SPLASH laughter SPLASH and the fish confused the bewildered fish your blue eyes are always full of tears now is that civility making its first appearance do you sense DIMLY DIMLY OBVIOUSLY dimly sense your criminality?

(The sword is clanged.)

You and the Romans oh unlucky you met me

(Pause.)

Me

(Pause.)

The last probably

(Pause.)

Cry for him then wet him with your weeping

(Pause.)

Yes

I call that grief and grief is beautiful

(A sound made by demolition.)

WIPE YOUR EYES WITH THAT ITS' CALLED A HANDKERCHIEF

(He is ripped from contemplation.)

Your brothers on the roof and every tile for smashing

(Exactly that occurs.)

There it goes we made those tiles we had a kiln down by the river

(More tiles are dislodged and shatter.)

The winter gales they blew half the roof away not last winter

(And shatter.)

the winter before no no it was last winter everybody lost a few the wind comes up the valley

NOT ONE OF YOU HAS THE VAGUEST

(A smash.)

VAGUEST IDEA HOW TO OPERATE A KILN HOW DO YOU THINK YOU

(Pause. A strange laugh comes from COPOLLA.)

You don't want a roof

Ha

ROOF WHAT'S A ROOF TO YOU

(He thrusts the child.)

Get over there

(The child trips.)

GET UP

GET UP

(The child is dragged over the floor. In their haste they tread on the tray. The tray tips up with a melancholy note, scattering the ashes.)

Oh God

Oh God I have

(He removes his foot. The tray settles with a second sound of infinite sadness…)

This

This

Terrible dishonouring of Thalia I

(A tile smashes.)

I sense is not entirely accidental you dropping her me treading in her your mischief my clumsiness no Thalia

(Pause.)

Thalia had it coming to her

(A tile again.)

I never liked her it gave me pleasure when she wept a secret pleasure yes I saw myself once in a mirror she was stretched out howling howling on a bed and I was standing helplessly beside her everything that could be said had been said and silence followed I lifted my eyes and in the mirror met myself oh I was so so

(With a spasm of rage he kicks the tray.)

THE SATISFACTION IN THAT GAZE

WHY DIDN'T I JUST

(He gropes for a meaning.)

Thrust her out my life?

(A tile crashes down.)

Kill her or

(And another…)

Have her killed there were slaves who would do that yes the woman disappeared not cheap of course out shopping

vanished a disused well a quarry I don't know I would
have said be gentle

(A shoal of smashing tiles.)

KILL GENTLY SILLY

(He mocks himself. The child laughs…)

A gentle killing we agree is silly

(Pause. COPOLLA contemplates the child.)

I'm thinking now of hanging you

(She laughs again.)

Yes it's comical the way I change my mind sword one
minute rope the next but the circumstances they change so
rapidly I am bewildered possibly my mind is not so supple
as it was

(The child laughs.)

POSSIBLY I SAY POSSIBLY POSSIBLY MY ARSE

(They both laugh…)

All the same it is not so very decayed and these events so
brilliantly orchestrated by your family send blood surging
into the abandoned quarters of my brain rather as sudden
storms flood buried cellars up come forgotten items
INSTINCT CUNNING RAGE

(The child laughs.)

Yes I am the archaeologist of my own personality

(Pause. They communicate… the villa creaks.)

It's their fault oh yes the brothers and the cousins one
wrong tactic after another by tearing off the roof they made
me think how we could be displayed to the best advantage
it is as if up there on the rafters they were perching on
the cheap seats of an auditorium and we we the actors

beautiful and dead were beneath them on the stage posed either side of a single fallen chair

(The child laughs.)

You like the sound of it good good I stipulate a single chair because when I snatch it from underneath your feet I will replace it under my own and topple it with the utmost care

THE ROMAN DOES NOT WASTE HIS SUICIDE

(The child laughs curiously.)

You like it

You like everything I say

(He laughs mildly.)

ROPES

(And again, louder.)

ROPES

(They both laugh now. A silence moves between them.)

How quiet it is

How quiet they can't have gone away

(He scrambles.)

I must tell you if some almighty power God or whoever it might be you pray to if you pray reached out and with nimble fingers played with my life as children play with dolls jamming the roof back on the house and throwing your whole tribe into a cupboard I would not thank him

I AM DYING TODAY

(He peers through the creaking shutter.)

They've gone

(He is more distraught.)

THEY'VE GONE NO THEY HAVEN'T THEY HAVEN'T

(He laughs weakly.)

There's more of them

Under the trees as usual and others on the road

You'd think it was a

Sullen

Idle

HUNDREDS

A melancholy race meeting

Joyless

Louche

Inert

A discharged army squatting in the dirt

WHAT'S DISCOURAGED THEM SURELY NOT ME

(He laughs.)

COPOLLA THE SOLITARY ROMAN WHOSE FINGER
SNAGGED THE LINE CALLED A TO B

No

Not solitary

Not solitary there is another

His spotless toga what a curiosity

They were expecting him

They surge

They jostle

A sudden volatility no wonder he looks apprehensive

(A terrible plunge.)

It's my boy…

10

The door tapped lightly.

COPOLLA: *(His mouth pressed to the hinge.)* I'M FULL OF
SUSPICION

(Pause. The tapping again.)

FULL OF IT

EUCLID: Father let me in

(COPOLLA is silent.)

Father I am here to

COPOLLA: Say hello to Aphrodite

EUCLID: What

COPOLLA: She's either side of you the head is on the left
don't confuse it with the postman the postman's on the
right my right your left OH YOU KNOW APHRODITE SHE
WIPED YOUR ARSE SHE MADE YOUR BED ONLY A SLAVE
HOWEVER have you said it?

EUCLID: Yes

*(Reluctantly, COPOLLA draws back the doorbolts. The sound of the
outside…)*

COPOLLA: I'm full of suspicion

EUCLID: Yes

*(EUCLID enters. COPOLLA slams the door and shoots the bolts. In
the following hiatus, the child laughs…)*

COPOLLA: She finds you funny so do I she finds the whole word funny her blue eyes look at them cold as my razor but she can cry she has cried and she is crying with more frequency this satisfies me in some way sadness is Roman

EUCLID: They love their children

COPOLLA: They love their children do they so did I and for my children's children I will break the hearts of those who made this child she let herself in she offered herself so to speak as a sacrifice who I am to quarrel with her ignorant yet possibly inspired decision?

EUCLID: I hardly recognize you father

COPOLLA: Is that so yet I am so much more myself

(A Beat.)

I AM FULL OF SUSPICION

(Pause.)

I thought you returned to the city your sickly child your urgent court case you couldn't wait to get away from here IT'S PROFOUNDLY SUSPICIOUS and you look conciliatory you have the pale and trembling mouth of the conciliator

(A Beat.)

Deny it

Deny to your father's face that is the reason you are here

(Before EUCLID can reply.)

I THINK TO INSINUATE YOURSELF INTO YOUR FATHER'S HOUSE THE HOUSE OF YOUR FATHER AND HIS FATHER AND HIS AND HIS AND HIS IN ORDER TO

EUCLID: May I speak?

COPOLLA: IN ORDER TO

(He gasps.)

USING YOUR PRECIOUS INTIMACY WITH HIM TO

(A gasp.)

THOSE BEAUTIFUL YEARS OF CHILDHOOD OUR LAUGHTER AND OUR TEARS IN ORDER TO

EUCLID: May I speak or not?

COPOLLA: TO WHAT TO WHAT TO WHAT TO LEVER HIM LIKE SOME RECALCITRANT MOLLUSC FROM ITS SHELL

(A Beat.)

Did you bring a sword?

EUCLID: A sword?

COPOLLA: A sword yes I can't see it under your clothes is it your weapon brilliantly concealed a sword to wield so as I lay dying on the threshold I would know my son kept them from desecrating my body at least until he fell also bleeding from the thrusts of fifty spears where is it the sword?

(A pause, a relief to COPOLLA also…)

EUCLID: I'll speak now and I have no sword

(Pause.)

Firstly I want to make it clear no one will come for you the army or the police they won't appear and drive these people off a decision has been arrived at and most reluctantly to abandon the outlying districts in order to concentrate our resources on protecting areas with a higher density of population this policy will be reviewed in a month or two and

COPOLLA: You are standing in your mother

(Pause.)

Thalia

(Pause.)

Thalia is a fine dust on your shoes

(The child giggles.)

We think that's funny yes we do

(He also laughs…)

EUCLID: *(Infinitely patient.)* All right

(Pause.)

Secondly

COPOLLA: FROM THAT DUST YOU GREW

(Pause.)

EUCLID: Secondly if you release the child they have guaranteed neither me nor you will come to harm all your books and all your pottery can be removed and taken to a place of safety they do not care for books but pottery they do like it is a considerable concession I think you

(He stops.)

You aren't listening

COPOLLA: *(At the window.)* I'm watching

EUCLID: *(A certain horror.)* You are not listening

COPOLLA: I'M STUDYING THE VIEW

(He defies EUCLID.)

And as I thought they are employing their time more sensibly than you they are creeping under the blanket of our conversation they are using you to mask an entirely predictable manoeuvre the child can smell it LOOK AT HER EYES HER EYES BURN BRIGHTER BLUE

(COPOLLA makes a swift move, toppling a chair in his haste. As he grabs the child she utters a cry.)

EUCLID: DON'T HURT HER DON'T HURT HER FOR GOD'S SAKE

(Pause.)

COPOLLA: Don't hurt her?

But she is a sacrifice

(A profound antagonism passes between them.)

EUCLID: I cannot leave without the child

COPOLLA: Tell them your father is a Roman and if they do not know what Roman is say I will show them

(A hiatus of repressed rage.)

EUCLID: I have a little girl

COPOLLA: Claudia

EUCLID: I have a little girl

COPOLLA: I know Claudia

EUCLID: DO YOU WANT MY LITTLE GIRL TO BE WITHOUT A FATHER?

(A pause.)

COPOLLA: I was full of suspicion

How right I was to be so full of suspicion

EUCLID: I CAME TO SAVE MY FATHER

COPOLLA: YOU DO NOT SAVE ME YOU DESTROY ME YOU BRING YOUR DEATH AND LEND IT TO MY ENEMIES IF YOU DIE YOU DIE

(He is mild.)

You have had your portion and so have I

EUCLID: I came because they told me they stopped me
on the road he is a mad dog in his house they said and
threatening a child not him I said not him

(Pause.)

Let me like Aeneas put my father on my shoulders and
leading the child by the hand walk out of Troy together
you have been magnificent they will fall to either side
dumbly admiring

(The plea fails.)

COPOLLA: Dumbly admiring possessors of the Roman land
how well my son corrupts me with his invocation of a
greater time it's good it's good but I decline to play another
man listen to me I am also a metaphor let the sculptors of
the future understand my beauty my sword in one hand
and a child's head in the other

ONE MORE ABIDING IMAGE OF THE CRISIS OF OUR
TIME

EUCLID: I'm taking this child

COPOLLA: *(A move.)* You may not have a sword I however do

EUCLID: You will not kill your own son

COPOLLA: If that is what you are I promise you I

EUCLID: *(Manoeuvring.)* IF THAT IS WHAT I AM

COPOLLA: If that is what you are yes if you if you

(The child giggles.)

THIS SHE FINDS PREPOSTEROUS ME TOO

(A false move.)

EUCLID: YOU HAVE CUT ME

(The child cries.)

LOOK

LOOK

COPOLLA: It's sharper than God's teeth I promise you

(A beat, then EUCLID weeps…)

I'M NOT SORRY I'M NOT SORRY

EUCLID: *(In despair.)* No you're not are you…

COPOLLA: *(Chanting now.)* THE LINE THE LINE FROM A TO B

EUCLID: Is there a bandage please?

COPOLLA: RUNS EVERYWHERE BUT NOT THROUGH ME

(He laughs wildly.)

EUCLID: Is there a bandage?

COPOLLA: Dead men require no bandages now get out your whimpering is discomforting the child the child who is preparing herself for what she knows will be briefly at least an unpleasant sensation

I SOUND LIKE THE DENTIST

Leave us

Leave us decently kiss something my foot or the hem of my toga you will not see me again my clever son

EUCLID: *(Bitterly.)* Never kiss you never

COPOLLA: All right don't of all the blessings that might have eased my death yours was the one I craved the least

NOW GET OUT FROM UNDER ME

EUCLID: *(Retreating to the door.)* GOD HATES YOU

COPOLLA: Possibly

(The door bolts are drawn. The world suddenly.)

Tell God from now on no roaming tribe of thieves will hold the Romans in contempt as they have been accustomed to

let them buy the land in blood mine and their children's
and if you perish CAN YOU HEAR ME remember the slave
who drew the line from A to B killed you not me

(The door is slammed again.)

HE WOULD NOT KISS ME KISS ME I SAID AND HE

(He seethes.)

Said no

Said no

Said no

(He breathes profoundly.)

Better isn't it better altogether we have only one another
Mr Copolla and Miss C

(A half-laugh, reflective…)

They may not execute him at least not immediately there
will be some horrible rehearsal let's not watch we saw it
all with Aphrodite didn't we we were horrified we forced
ourselves to witness it but oh I think once is enough and
you particularly

*(An awful cry… a blade of silence falls between COPOLLA and the
child…)*

You particularly shouldn't be

*(COPOLLA hears his son call for him. As he suffers, the child cries.
COPOLLA does nothing to stop her tears… he walks to a chair and
sits…)*

It's music

(His son wails distantly. The child wails close.)

Did any man hear such a music any man in history?

She counterpoints him

(It goes on, altering, as if in movements.)

The only missing instrument is me

(He heaves a visceral cry.)

But I must not

OH I MUST NOT

(He drags a breath from himself.)

SIT THERE

SIT THERE

(The child is forced onto the chair. The sound of the iron sword lifted…)

And Thalia went on journeys

(He scoffs.)

Oh the paltry nature of her curiosity was her husband not sufficiently exotic

THE BLUE EYES OF A CHILD SHRINK AT THE SIGHT OF ME

(A Beat.)

I have never done hurt to a living thing never never oh fish you say fish yes fish possibly and birds a bird or two birds yes

LOOK AT MY MOUTH WHAT IS WRITTEN IN MY MOUTH A LOATHING OF BRUTALITY

(His vehemence causes the child to whimper.)

I am sorry

I am so sorry

There never was a man who could not murder and those who bawl the loudest their placidity excuse their savagery

by rage they swagger in their rage as if it were a cloak I
DID NOT KNOW MYSELF IT WASN'T ME

(A Beat.)

This is me

I have no rage it is decision

(He swallows. At last he is perfectly calm.)

There is before the act and after the act who I was before
the act will cease to be

(The sword mutters a faint ring as COPOLLA lifts it.)

CHILD: Vivam tibi supplico

(Her first word stops COPOLLA. His frown is audible.)

COPOLLA: Let you live?

(He is filled with wonder.)

The child of the barbarians has a single Latin phrase and
she does not waste it

THE CHILD: Supplico

Supplico

COPOLLAR: *(Ravished.)* Beautiful is my language do you not
think so?

THE CHILD: Supplico

COPOLLA: The eyes

The words

Together and the moment infinitely oh infinitely calculated
to wither me I cry the beauty and the skill of it I cry

(A breath.)

I talk of civility and still I kill

How is it possible

I do not know

I will however

Oh I will

(A Beat.)

I will do this little one to the best of my ability my ability being

(A breath.)

Neither of us knows the extent of my ability

(A Beat.)

WE SHALL SOON SEE

(A beat, COPOLLA thrusts the sword violently into the CHILD. It passes through her frail chest and fixes into the wood of the chair behind her. A note, high-pitched, which fades. Only the breath of COPOLLA remains, inhalation exhalation, inhalation…)

Must not run now not run but sit a chair beside her chair so as they burst in it

(He breathes precisely as before.)

It is a spectacle an enduring spectacle of

(And again.)

We live by such

(He goes to a chair, drags it over the floor.)

Contrivances

(He sits…)

Open the shutters possibly yes why not why not open them the door the whole lot open them

(He gets up. He unshutters one set after another. They crash back. The world enters…)

And sit

And sit

(He sits…)

No further back so when they crowd in it's her they see they see her first pinned to the chair the sword jutting the jutting sword which holds her there and only afterwards do I appear alive but still entirely still I lift my eyes and in their rage they spear me I say nothing I try to say nothing she said nothing but they might enter by the other door in which case

(He drags the chair over the tiles.)

I'd be better placing my chair here

THIS IS SILLY

Silly but I have an eye for these things an educated eye

(He shifts it again.)

They don't of course so what I do

(He sits. Birdsong travels from the gardens.)

I do

I do

I do have an eye for

(The chair is dragged again.)

Eloquent gestures

(He sits. Time elapses. He fidgets.)

How typical of my son to have recalled to me the tableau of Aeneas quitting Troy for a brief moment I was seduced only a brief moment

No

(A Beat.)

No that was Rome's beginning this is the end an altogether harder metaphor I don't pretend it's

WHERE ARE THEY

(A Beat.)

Got the charm of Virgil

THE BROTHERS AND THE UNCLES WHERE I CAN'T SIT IN THIS CHAIR ALL DAY

(A Beat.)

Oh listen

(An idyllic sound.)

The frail music of the fountain ha the hours I spent manipulating the lead pipe too wide an aperture produces noisy torrents conversely if the aperture is tight the slightest breeze spills it it frets it stutters like

(A Beat.)

AN OLD MAN IN A CHAIR WHERE ARE MY KILLERS

WHERE

(A Beat.)

There is a moment and it is brief when what so cries out to be done must be done that moment is passing even now I hear it pass

IT'S GONE

IT'S GONE

THE MOMENT'S GONE

(He staggers out of the chair.)

Relying on one's enemies to complete a gesture is not wise

I'M GOING OUT

I boast

I'M GOING OUT

This boasting has to stop speak simply Copolla speak only
what is the case and not what was the case and is no longer
for example going out my desire is I think authentic at least
I have no reason to doubt the authenticity of this wish it is
however a wish which certainly will be frustrated before it
can be converted into action so to say

I'M GOING OUT

is frankly preposterous we know how far this wish will get
me do we not it will get me to the threshold the threshold
also is

(An artificial laugh.)

THE THRESHOLD OF THE WISH

*(A wave of nausea engulfs him. Through his despair, the fountain's
little music…)*

The music of civility

Ha

It's why you're dead and why any second I will be

(The fountain…)

Or is it laughter some nights I think that fountain finds me
comical it's mocking me a laughter not without a certain
sympathy but

(A Beat.)

The laughter of a

(A Beat.)

Bad girl

(A gasp. A horror.)

OH HERE COMES SOMEBODY

(The crashing of furniture, collisions and a fine note left in silence…)

*

JUDITH

A PARTING FROM THE BODY

Characters

JUDITH
A Widow of Israel

HOLOFERNES
A General of Assyria

THE SERVANT
An Ideologist

The tent of a general. HOLOFERNES alone.

HOLOFERNES: Tonight I must talk about death. For example, its arbitrary selections. This I find impossible to assimilate. This I find agony to contemplate. Its fingering of one. Its indifference to another. Its beckoning to one. Its blindness to another. This haunts me, this casualness. This gnaws my curiosity. I might say this quality in death has governed my emotions and made battle precious. Come in. For while victory is the object of the battle, death is its subject, and the melancholy of the soldiers is the peculiar silence of a profound love. Do come in, I detest the way some hover round the door, do you think I am deaf? This certainly lends me a quality which some describe as tenderness. Because I walk among the dead they will ascribe to me feelings of shame or compassion. This is not the case. Rather, I am overcome with wonder. I am trembling with a terrible infatuation. Come in, I said.
(JUDITH enters, kneels.)
This sensitivity they find hard to reconcile with cruelty, for which I also have a reputation. But cruelty is collaboration in chaos, of which the soldiers are merely the agents. It is not without philosophy. And some generals talk of necessity. They talk of limited objectives. There are no limitations, nor is there necessity. There is only infatuation. I hate to be bothered when I am thinking about death. Come in!
(A SERVANT WOMAN enters, kneels.)
What a racket even bare feet make for the contemplative mind. Tomorrow the dead will clog the ditches, so I must think. It is perfectly natural to think, however little thought affects the outcome.
(Pause. JUDITH produces a bottle. She uncorks it, with a characteristic sound. Pause.)
I do not drink, which if you were not a stranger, you would know. Obviously you believe in rumours, for example, the rumour that cruel men are degenerate. The opposite is the case, I promise you.

(A long pause.)

THE SERVANT: I heard – futile now, I see – I heard – you
liked women. *(She looks at JUDITH.)* Don't you like women
either?

HOLOFERNES: Tonight I must talk about death.

THE SERVANT: She talks about death! *(She looks at JUDITH.)*
Don't you? All the time she does. Death this, death that. I
say to her, you melancholy thing, I don't know what made
you like it. No, she is utterly morbid. Aren't you?
(Pause. JUDITH stares at the ground.)

HOLOFERNES: I think you are a poor liar, and she is shallow.
I think you have brought me a bitch as a present, a thing
that giggles. On some nights I should certainly not cavil,
but tonight is different. Tonight –

THE SERVANT: You want to talk about death! Of course you
do, and she can, can't you, she's shy, that's all. I promise
you on this particular subject she can spout on for hours,
can't you, go on, show the gentleman how much you. Go
on. How well you. Judith. Show him.
*(Pause. Suddenly HOLOFERNES seizes the SERVANT, fixing her
tightly in an upright posture, between life and death. Pause.)*

HOLOFERNES: Those who die tomorrow, let us think of them.

THE SERVANT: Yes –

HOLOFERNES: The speed of their final thoughts, the torrent of
their last reflections.

THE SERVANT: Yes –

HOLOFERNES: We ache for the pain of our companions, I am
certain of it, soldiers nourish the secret hope their friends
will die, does that horrify you, I only – *(The SERVANT
chokes.)* – seek the truth of battle, does that horrify you, I
only probe the ecstasies of pain –

JUDITH: You are killing my property. *(HOLOFERNES is still, rigid.)* My property can't breathe. *(Pause.)*

HOLOFERNES: I do not wish to fuck tonight.

JUDITH: No. You wish to talk.

HOLOFERNES: And anyway, this area is out of bounds, didn't you know, it is forbidden to civilians.

JUDITH: Yes.

HOLOFERNES: There are notices everywhere, or can't you read? What possible use are you to me if you can't read, tonight of all nights, when I must argue death, what use is the company of the illiterate?

JUDITH: I could be illiterate and still –

HOLOFERNES: Converse?

JUDITH: I might –

HOLOFERNES: There is no wisdom in the illiterate, I assure you, none –

JUDITH: Oh, I don't know –

HOLOFERNES: No, listen, don't repeat untruths which are merely sentimental –

JUDITH: I wasn't being sentimental, only –

HOLOFERNES: It is a fallacy that ignorance can harbour truth, and you are SO UNWELCOME, take this away! *(He releases the SERVANT, who slides onto her knees. JUDITH does not move. The SERVANT breathes deeply in the silence.)* I do like women, but for all the wrong reasons. And as for them, they rapidly see through me. They see I only hide in them, which is not love. They see I shelter in their flesh. Which is not love. Now, go away. *(Pause.)*

JUDITH: Let me speak. I cannot promise anything I say will be original. But I am not unread. And if I say things that don't accord with your experience, it may serve to sharpen

your own perceptions. No one can always engage with his
equals, sometimes it's beneficial to hear an unsophisticated
point of view. And anyway, how do you know you have an
equal?

HOLOFERNES: I have no equal in the field I've made my
speciality.

JUDITH: Which field is that? Murder or philosophy? *(She is
suddenly pained at her cleverness.)*
No, that was –
Give me another chance to –
That was –

*(HOLOFERNES, as if oblivious to her, sits in a canvas chair, looking
away, as if in thought. In the silence, the cry of a sentry in the
night.)*

HOLOFERNES: It is of great importance that the enemy is
defeated.

JUDITH: Oh, yes!

HOLOFERNES: Or is it? Perhaps it only seems so.

JUDITH: Seems so?

HOLOFERNES: Always the night before the soldiers die I
think – perhaps this is not important, after all. Perhaps it
would be better if the enemy defeated us. I mean, from
a universal point of view. Perhaps my own view is too
narrow.

JUDITH: *(Thoughtfully.)* Yes…

HOLOFERNES: Fortunately this consideration only occurs to
me after I have made the plan of battle, never before. It is
as if the thought were released by the certain knowledge I
shall win.

JUDITH: Yes, but is it certain?

HOLOFERNES: Yes. No matter what the preparations of the enemy we shall win. For one thing, they believe we shall win, which alone ensures that they will lose. Take your clothes off now. As for this gnawing sense I have described that victory lacks authenticity, this disappears with the sunrise.

JUDITH: Take my clothes off… ?

HOLOFERNES: I think it is the persistence and proximity of Death, who lurks in all the interstices of life and cannot be abolished, which justifies the military profession. I think it is abhorrent only to those who lack the intellectual courage to recognise it for what it is – the organization of a metaphor. Did you not want to take your clothes off? What else did you come for? Hang them on a chair. I long to be married, but to a cruel woman. And as I lay dying of sickness in a room, I would want her to ignore me. I would want her to laugh in the kitchen with a lover as my mouth grew dry. I would want her to count my money as I choked.

JUDITH: *(In confusion.)* I cannot. *(She shakes her head.)* I cannot – simply –

HOLOFERNES: No.

JUDITH: As if –

HOLOFERNES: No.

JUDITH: If you would –

HOLOFERNES: Yes?

JUDITH: Just – touch – or –

HOLOFERNES: Touch?

JUDITH: Or –

HOLOFERNES: Murmur?

JUDITH: Something – just –

HOLOFERNES: I can see how difficult it is for you. Unfortunately I only wish to talk about death. It is you who came to be naked.

JUDITH: Yes, but – naked lovingly.

HOLOFERNES: Lovingly naked?

JUDITH: Yes.

HOLOFERNES: Tomorrow many will be naked. And so humiliated in their nakedness. So cruelly naked and smeared with excrement.

JUDITH: I CAN'T UNDRESS WITH YOU –

HOLOFERNES: Their arses, their silly arses show –

JUDITH: THIS IS SO MUCH HARDER THAN I THOUGHT.

HOLOFERNES: Yes, and you have hardly begun. *(Pause. She glares at him. She controls her panic. She turns to the SERVANT.)*

JUDITH: Take my clothing.

THE SERVANT: *(Smiling.)* I've done this before. For Judith. And not only Judith!

JUDITH: He wants me naked. So.

THE SERVANT: All sorts of girls.

JUDITH: *(Undressing.)* Naked I must be.

THE SERVANT: *(Taking a garment and laying it over her arm.)* Some could and some couldn't.

JUDITH: Naked and unashamed.

THE SERVANT: Because undressing is an art.

JUDITH: As if I were before the mirror and not before – *(She freezes.)* I CAN'T *(Pause.)*

THE SERVANT: You've done it before.

JUDITH: Still, I can't

THE SERVANT: Whyever not? Silly! *(Pause. The SERVANT looks to HOLOFERNES.)* She can't… I'm sorry… she is very sensitive… Idiot! No, she is though. She is magnificent but. *(She shakes her head.)* There you are, people are like that, one day flinging it all off and another – it must be you. It must be your. Whatever you have got. That's doing it. I mean. You are the most peculiar man, and I say that with all respect, with every admiration, you throw a girl off her – you would make a prostitute uneasy – and that's not as difficult as you would think, it really isn't, I've known exasperated prostitutes. *(She turns to JUDITH.)* Put this on again, you'll –

JUDITH: No. *(Pause.)* I'll stay like this. Half-naked. *(Pause.)* I am a widow, I don't know why I mention that. To earn your sympathy, perhaps.

HOLOFERNES: I have no sympathy.

JUDITH: No, I didn't think –

THE SERVANT: Why should he?

JUDITH: I suppose I –

THE SERVANT: He never knew your husband, why should he –

JUDITH: *(To the SERVANT.)* JUST GET OUT. (*Pause. The SERVANT prepares to go.)*

HOLOFERNES: No. Stay. *(The SERVANT looks to JUDITH.)* Wouldn't you prefer to stay? Admit that you would prefer that.

JUDITH: Perhaps she would, but I –

HOLOFERNES: No, no, it's me that has to choose, surely? It is my night, not yours. Tomorrow I. Tomorrow they. Flesh on all the hedges. No, it's me surely? *(Pause. The cry of a sentry in the night.)* I am a man who could never be loved I am a man no woman could find pitiful. Pity is love. Pity is passion. The rest is clamour. The rest is just

imperative. *(The SERVANT looks at JUDITH. A silence.)* When I see my soldiers drag a woman in the thorns, her white legs thrashing the air and her squeals oddly harmonious with the squeals of passing transport, I ask myself who is the most pitiful, knowing as I do how sorry for themselves all soldiers are, and how they smother misery among the clods and nettles and disordered clothing of their victims. I find it hard to reprimand them. After all, what is an army? It is the mad life licensed. It is not harmony is it? It is not harmony on the march.
(Pause.)
When a woman loves a man, it is not his manliness she loves, however much she craves it. It is the pity he enables her to feel, by showing, through the slightest aperture, his loneliness. No matter what his brass, no matter what his savage, it creeps, like blood under a door… *(Pause.)*

THE SERVANT: It's going to be difficult tonight. I felt as we came in here, it's going to be difficult tonight.

JUDITH: I must admit, Holofernes is not what I expected. I am neither awed nor intimidated, and I can say in perfect honesty, he is not what I expected. It makes things different. It doesn't make them worse. I should dress, in order that –
(She goes to reach for her clothes.)

HOLOFERNES: No.

JUDITH: *(Stopping.)* I think if we are to engage with one another in –

HOLOFERNES: No.

JUDITH: It is very hard to be – to collect one's thoughts and –

HOLOFERNES: I also will be naked. *(Pause.)*

JUDITH: Yes. Well, that would – that might –

THE SERVANT: This isn't what we expected. Is it? This is far from what –

JUDITH: Be quiet. *(Pause.)*

It doesn't help. *(Pause.)*

Be quiet.

(HOLOFERNES gets up. The SERVANT goes to receive his clothes. He removes them item by item.)

THE SERVANT: *(Laying them over her arm.)* What lovely stuffs…

HOLOFERNES: Dead men's stuffs.

THE SERVANT: Oh, really?

HOLOFERNES: An army is not honourable, is it?

THE SERVANT: I wouldn't like to say if it is honourable or –

HOLOFERNES: No, it is not honourable, so I make no pretence at honour.

THE SERVANT: I respect that, I really do, and that's a nice piece, too, dead men's, is it? Lovely weave. *(She looks at him.)* You're not that strong, are you? You're not what I'd call powerful. But wiry, are you? Probably you're very fit?

JUDITH: You talk too much.

THE SERVANT: Do I? It's nerves. *(To HOLOFERNES.)* You're stopping there, are you? That's it? *(HOLOFERNES is lightly clad. He does not reply.)* That's it. *(She goes to lay out the clothes.)*

JUDITH: Tomorrow, when you have defeated Israel, as you say you cannot fail to do, how much will you destroy?

HOLOFERNES: All of it.

JUDITH: And the children?

HOLOFERNES: Them I'll enslave.

JUDITH: And the men, you'll –

HOLOFERNES: Cut their throats.

JUDITH: The old men, and the –

HOLOFERNES: If they have throats –

JUDITH: You'll cut them.

HOLOFERNES: Some of this cutting I will do myself.

JUDITH: That's no less than I expected.

HOLOFERNES: I do not distinguish myself from the army. I am cleverer than the army, but not better than the army. I do things they could never do, such as to plot the dispositions. But this does not relieve me of my compact with their vileness. If vileness it is.

JUDITH: *(Shrugging complacently.)* Some would say so.

HOLOFERNES: Some would. I never pay regard to some's opinion. Neither do I laugh at myself. Sometimes, like tonight, I think I want to see a woman naked, but usually, seeing her, I realise that it is not what I wanted at all. Generally speaking, I am unhappy until I see the happy, and then I understand the reason for my condition. If I had allowed you to be naked, or you had allowed yourself, I should have dismissed you long before now.

THE SERVANT: Lucky, then! Lucky you –

JUDITH: *(Hissing.)* YOU – MAKE – THIS – SO –

THE SERVANT: Sorry –

JUDITH: PITIFULLY – MUNDANE – AND –

THE SERVANT: Sorry –

JUDITH: SIT – AND – WATCH. *(The SERVANT obeys. A pause.)* I also am unhappy. I believed I was unhappy because I was widowed. But my widowing merely licensed me to show myself for what I am. Everyone else must laugh and smile and greet each other, hoisting their children into the air and acting the perfect neighbour, whereas I am privileged to wear a melancholy face. Many envy me for this, and men are drawn to unhappy women, as perhaps you know, being subtle. I'm subtle, too. None subtler. She's right, however, you are not well-built Your power comes form elsewhere obviously. Am I talking too much? You have revealed so much I feel I should also, but perhaps that's wrong. You might wish me to be silent. You might wish to imagine me rather than to know me. That is the source of desire, in my view. Not what we are but the possibilities we allow others to create us. Silence, for example. Might be judged as mystery. *(Long pause. They look at one another.)*

HOLOFERNES: I can't be loved.

JUDITH: So you said.

HOLOFERNES: So if you were thinking of loving me, you would do well to reconsider. *(Pause.)*

JUDITH: Yes… *(Pause.)* Yes… I came here thinking… what did I think… I –

THE SERVANT: You thought –

JUDITH: I SAID TO BE QUIET, DIDN'T I? *(Pause.)*
I came here thinking – obviously – thinking – I love – I – *(Pause.)* Never mind, love will do – (*Pause.*) Love the – object – may I call you an object – the object Holofernes – the strategist, the general, the theorist, the murderer, the monster, the hero Holofernes. All those things, which are easy to love. Which are almost a substitute for love. But love is more difficult, it's – PLEASE DON'T MAKE ME GO YET. *(Pause. The SERVANT looks anxiously from JUDITH to HOLOFERNES. The cry of the sentry. Pause.)*

HOLOFERNES: Let us talk about death.

JUDITH: Yes.

HOLOFERNES: Its ridiculing of life.

JUDITH: Yes.

HOLOFERNES: Its mockery of purpose, its humiliation of –

JUDITH: Yes, yes. *(Pause. HOLOFERNES looks at her, while JUDITH stares at the ground.)*

HOLOFERNES: We exist for one reason.

JUDITH: One reason? I thought we existed for no reason at all.

HOLOFERNES: To reproduce ourselves. *(Pause. She affects a gasp.)*

JUDITH: That's odd! That – coming from you – is particularly odd because – the pain you've given – and the things you've – to people who have never – and now you say – it is odd. Really it is odd. I think you have such a beautiful manner. Quite unpredictable.

HOLOFERNES: Given we have no purpose but this eminently absurd purpose it would seem to me it is neither more creditable, nor more dishonourable, to slaughter than to kneel on the cold floor of a monastery. Naturally, I speak from Death's perspective. What other perspective is there?

JUDITH: Yes, but if life is so very – is so utterly – fatuous, should we not comfort one another? Or is that silly? *(Pause.)* You think I'm silly. You're right, I'm only saying this to – I'm spewing the conventional opinion because – when this is such a special night, I really should forbid myself the conventional opinion, even if it is correct, which it may be, even so, however conventional it might be – AND ALL I WANTED WAS TO LIE WITH YOU. *(Pause.)*

HOLOFERNES: And would that be easier?

JUDITH: Not easier, but. *(Pause.)* Not easier at all. *(She draws her garments round her.)*

THE SERVANT: I always said, with love don't ask too many questions. Love's silent, I said. Or it speaks in rather ordinary words.
(She turns to HOLOFERNES.)
Tomorrow you'll be different! You'll have done the killing of a lifetime! Tomorrow you won't know yourself! 'Did I go

on about death?' 'Was I miserable?' OFF WITH YER SKIRT, DARLING! *(She chuckles.)* No, I've seen it. We picked the wrong night.
(JUDITH, with a surge of bravado, gets up.)

JUDITH: All right, let's fuck.

THE SERVANT: Oh, dear…

JUDITH: I mean, all this – what is all this? You're a general, I'm a widow, so what? You kill thousands, I stay at home, so what? Don't think I haven't met your type before. I have. You want me to plead and pander. I will do. I can do that. You want me to say how much I, how magnificently you, all right, I will do, I'm far from educated, so I'll stop pretending, and anyway, nothing you say is original, either. Do I insult you? Do I abolish your performance? It needs abolishing.
(Pause. The SERVANT turns away in despair. HOLOFERNES stares at her, without emotion. The pressure in JUDITH dissipates. She shrugs.)
I am reckoned to be the most beautiful woman in the district. So I thought I had a chance.
(She goes to pick her clothing off the floor. She stops, and lets out a scream. The scream ceases. She remains still.)

THE SERVANT: I said to Judith, are you really up to this? Yes, she said. It'll hurt you, I said, one way or another. I know, she said. You'll never be the same, I said. I know that, too, she said. But you can know a thing and still not know it. Now look at us. *(Pause.)*

HOLOFERNES: And yet I want to be. *(Pause.)* I, the impossible to love, require love. Often, I am made aware of this. *(Pause.)*

THE SERVANT: You are? *(Pause.)*

HOLOFERNES: This lack.

THE SERVANT: You are, are you?

HOLOFERNES: This lack asserts itself in a distinctive way.

THE SERVANT: Yes?

HOLOFERNES: DO YOU THINK I CAN'T SEE YOU? *(The SERVANT is transfixed.)* YOUR MASK. YOUR FOG. DO YOU THINK I CAN'T SEE YOU? *(Pause.)* The way in which it asserts itself is as follows. Frequently I expose myself to the greatest danger. I court my own extinction. Whilst I am exhilarated by the conflict I am also possessed of the most perfect lucidity. So absolute am I in consciousness, yet also so removed from fear of death, I am at these moments probably a god. Certainly that is how the enemy perceives me. It is only when the action is over, and I am restored to the weary and sometimes damaged thing that is my body, that I sense a terrible need; not for praise, which I receive in abundance, but of that horror in another that I might have ceased, and had I ceased, she also could not have but ceased. I am not the definition of another's life. That is my absent trophy. I think we live only in the howl of others. The howl is love. *(Pause.)*

THE SERVANT: I think, with you, the problem is your strength. Do you mind this? Do you mind if I lecture? I think you probably are perfect. You know too much, which is like armour. Shall I go on? I've seen the hardest whore panic when she could not detect a weakness in the customer. You must give people rights. You must give them power over you. Like I step off the pavement for a beggar if he curses me. What has he got? Nothing. Nothing but his curse. So I yield him that. I give him his paltry power. So with you, you must give the woman something to hold over you. You are too perfect. There! End of lecture! *(She turns to JUDITH.)* Are you feeling better, darling? She is not a whore. She is a widow and not a whore. Only with you around, she felt like whoring!
(She laughs. A silence. The cry of the sentry. Suddenly HOLOFERNES clasps the SERVANT in his arms, desperately, sobbing quietly. The SERVANT looks to JUDITH. As suddenly, HOLOFERNES releases her.)

HOLOFERNES: You say I am not weak. I was weak once. None weaker. I crept through life. I staggered from sickness to sickness.

THE SERVANT: I didn't mean that kind of –

HOLOFERNES: I ran from other boys and hid in corners. I sought no company, or the company of girls whose games appeared less brutal, falsely, but. I stammered with shame when asked to speak, even though my mouth was full of language. I lived always in the shadows, hating the sun's glare because it exposed me to the scrutiny of others. There was none weaker than me. *(Pause.)* But being weak, I discovered cunning. I learned to say one thing, knowing it would satisfy the expectation, whilst carrying on a second and more secret conversation with myself. I led people away from my true intention, my speech became a maze, I used speech to trap my enemies, my speech was a pit, I lived in speech making it a weapon. And also I learned to run. I practised running, so when speech failed, I could out-distance them. That is how I, the runt, became a general. The mind of the weak-bodied is so terrible, is so outlandish and so subtle. He has made a spiked thing of it, to impale your innocence.

(Pause.)

JUDITH: You mean, nothing you say is true? *(He looks at her.)* I don't mind that. I am perfectly able to lie myself. I AM ALMOST CERTAINLY LYING NOW IN FACT. *(Pause.)* No, that's –
I'm glad because –
That puts my mind to rest – *(She laughs.)*
Excellent! Because so much is false when men and women are together, so much! I have always thought, when men and women are together, all this is false! And you say – you confess – all is trickery, all is deception, façade and affectation! Excellent! Forgive my hysteria, it was the pressure, the sheer suffocating pressure of sincerity. And now I am light! I am ventilated! A clean, dry wind

whirls through my brain! I intend to kill you, how is that for a lie? And that must mean I love you! Or doesn't it? Anything is possible! I think, now we have abandoned the search for truth, really, we can love each other! *(She looks to the SERVANT.)* The relief! *(She laughs again.)* The relief of knowing you are simply an element in a fiction! I think before this moment I was never equipped to love. *(She extends her hand to HOLOFERNES.)* Take my hand! Take my widow's hand in your murderer's hand, my mothering hand in your massacring hand! *(He extends his. She holds it, looks at it.)* It's so white! It's so well cared for. Poets are much grubbier, but they also murder. *(Pause. She kneels beside him.)* Do you like me at all? Of course your reply will be a pack of lies, but. Say anyway. *(Pause.)* I spent hours on this get-up. Like a bride. Which is another lie. My lips are not in the least bit red, I am rather pale-mouthed actually. Lies everywhere! Do you like me, though? When you told me you could not help yourself lying I fell in love with you. That was the moment. My husband betrayed me all the time, with girls, but this will be different, won't it? Why girls? Was he ashamed of something? Lie, do lie! *(Pause.)*

HOLOFERNES: I know why you're here. *(Pause. The SERVANT stares.)*

JUDITH: I know why I came.

HOLOFERNES: I know what you intend.

JUDITH: I know what I intended.

HOLOFERNES: I know it all.

JUDITH: I knew it all *(Pause.)* I knew it all. And now I know nothing. *(He looks into her.)*

HOLOFERNES: We love, then.

JUDITH: Yes.

HOLOFERNES: And I, who is unlovable, I am loved.

JUDITH: My dear, yes… *(Pause.)*

THE SERVANT: One of them is lying. Or both of them. This baffles me, because whilst Judith is clever, so is he. Whilst Judith was renowned for being subtle, what else is he? And only six hours to the battle! *(She comes forward.)* The battle begins at dawn. It begins with shouting. They shout for twenty minutes. Yes, a twenty-minute shout! Then they let fly the javelins. Then they shout again. I've seen it. Four times I've seen it. Four times I've run for my life. Our General says we will learn from our mistakes. He says this with monotonous regularity. We have learned, say the soldiers. We've learned to run the moment we see Holofernes. They look for him. His little form. They see him move his staff – like this – and this – and every movement of his staff brings down an unexpected blow. I run. I jump on the nearest wagon. I whip the horses. Off I go. Fuck the war and fuck the wounded. The whores are miles ahead. The sign of a lost battle is the fleeing whore-carts. Sometimes they pass through towns hours before the army. That's the signal to pack up and go. The whores outrun the cavalry! What strategists they are! What sensibilities! *(To JUDITH and HOLOFERNES.)* Shall I leave you, or –
(She sees they are embracing.)
Oh, one of them is lying, but which!
(Pause. She looks for a safe distance, sitting on a pile of clothes.)

JUDITH: You kiss strangely. I don't criticize, but how strangely you kiss!

HOLOFERNES: And you.

JUDITH: Me?

HOLOFERNES: Your mouth smothers mine, as if it were a hunger. But it might also be – a violence.

JUDITH: And yours is hard. You keep your lips tight-sealed, which might be wonder, or perhaps, are you ashamed? Don't be ashamed. I like your lips.

HOLOFERNES: I can't be loved…!

JUDITH: You are! You are loved!

THE SERVANT: How brilliant she is! How ecstatic she is! She convinces me! But she must be careful, for with lying, sometimes, the idea, though faked, can discover an appeal, and then we're fucked! It's true! I've seen it! I've seen everything!

JUDITH: Shh! *(The SERVANT sit again.)* He wants to sleep. *(The SERVANT looks puzzled.)* Don't you? You want to sleep…

HOLOFERNES: Yes.

JUDITH: And I know why… *(To the SERVANT.)* I do know why! Dear one, you want to sleep because this is also has been a battle. Tomorrow we will make love. *(She turns angrily on the SERVANT.)* It has been a battle for him!

THE SERVANT: Yes…

JUDITH: A terrible battle for him. To love. To give. *(To the SERVANT.)* And you stare, because he does not pull me to the floor. I hate the way you stare! You do hate men! How you hate them!

THE SERVANT: Me?

JUDITH: Yes. For you they have no modesty, their modesty is a sign of impotence. I do hate the way your lip is half-bent in laughter, in contempt, whore!

THE SERVANT: *(puzzled.)* Who's stopping him sleeping? I'm not!

JUDITH: Whore!

THE SERVANT: Abuse away, dear –

JUDITH: That is real whoring, it is real whoring when a woman mocks the modesty in a man!
(Pause. In the silence, the sentry cries, and HOLOFERNES, wrapped in JUDITH's arms, sleeps. A long pause, without movement.)

THE SERVANT: *(Abandoning her persona.)* Judith…

JUDITH: Shh… *(Pause.)* Listen, his breathing, like returning tides…

THE SERVANT: Judith…

JUDITH: Shh… *(Pause.)* His moving, like slow cattle on the road…

THE SERVANT: Judith… his sleep is restoring him for slaughter… his strength is the extinction of our race… Judith… his breath is our oblivion… his dreams are our pain… get the sword down, Judith… his luxury is our murder… Judith… his tranquillity is our scream… the sword's up there…

JUDITH: I've seen the sword.

THE SERVANT: Good. Unsheath it.

JUDITH: I hear you. I hear you very clearly.

THE SERVANT: You have a child.

JUDITH: I have a child, yes.

THE SERVANT: Take the weapon down, then.

JUDITH: Yes.

THE SERVANT: Your child sleeps also. Her last sleep if you –

JUDITH: I am not hesitating.

THE SERVANT: You aren't hesitating? What are you doing then?

JUDITH: I don't know, but you need not urge so. I am not hesitating.

THE SERVANT: You say you are not hesitating, but it looks like hesitation. Take the sword down or I will.

JUDITH: I am absolutely not hesitating.

THE SERVANT: No, but – *(She goes to reach for the sword.)*

JUDITH: DO NOT TAKE THE SWORD DOWN.

THE SERVANT: Israel commands you. Israel which birthed
you. Which nourished you. Israel insists. And your child
sleeps. Her last sleep if –

JUDITH: I AM WELL DRILLED. (*She glares at the SERVANT. The
sentry cries. Pause. JUDITH goes to the sword.)*

THE SERVANT: Excellent. *(JUDITH unsheaths it.)*
Excellent.
My masterful.
My supreme in.
My most terrible.
My half-divine. *(JUDITH raises the weapon over HOLOFERNES.)*

HOLOFERNES: *(Without moving.)* I'm not asleep. I'm only
pretending. *(Pause. The sword stays.)*
My dear.
My loved one.
I'm not asleep. I'm only pretending. *(Pause. JUDITH closes
her eyes.)*

JUDITH: Why?

THE SERVANT: Don't discuss!

HOLOFERNES: Because, I must win everything.

THE SERVANT: Oh, don't discuss! Israel dies if you discuss!

HOLOFERNES: I can win battles. The winning of battles is, if
anything, facile to me, but.

JUDITH: My arm aches!

HOLOFERNES: But you.

JUDITH: Aches!

HOLOFERNES: Love.

JUDITH: My arm aches and I lied!

HOLOFERNES: Of course you lied, and I lied also.

JUDITH: We both lied, so –

HOLOFERNES: But in the lies we. Through the lies we. Underneath the lies we.

THE SERVANT: OH, THE BARBARIC AND INFERIOR VILE INHUMAN BESTIAL AND BLOODSOAKED MONSTER OF DEPRAVITY!

HOLOFERNES: Judith.

THE SERVANT: OH, THE BARBARIC AND INFERIOR VILE INHUMAN BESTIAL AND BLOODSOAKED MONSTER OF DEPRAVITY!

HOLOFERNES: Judith…!

JUDITH: OH, THE BARBARIC AND INFERIOR – *(Seeing JUDITH is stuck between slogan and action, the SERVANT swiftly resorts to a stratagem, and leaning over HOLOFERNES, enrages JUDITH with a lie.)*

THE SERVANT: He is smiling! He is smiling! *(With a cry, JUDITH brings down the sword.)* Goddess! *(JUDITH staggers back, leaving the sword in place. The SERVANT leaps to it and saws energetically.)*
Immaculate deliverer!
Oh, excellent young woman!
Oh, virgin!
Oh, widow and mother!
Oh, everything! *(She saws in ecstasy.)*
Fuck this! Hard going, this!
(JUDITH groans, crawling along the floor, and shaking her head from side to side like an animal trapped in a bag. The SERVANT ceases her labours. She takes deep breaths. JUDITH stops. Long pause.)
Have you got the bag? *(Pause.)*
Judith? *(Pause.)*

The bag? *(Pause. She sits, wearily.)*

I do apologize, I thought for – I really do – for one moment, I thought – she won't – she can't – I do apologize - *(Pause.)* I will put it in the bag. You needn't. *(Pause.)* Ever see it again.

(JUDITH gets up with a strange energy. She dusts off her hands.)

JUDITH: I was silly there.

THE SERVANT: Oh, I don't know, you –

JUDITH: I was. So fucking silly. Nearly fucked it, didn't I? Nearly fucked it with my. No, I was a silly cunt there, wasn't I?

THE SERVANT: Well, you –

JUDITH: Oh, fuck, yes a proper slag and bint there –

THE SERVANT: In your pocket I think there's a –

JUDITH: A right bitch cunt, I was, nearly bollocked it, eh, nearly – *(She staggers.)* OH, MY DARLING HOW I – *(She recovers.)* Nearly poxed the job, the silly fucker I can be sometimes, a daft bitch and a cunt brained fuck arse – *(She staggers.)* OH, MY – OH, MY –

THE SERVANT: The bag, Give me the bag.

JUDITH: OH, MY – OH, MY –

THE SERVANT: GIVE IT TO ME, THEN. *(Pause. JUDITH stabilizes herself.)* We take the head because the head rewards the people. The people are entitled symbolically to show contempt for their oppressor. Obviously the spectacle has barbaric undertones but we. The concentration of emotion in the single object we etcetera. So. *(JUDITH is still.)* All right, I'll wrap it in a sheet. *(She pulls a cloth from the bed and begins with a will to wrap the severed head.)*

JUDITH: I want to fuck. *(Pause. The SERVANT stops.)*

THE SERVANT: Lie down. Rest for a little while, then we can –

JUDITH: No, I must fuck. I must. *(Pause.)*

THE SERVANT: With who do you –

JUDITH: I want to fuck with him. *(Pause.)*

THE SERVANT: You are in such a state, my dear, and I do understand, but –

JUDITH: I can arouse him. He is still warm, so obviously I can arouse him. *(She moves towards the body.)*

THE SERVANT: Sit down, and count to a hundred –

JUDITH: You count to a hundred, I'll arouse him. Look! *(She draws back the cloths, exposing him to herself.)* Oh, look…!

THE SERVANT: GET AWAY FROM HIM.

JUDITH: *(Touching him with innocence.)* It curls… it moves like weed in the slow current of my gaze…

THE SERVANT: VILE AND DISHONOURABLE –

JUDITH: Shh! Shh! Do look, the strange and mobile nature of him here, a landscape, look, I never saw my husband so revealed, so innocent and simple, I must arouse him.

THE SERVANT: *(Attempting coolness.)* Don't do that with an enemy –

JUDITH: An enemy?

THE SERVANT: It demeans your triumph and humiliates our –

JUDITH: How can he be an enemy? His head is off.

THE SERVANT: ENEMY. VILE ENEMY.

JUDITH: You keep saying that… ! But now the head is gone I can make him mine, surely? The evil's gone, the evil's in the bag and I can love! Look, I claim him! Lover, lover, respond to my adoring glance, it's not too late is it? We could have a child, we could, come, come, adored one, it is only politics kept us apart!

THE SERVANT: I think I am going to be sick…

JUDITH: No, no, count to a hundred…

THE SERVANT: I will be made insane by this!

JUDITH: You weren't insane before. Is it love makes you insane? Hatred you deal admirably with. Come, loved one… !
(She lies over HOLOFERNES's body. The SERVANT is transfixed with horror.)
He doesn't move…
He doesn't move… !
(Slowly, reluctantly, she climbs off the body. She sits among the wreckage of the bed. The cry of the sentry. A long pause. The SERVANT looks at JUDITH.)

THE SERVANT: Judith…

JUDITH: Yes…

THE SERVANT: I think we must –

JUDITH: Yes –

THE SERVANT: Or it'll be –

JUDITH: It will be, yes –

THE SERVANT: Dawn and –

JUDITH: Exactly. *(Pause. JUDITH doesn't move. The SERVANT kneels beside her.)*

THE SERVANT: I will find you a husband. Such a fine man and he will make you laugh but also fill you with admiration. He will have both wit and intelligence. And the wit will not demean him, nor the intelligence make him remote.

JUDITH: Difficult…

THE SERVANT: Difficult, yes, but I will find him. And he will give you children. He will be a child with them and a man with you. And his childishness will never mock his manliness, nor his manliness oppress the child.

JUDITH: Difficult…

THE SERVANT: Difficult, yes, but I will discover him. And old women will smile at your radiant delight, and silences will fall between you born of perfect understanding, so deep will be your mutuality speech will be redundant, such a bond, oh, such a union, the plants will thrive on your allotments form your tender touch, get up now. *(Pause.)*

JUDITH: I can't. *(Pause.)*

THE SERVANT: You can't… ?

JUDITH: Move.
(Pause. She stares at the SERVANT in horror.)

THE SERVANT: Judith –

JUDITH: CAN'T MOVE! *(Pause. The SERVANT subdues her irritation.)*

THE SERVANT: What are you saying? I'm full of patience but. All sympathy and tolerance but. A hard night this, admittedly but. IF THEY CATCH US IT'S WOMBS TO THE ALSATIANS, BITCH! *(Pause.)*

JUDITH: Listen –

THE SERVANT: All right –

JUDITH: Are you listening –

THE SERVANT: Yes –

JUDITH: Because, I have no more wish to be –

THE SERVANT: All right –

JUDITH: Than you have –

THE SERVANT: All right, all right –

JUDITH: I am fixed to the ground, do you follow me, I am unable to move, I have the will but not the power –

THE SERVANT: Yes –

JUDITH: I'm stuck, I'M STUCK.
(Pause. The SERVANT looks around, anxiously, then with resolution, goes to lift JUDITH. JUDITH lets out a cry of pain.)

JUDITH: It hurts!

THE SERVANT: What, what hurts?

JUDITH: Don't touch me, please!

THE SERVANT: Don't touch you?

JUDITH: Please, don't touch me again… ! *(Pause. The SERVANT wipes her palms on her skirt, nervously. She walks swiftly up and down, stops.)*

THE SERVANT: God's punished you. *(Pause.)*

JUDITH: What.

THE SERVANT: God has.

JUDITH: Why.

THE SERVANT: Obviously.

JUDITH: Why.

THE SERVANT: For –

JUDITH: What!

THE SERVANT: Just now. With him.

JUDITH: Punished me?

THE SERVANT: You have offended Him! *(Pause.)* I can't come near you, in case – can't possibly – in case – He might – *(JUDITH emits a long wail.)* Obviously you're judged and – *(The wail rises.)* Plead! Plead with Him! *(She stares at*

JUDITH. *Pause.)* All right, I will. *(She kneels.)* And if it fails, I have to go, forgive me, but –

JUDITH: No, don't do that, I –

THE SERVANT: HAVE TO OBVIOUSLY. *(She stares at JUDITH.)*
Take the head and. *(Pause.)*
Obviously. *(Pause.)*
You will be honoured. All Israel will. And streets will be. And parks. Great thoroughfares. Whatever you suggest. *(Pause.)*

JUDITH: Plead! *(The SERVANT concentrates.)* Louder!

THE SERVANT: I am, but –

JUDITH: Louder, then! *(The SERVANT rocks to and fro on her knees, then stops. She scrambles to her feet.)*

THE SERVANT: I think you must do it.

JUDITH: He wants me to die!

THE SERVANT: I don't think we can make assumptions of that sort but –

JUDITH: Yes! Hates me and wants me to die!

THE SERVANT: I'm sorry but –
(JUDITH lets out a profound cry of despair as the SERVANT, clasping the head, goes to the door. She stops. She looks back at JUDITH. Pause.)
I say God. I mean Judith.
(Pause.)
I say Him. But I mean you.
(Pause. The cry of the SENTRY is heard. The SERVANT places the head on the ground, and comes back to JUDITH. She kneels before her, and leaning on her knuckles, puts her forehead on the ground. Pause. JUDITH watches.)

JUDITH: You are worshipping me.
Aren't you? Worshipping me?
Why are you doing that?

THE SERVANT: Not for what you are.

JUDITH: No?

THE SERVANT: For what you will be.

JUDITH: When?

THE SERVANT: When you stand, Judith.

JUDITH: I can't stand… *(Pause.)*

THE SERVANT: Firstly, remember we create ourselves. We do
not come made. If we came made, how facile life would
be, worm-like, crustacean, invertebrate. Facile and futile.
Neither love nor murder would be possible. Secondly,
whilst shame was given to us to balance will, shame is
not a wall. It is not a wall, Judith, but a sheet rather,
threadbare and stained. It only appears a wall to those
who won't come near it. Come near it and you see how
thin it is, you could part it with your fingers. Thirdly, it is a
facility of the common human, but a talent in the specially
human, to recognise no act is reprehensible but only the
circumstances make it so, for the reprehensible attaches
to the unnecessary, but with the necessary, the same act
bears the nature of obligation, honour and esteem. These
are the mysteries which govern the weak, but in the strong,
are staircases to the stars. I kneel to you. I kneel to Judith
who parts the threadbare fabric with her will. Get up, now.
*(Pause. JUDITH cannot move. The SERVANT counts the seconds.
She perseveres.)*
Judith, who are these we worship? What is it they possess?
The ones we wrap in glass and queue half-fainting for a
glimpse? The ones whose works are quoted and endorsed?
The little red books and the little green books, Judith, who
are they? Never the kind, for the kind are terrorized by
grief. Get up now, Judith.
(Nothing happens. Pause.)
No, they are the specially human who drained the act
of meaning and filled it again from sources fresher and
– *(JUDITH climbs swiftly to her feet.)*

JUDITH: You carry the head until we reach the river. Then I'll carry it. *(She busily goes to the sword.)* The sword I'm taking with us. *(The SERVANT, amazed and gratified, starts to scramble to her feet.)* WHO SAID YOU COULD GET UP. *(Pause. The SERVANT smiles, weakly.)* Beyond the river, you walk behind me. Ten yards at least.

THE SERVANT: Yes. Good. *(She starts to rise again.)*

JUDITH: WHO SAID YOU COULD GET UP. *(The SERVANT stops.)* And any version that I tell, endorse it. For that'll be the truth.

THE SERVANT: Absolutely – *(She moves again.)*

JUDITH: WHO SAID YOU COULD GET UP. *(The SERVANT freezes, affecting amusement.)*

THE SERVANT: I was only thinking –

JUDITH: Thinking? I do that.

THE SERVANT: Wonderful!

JUDITH: In fact, looking at you as I do, I find your posture contains so many elements of mute impertinence.

THE SERVANT: Honestly?

JUDITH: Honestly, yes. Your head, for example, presumes the vertical.

THE SERVANT: I'll stoop. *(She lowers her head. Pause. JUDITH comes close, kneeling beside her.)*

JUDITH: I shall so luxuriate in all the honours, I do not care what trash they drape me with, what emblems or what diadems, how shallow, glib and tinsel all the medals are, I'LL SPORT THEM ALL – *(The SERVANT goes as if to embrace her.)* DON'T SHIFT YOU INTELLECTUAL BITCH! *(The SERVANT stoops again, laughing with delight.)* No, I shall be unbearable, intolerably vile, inflicting my opinions on the young, I shall be the bane of Israel, spouting, spewing, a nine-foot tongue of ignorance will slobber out of my mouth and drench the populace with the saliva of my prejudice, they will wade through my opinions, they will wring my accents out their clothes, but they will tolerate it, for am I not their mother? Without me none of them could be born, HE SAID SO. *(Pause.)*

THE SERVANT: Yes. To everything. Shall I get up?

JUDITH: No, filth.

THE SERVANT: I was only thinking –

JUDITH: Thinking? I do that.

THE SERVANT (*With a short laugh.*): Yes! I forgot! But it occurs to me, time is –

JUDITH: No hurry, filth. Sit still. *(Pause. The SERVANT stares at the ground. JUDITH walks round her, holding the sword.)* Filth –

THE SERVANT: Do you have to call me –

JUDITH: Filth, put your teeth against my shoe. *(A black pause.)* Filth, do. *(The SERVANT inclines her head to JUDITH's foot, and is still.)* I think I could cut off a million heads and go home amiable as if I had been scything in the meadow. Clean this. *(She holds out the weapon. The SERVANT goes to wipe the blade on a cloth.)* No, silly, with your hair. *(Pause.)*

THE SERVANT: Now, listen –

JUDITH: You listen.
(The SERVANT anxiously regards the door. She takes the weapon and cleans it with her hair. She lays the weapon down, goes to stand. JUDITH's foot constrains her. Pause.)
Your hair's vile.

THE SERVANT: Obviously, I have just –

JUDITH: Cut it off, then. *(With a weary movement, the SERVANT, affecting patience, leans forward on her hands.)*

THE SERVANT: Judith…

JUDITH: Must! Must! *(Pause. The SERVANT lifts the weapon again.)* To kill your enemies, how easy that is. To murder the offending, how oddly stale. Real ecstasy must come of liquidating innocence, to punish in the absence of offence You haven't done it yet that must be the godlike act, when there is perfect incomprehension in the victim's eyes I will if you won't!
(The SERVANT, in an ecstasy of disgust, hacks her hair. She is still again.)
Later, we'll crop it. What you've done is such a mess.

THE SERVANT: Yes…

JUDITH: Well, isn't it?

THE SERVANT: Whatever you say.

JUDITH: Whatever I say, yes.
(Pause. JUDITH walks over the stage, looking at the still form of the SERVANT. She walks back again, stops.)
I'm trying to pity you.
But it's difficult because.
Because for you nothing is really pain at all.
Not torture. Death. Or.
Nothing is.
It's drained, and mulched, and used to nourish further hate, as dead men's skulls are ground for feeding fields …

THE SERVANT: Whatever you say.

JUDITH: Whatever I say, yes.

THE SERVANT: *(Seeing the slow spread of light.)* There's light under the flaps. It's dawn, Judith.

JUDITH: Dawn! Yes! This is the hour sin slips out the sheets to creep down pissy alleys! Morning, cats! Did you slither, also? Morning, sparrows! Rough night? Hot beds cooling. The running of water. Well, it has to end at some time, love! But its smell, in the after hours… Magnificence! *(She laughs, with a shudder. A cracked bell is beaten monotonously.)*

Israel!
Israel!
My body is so
Israel!
My body has no
Israel!
Israel!
My body was but is no longer
Israel
Is
My
Body!

(The cracked bell stops. Sounds of naturalistic conversation, the clatter of pots, the rising of a camp. The SERVANT gets up. She goes to JUDITH and kisses her hands. Taking the head in the bag, she slips out of the tent. JUDITH does not follow at once.)

LOT AND HIS GOD

Characters

DROGHEDA
An Angel

SVERDLOSK
The Wife of Lot

LOT
A Citizen of Sodom

WAITER
An Object of Contempt

I

An angel seated in a café.

DROGHEDA: I came to the city. I saw the people were filthy.
And those who were not filthy were still filthy. The filth
of those who were not filthy was not in their acts or even
in their thoughts but in their permission, for permission is
filthy if the thing permitted is filthy. And I saw no one and
heard no one who withheld this permission. Therefore the
filth was divided equally between those who practised filth
and those who looked on filth without revulsion. I reported
this and was praised for my report…

*(A woman enters. She sits swiftly at the table. She casts a glance
about her…)*

SVERDLOSK: I'm not leaving…

(She bites her lip)

Leave leave all you hear is leaving perhaps people should
leave less perhaps less leaving altogether would be nice
I-don't-like-it-I'm-leaving well you can't you can't leave try
staying instead staying and fighting or not fighting I don't
care what are you anyway a rat rats leave rats are famous
for it be a rat for all I care but don't ask me to be one pack
your bags you say so casually pack your bags do I look like
a woman who packs her bags look at me the hat the gloves
the

(DROGHEDA appears absent-minded…)

I'm talking to you the hat the gloves I'm talking to you I'm
talking to you

(DROGHEDA drags his gaze back to SVERDLOSK.)

The shoes they match my husband collects books five
thousand books he has some from the fourteenth century
the fourteenth century fragile and priceless fourteenth

century books and you say pack your bags that look I
hate that look that exasperated look no I'm not going
anywhere too bad if it exasperates you is he supposed to
burn his books and me I live for shoes do you know the
more offended you look the more pleasure I discover in
offending you pack your bags tell them pack theirs does
anybody serve you here why do you always sit in dirty
cafes there is a clean one over there perfectly clean and
they like to serve good-morning they say and they serve
I thought when I first set eyes on you he has a certain
tolerance for dirt not squalor dirt used things smeared
things to touch the unclean scarcely troubles him whereas
I already I want to wash my hands I'm wearing gloves but
still I want to wash my hands

(She stands swiftly.)

Is there a sink here you would know no no

(She sits as swiftly.)

It doesn't matter no imagine the sink imagine the soap the
cracked and sordid soap a perfect culture for pathogens
as for the towel imagine it not that I ever use the towel
however pristine is the towel still I ignore its blandishments
shaking my wet fingers in the air I do so love to embarrass
you the woman's mad the hatted woman the woman in
the hat and gloves quite mad he must be in love with
her a servile love not nice not healthy and she smacks
him probably the point is I am not leaving neither is my
husband

*(She looks at the ground. Her foot bounces… DROGHEDA gazes at
her… time passes…)*

DROGHEDA: My feelings with regard to you are complicated
on the one hand I despise your obsessive and frankly
pitiful self-regard but on the other I have to confess to a
certain admiration for the stubbornness with which you
cling to it it is not as if you were oblivious to the futility
of the life you have just described the gloves the shoes

the hats etcetera you are perhaps incapable of shame apology or even mild regret a thing oddly attractive to me and not me only many men I notice stare at you though these lingering regards are tainted with an apprehension you might drag them to their deaths death is not a dread of mine but humiliation might be as for packing bags in saying pack your bags I was excessively considerate you should go in what you stand up in or nothing at all yes go naked you degraded bitch the dirty cafes I choose for our rendezvous complement your character

(His gaze is fixed on her…)

SVERDLOSK: You do love me

(She leans back in her chair, plucking her skirt…)

You love me and it drives you mad I am not driven mad by you still no service how long have we been here perhaps if you were less taut less stiff less bitter less everything in fact some slovenly individual might pluck up courage and take our order we are giving wittingly or unwittingly the impression of a desperately unhappy couple no wonder no one intervenes we are not an unhappy couple we are not a couple at all you love me and I love my husband that's it that's it that's all there is to it

(She plays with a glove…)

Call me bitch again degraded bitch say it again go naked dirty bitch say

(DROGHEDA is unwilling…)

A funny couple we would be you a little filthy me scrupulously clean your filth as artificial as my cleanliness as for the disparity in our ages why won't you say it naked bitch either you meant to say it or you did not if you meant what you said surely it can be said again if you were simply irritated if those words were so to speak expletives then apologize

(She challenges DROGHEDA with her gaze.)

Here he comes no he doesn't

(She looks askance.)

He doesn't

He doesn't

That woman came in after me long after me you see he
skirts our table anyone would think we suffered from some
communicable disease and frankly you look unhealthy
an affectation obviously but how should he know that
apologize or call me bitch degraded bitch one or the other

(Pause.)

You would like to say the words again but because I want
to hear the words the words have lost their charm for you
very well invent some other words worse words preferably
degraded bitch I liked but how mild that is mild abuse is
silly and what might have satisfied me only minutes ago
could only disappoint me now so very altered are our
circumstances my husband look my husband searching
for us no we have entered a crueller sphere you and I
harder and crueller altogether call him he is short-sighted
the consequence of reading documents printed in the
fourteenth century he's seen us he's seen us pull up another
chair

(DROGHEDA fetches a third chair as LOT enters.)

Darling

(She kisses LOT's cheek.)

We are quarrelling Mr Drogheda and I quarrelling in an
amicable way at least it was amicable to begin with it is
less amicable now he began by urging me to pack my bags
I recoiled from the suggestion whereupon he called me
a degraded bitch I was both shocked and charmed and
begged him to repeat it he declined to so you see your

arrival is timely things might have got a lot worse there is a friction between Mr Drogheda and I possibly of a sexual nature I say possibly it's obvious he used the word naked naked naked he said and the service here is terrible by terrible I mean non-existent

(SVERDLOSK opens her handbag. She takes out a compact. She looks at herself in the mirror. At last LOT sits in the chair proffered by DROGHEDA. DROGHEDA does not sit at once but leans with his hands on the back of his own chair…)

DROGHEDA: Your wife infuriates me

(SVERDLOSK lets out a bemused cry. She plucks at a stray hair…)

My announcement of the imminent destruction of this place and every single one of its inhabitants provoked in her a perverse and frankly infantile reaction a reaction which even on a brief acquaintance might have been predicted what was less predictable was my own equally perverse and infantile frustration with her intransigence I admit that under extreme provocation I described your wife in terms I now regret terms to which she ascribes a sexual character

(SVERDLOSK lets out a further cry of mockery.)

Fortunately your appearance puts an end to any further deterioration in the situation I am a messenger a complacent messenger perhaps given I assumed my warning could have only a single consequence namely that the pair of you would pack your bags and quit the city in this confidence I was naïve perhaps perhaps I say perhaps I am reluctant to admit a weakness certainly I was naïve here comes a waiter no he doesn't

(Pause. He sits… at last LOT speaks.)

LOT: We like it here

(DROGHEDA regards LOT with a certain disdain.)

DROGHEDA: Here?

You like it here?

SVERDLOSK: He doesn't mean here when he says here he
means Sodom he does not mean here how could anybody
like it here obviously not here you did not mean here did
you not this squalid parody of a café you meant the city
didn't you he meant Sodom

(SVERDLOSK snaps shut her compact.)

LOT: I meant Sodom

(Pause.)

I meant Sodom on the other hand I think I have to say
it would be inconsistent of me to declare as I have to Mr
Drogheda that I liked the city of Sodom but in the next
sentence to affect a revulsion for this filthy café which in
its every aspect expresses Sodom not least in its filth I
think we could safely say of this place that its ugliness its
decrepitude and the slovenliness of its waiters is scarcely
accidental rather these are aspects of a perverse fashion

(Pause. SVERDLOSK is gazing at DROGHEDA…)

SVERDLOSK: He is too clever for me

LOT: I am not too clever for you and you are a liar to say so
it is a lie you have played with for forty years never mind
every man must have his lie and every woman

SVERDLOSK: I love you

LOT: Of course you do and here comes the waiter

(He casts a glance off…)

In accordance with what I have just described he will
demonstrate a reluctance to accept our order if he wipes
the table at all it will be with a disgusting cloth and at no
point in the transaction will he meet our eyes all in all he
will exert himself to be unremittingly offensive strangely
this entails more effort than common politeness would but
this is Sodom you talk to him I won't

300

(A WAITER appears, young and slovenly. He proceeds to justify every one of LOT's speculations, beginning with a cursory wiping of the tin table. They watch him in silence. At last he indicates a willingness to take their order but DROGHEDA stands abruptly, accidentally toppling his chair in his resentment…)

DROGHEDA: *(Bitterly.)* I'm blinding you

(The WAITER lifts his gaze to DROGHEDA, a gaze full of contempt. SVERDLOSK acts swiftly to end the confrontation.)

SVERDLOSK: Three coffees coffee is it coffee darling three coffees and cold milk the cold milk separately

(DROGHEDA retrieves his chair. The WAITER idles and departs. DROGHEDA sits…)

LOT: Don't blind him

DROGHEDA: Too late he's blinded

LOT: You are impetuous Mr Drogheda and as a consequence we shall never be served though it has to be said that were we to be served we might have cause to regret it

(An appalling cry from a distance… DROGHEDA stares at the table. SVERDLOSK bites her lip, her gaze fixed on DROGHEDA. LOT looks over his shoulder in the direction of the cry.)

If I have learned one thing from living as we have for thirty years in such a place as Sodom it is this that however unregulated things seem eventually they are regulated you are of course the regulator

DROGHEDA: He offended me

LOT: Yes

DROGHEDA: Precisely as you described

LOT: Yes

DROGHEDA: He is a waiter and he claimed ascendancy over me

LOT: He did his whole manner was insubordinate even his way of standing

DROGHEDA: As for the cloth

LOT: Filthy

DROGHEDA: And the way he moved the cloth

LOT: Calculated to humiliate the customer do you intend to blind the others they are animated suddenly like a swarm of bees

DROGHEDA: Yes

LOT: And some have kitchen knives

SVERDLOSK: *(Apprehensive.)* Blind them

LOT: It is one of the characteristics of Sodom that whereas the citizens seem for the most part to exist in a condition of self-induced torpor

SVERDLOSK: *(Alarmed.)* Blind them

LOT: It takes surprisingly little to induce them to erupt into a frenzy

SVERDLOSK: Blind them darling

LOT: Knives guns bottles clubs the official description of Sodom as a place of pleasure and civility is routinely contradicted as you see

SVERDLOSK: *(Rising from her chair in her terror.)* DARLING BLIND THEM PLEASE

(A torrent of cries and curses… SVERDLOSK resumes her seat.)

Darling I said Mr Drogheda is not darling to me I called him darling presumably because

(The whimpering of stricken men…)

Because

Because a woman exposed to danger inevitably invokes the prospect of intimacy with whomsoever possesses the wherewithal to save her in this instance this individual was Mr Drogheda it was instinct instinct and expediency on the other hand

(She falters…the WAITERS are mournful…)

I am attracted to Mr Drogheda

LOT: Obviously and his angelic powers lend him a charm which surely abolishes any reluctance a woman might have entertained given his self-neglect though that too might be an inducement to an immaculate and pristine woman such as you

(To DROGHEDA.)

Do you intend to leave them like that?

(DROGHEDA shrugs.)

Crawling crying for their mothers apologizing and so on in a minute they will find our feet and slobber over them and after feet it will be knees it's unedifying don't you think?

(DROGHEDA regards the spectacle with indifference…)

DROGHEDA: I am not here to save them I am here to save you

LOT: I should like to explain why that is not the simple matter it seems to be to you but the complaints of these

DROGHEDA: I'll silence them and then we must get on

LOT: No please

(DROGHEDA casts a glance at LOT.)

I mean let us get on but I would prefer it if you refrained from adding to their suffering by inflicting them with whatever

SVERDLOSK: Dumbness

LOT: Dumbness for example yes

DROGHEDA: They're as good as dead

(Pause.)

LOT: Yes

Yes

And so are we only

(A sudden silence falls over the cafe…)

I should not have interceded for them

(DROGHEDA shrugs…)

My pity condemned them to a further swathe of agony I must learn to keep my mouth shut when there are angels in the room whatever an angel may or may not be we can be sure of one thing he is not inhibited by considerations of humanity and why should he be since he is not human now they are waving their arms in the most pitiful way like waterweed in currents much worse I think to behold than their wailing was to listen to BUT I SAY NOTHING I ASK NOTHING IGNORE MY LITTLE TWITCH OF SYMPATHY

(DROGHEDA regards LOT with contempt…)

DROGHEDA: Your vanity is preposterous

LOT: Is it?

Possibly

Possibly I'm vain

My wife has made similar complaints of me

DROGHEDA: Neither of my actions either in blinding or making dumb the insolent waiters was inspired by the desire to frustrate your kindness

LOT: I apologize

DROGHEDA: If it was kindness

LOT: I think it was but it may not have been

DROGHEDA: As you say it may not have been you perhaps might wish to consider the paradox of kindness in the solitude of your library if you ever again enter your library which you may you may prefer your library to the will of God sadly you will not have long in which to enjoy it let alone resolve paradoxes of this magnitude I am here to urge you to pack your bags that's all just pack your bags and go that's all why I have lingered here so long I do not know

SVERDLOSK: You know perfectly well

DROGHEDA: Do I?

SVERDLOSK: Yes

It's me

DROGHEDA: It is you yes I was being disingenuous and the more you insist on it the more convinced I become that I cannot leave until I have enjoyed some intimacy with you what kind of intimacy I don't know what kind of enjoyment I don't know either perhaps no enjoyment at all the fact you state these things out loud before your husband is

SVERDLOSK: He's used to it

DROGHEDA: Is

SVERDLOSK: Thirty-seven years I have loved my husband

DROGHEDA: Is

SVERDLOSK: Thirty-seven

DROGHEDA: A calculated provocation obviously I am not naïve but still the provocation works I am aroused and he looks suitably long-suffering his mouth is shaped by pain and certainly if he were not in pain we both know none of this could satisfy me

(LOT suddenly rises from his chair, indifferent to DROGHEDA's discourse but shaken by the wretched appearance of the WAITER who, blind and dumb, is crawling over the floor...)

All of which causes me to wonder if I am not the subject of some domestic game marriage is an unpredictable and frequently delinquent institution but if you are playing with me I have succumbed the only question is

LOT: *(Staring at the WAITER.)* Put him out of his misery why don't you

DROGHEDA: What happens next?

LOT: *(To DROGHEDA.)* YOU ARE TORTURING THIS MAN

SVERDLOSK: Not a man

LOT: THIS YOUTH YOU ARE TORTURING THIS YOUTH

DROGHEDA: All the time you resort to exaggeration have you noticed that exaggeration and hyperbole?

SVERDLOSK: And he is a scholar with books dating from the fourteenth century

DROGHEDA: The scholar exaggerates

SVERDLOSK: I blame the library

DROGHEDA: Why?

SVERDLOSK: He sits alone in there day after day don't you darling you see no one?

LOT: I see you

SVERDLOSK: You see me but very few others and this I think contributes to a certain sense of unreality everything disturbs you

LOT: I AM DISTURBED BY CRUELTY I AM DISTURBED BY TORTURE

DROGHEDA: It is not torture it is punishment a man of your distinction can surely discriminate between the two?

SVERDLOSK: He can't

DROGHEDA: Perhaps he can't and certainly it is one of the characteristics of Sodom I have found the most irritating worse even than the universal depravity but they are contingent one upon the other are they not if one cannot distinguish between words

(The stricken WAITER dimly grasps the air…)

how might one distinguish between values it's not possible

LOT: *(Rising from his chair.)* I cannot sit and watch this

SVERDLOSK: Sit down

LOT: I will not sit down

DROGHEDA: All right stay standing but before you become any more shrill in your indignation perhaps you should recollect who it was initiated all these actions the consequences of which you now pretend to find intolerable

LOT: I don't pretend and they are intolerable

DROGHEDA: It was you

LOT: NEVER DID I

DROGHEDA: Recollect I said

LOT: NEVER WOULD I

DROGHEDA: Never would you speak the words but all the same you know perfectly well who it was encouraged me

SVERDLOSK: It was me

DROGHEDA: It was you but your husband was no less responsible

SVERDLOSK: He has a tone

DROGHEDA: A tone yes you could call it a tone

SVERDLOSK: The tone adopted by my husband enabled me
to issue the command it's strange how that happens the
blinding and the dumbing certainly were done by you but
the atmosphere in which this blinding could be perpetrated
was created by my husband his wit contempt disdain
etcetera on reflection in giving the order to blind I feel I
was the least reprehensible if any of us is reprehensible at
all he is holding my foot he is weeping and holding my
foot such a different attitude he was menacing ten minutes
ago now he's

(She laughs…)

YOU'RE TICKLING ME

(LOT stares at the spectacle of his wife and the WAITER…)

DROGHEDA: Let's talk about God's will for a minute I say a
minute it need not take that long

SVERDLOSK: *(To the WAITER.)* STOP IT

DROGHEDA: I think you know what His will is the only
question is when and if you are conforming to it it's funny I
really want a coffee now possibly because I know I cannot
have one of course we could go somewhere else there is a
café over there where when they wish you good-morning it
is sincere apparently

LOT: No

DROGHEDA: You see you like conditions to be sordid mildly
sordid mildly chic I am beginning to understand you your
wife is more complicated

LOT: It isn't chic here it is horrible

DROGHEDA: All the more reason to go elsewhere

LOT: We have inflicted awful things on these

SVERDLOSK: *(Standing.)* I have to move

LOT: These harmless and

SVERDLOSK: *(To the WAITER.)* LET ME GO LET ME GO

LOT: Inoffensive

SVERDLOSK: *(Lifting her chair and moving it a few feet.)* They are inoffensive now they were not inoffensive twenty minutes ago

LOT: I AM NOT MOVING

(He sits. He bites his lip…)

Look at them, oh look…

(He shakes his head…)

DROGHEDA: When I urged your wife to pack her bags she was knowingly or unknowingly profoundly seductive in the vehemence with which she repudiated the proposition and I confess the erotic character of our quarrel still influences me or I should have left here long ago after all what I have to say is scarcely complicated her attitude to the waiters for example is in stark contrast to your own if she has pity for them she does not advertise it whereas you

SVERDLOSK: *(To DROGHEDA.)* Kiss me

(Pause. DROGHEDA looks at SVERDLOSK without moving.)

LOT: In requiring my wife and I to abandon Sodom God was possibly and I hesitate to interpret Him possibly rewarding my fidelity to Him and I am thankful there are other considerations however considerations unrelated to my library or any other property property is not the issue

DROGHEDA: *(To SVERDLOSK.)* Kiss?

LOT: So what if the books date from the fourteenth century decay is decay no it's not the books

SVERDLOSK: *(To DROGHEDA.)* You don't want to kiss?

DROGHEDA: I don't know

LOT: Please confirm to God that Lot for all his love of
literature was not constrained by it no this is a matter of
ethics not property

DROGHEDA: Your ethics are paltry

LOT: Possibly

DROGHEDA: A self-indulgence

LOT: Possibly

DROGHEDA: And of negligible interest to God I don't know
why the invitation to a kiss is not more compelling to
me obviously of all the intimacies available to us the
kiss must always be appreciated as the greatest as well as
conventionally the first nothing that occurs subsequently
replicates the splendour of the kiss except a further kiss all
the same I

(He makes a futile gesture.)

No let's start with the kiss

SVERDLOSK: Wait

Wait

(She opens her handbag…)

Your meditation on the theme of kissing has abolished
any spontaneity that might have lingered in the obscure
channels of our relationship Mr Drogheda on the other
hand I am not so infantile as to think spontaneity is
evidence of desire on the contrary desire is frequently
constrained by its integrity all the same I feel licensed by
your thoughtfulness to admit my own equivalence

(She takes out a mirror and lipstick.)

My lips for such a kiss

(She pouts. She applies the lipstick.)

LOT: *(Who has watched the waiter's ordeal.)* Oh my poor boy oh my poor poor boy

(He stands. He takes the WAITER and assists him into his vacant chair.)

Sit

Sit

SVERDLOSK: My lips require this imitation of perfection

LOT: He hears us he hears everything

DROGHEDA: Imitation?

SVERDLOSK: I am fifty Mr Drogheda

DROGHEDA: And how does that detract from their perfection since your age is your form and your form is the subject of my fascination?

LOT: *(Bitterly.)* HE HEARS THIS HE IS NOT DEAF HE HEARS ALL THIS

DROGHEDA: Then let him sit in silence

LOT: *(A terrible intuition.)* No

No

(The WAITER writhes as he is stricken with deafness.)

No

DROGHEDA: Everything you say contributes to his misery

LOT: Then punish me since it is I who offends you

DROGHEDA: God loves you

(The WAITER, grasping his altered condition, staggers to his feet, toppling the chair as he does so…)

Which is not to say you are immune from His resentment

LOT: *(Assisting the WAITER, who shakes his head and streams tears.)*
It's all right it's all right it's all right

SVERDLOSK: It's not all right is it not really all right he is blind
deaf and dumb how is that all right?

(She shuts her bag with a click.)

DROGHEDA: This resentment is understandable given your
reluctance to obey Him

LOT: *(To the WAITER.)* Sit

Sit

*(He picks up the fallen chair. SVERDLOSK kisses DROGHEDA, one
hand lifted to his face…)*

Sit you poor boy

(He assists the WAITER into the chair.)

Perhaps I am reluctant yes certainly I am it's obvious I am
reluctant to obey Him and these acts of wanton cruelty
by you His agent and His angel incline me to think my
reluctance is entirely justified

(To the WAITER.)

Oh how terrible it is this silent weeping

(To SVERDLOSK.)

A handkerchief darling darling a handkerchief

(He extends a hand, unaware of SVERDLOSK's preoccupations.)

Handkerchief

*(He turns, sees her lingering kiss. He watches it. He moves away from
the table to observe the kiss from a new perspective. He is filled with
awe… the kiss ends, and SVERDLOSK, opening her handbag again,
removes her compact and sets about restoring her face. DROGHEDA
is pensive.)*

Sodom has its attractions Mr Drogheda even for one who purports to recoil from it apparently

SVERDLOSK: Shh

LOT: Not that we dare expect this brief transaction to diminish in the slightest your determination to destroy this city and all of its inhabitants

SVERDLOSK: Shh

LOT: Including presumably the woman with whom you have enjoyed this brief intimacy

SVERDLOSK: Shh I said

LOT: On the contrary

(The WAITER rotates in his chair, his face taut with incomprehension…)

I have no doubt this lapse from your own high standards will only intensify your contempt for us

(The WAITER tumbles off the chair, sprawling…)

SVERDLOSK: *(Snapping shut her compact.)* I wish you did not waste yourself

LOT: Waste myself?

(He goes to assist the WAITER onto his feet, but hesitates, sensing the futility of it.)

How do I waste myself?

SVERDLOSK: Always you argue always you dissent

LOT: Possibly

SVERDLOSK: Your gaze is like a reprimand and always you frown the frown is permanent I love you but you will not live long

(She turns her gaze to DROGHEDA.)

He knows no peace my husband neither in sleep nor in between my legs it is scarcely a compliment to a woman and it gives me no satisfaction to announce it but he never knows that loss that sublime loss of self that's love do you darling know the loss of love I don't know why I tell you this presumably because I am a faithless wife and the faithless wife betrays to tell you the deepest secrets of our marriage is a gift to you Mr Drogheda do you appreciate the gift I wonder I will mock him if you ask me to mock jeer or scorn his acts what I cannot do I think is cease to love him our kiss was the beginning I assume let me wipe your mouth the kiss left lipstick stains shall I?

(She holds up a clean handkerchief. DROGHEDA seems paralyzed with introspection…)

Do it yourself if you prefer

(DROGHEDA lifts his gaze to SVERDLOSK. She falters…)

Or don't do it

(He looks. SVERDLOSK recovers.)

It's incongruous I daresay but whilst one is inevitably drawn to a man who has recently come from a woman the visible evidence of the fact in the form of lipstick smears renders him ridiculous and annihilates the sexual authority he might otherwise have enjoyed strange strange isn't it

(She looks to LOT.)

Do you find that strange?

(And back to DROGHEDA.)

Please take it off

(She holds out the handkerchief again. Her eyes fix his. At last DROGHEDA takes the handkerchief. SVERDLOSK opens her bag and holds up the compact mirror for him. He dabs his mouth…)

LOT: I know nothing about

SVERDLOSK: Liar

LOT: Sexual love and its

SVERDLOSK: Liar

LOT: Ambiguities

SVERDLOSK: Lying

Lying

Liar

(She laughs briefly.)

My lie is I am not clever yours is you are ignorant of sexual
love from these preposterous fallacies we have made a life
a life which thanks to Mr Drogheda is coming to an end a
woman who has been intimate with an angel presumably
cannot simply return to the marriage bed a little soiled
a little bruised a little absentminded as she is used to
doing when returning from the passion of a mortal man
impossible I should have thought Mr Drogheda already I
want to kiss you again already

*(DROGHEDA is still, the handkerchief clutched in his hand… at
last he looks up)*

DROGHEDA: Wonderful is the wife of Lot

*(SVERDLOSK is moved by DROGHEDA's compliment. She is briefly
honest.)*

SVERDLOSK: Thank you

(She lowers her eyes.)

Thank you

(Pause. She lifts her eyes again.)

To find me wonderful is not incompatible I think with the
sadness I know you are experiencing not incompatible
at all you sense your passion for me will damage your

life but at the same time you long to be damaged I know this agony I have been where you now find yourself not once but many times and what is worse for you you find me cruel and self-obsessed apprehensive is Mr Drogheda when he contemplates the wife of Lot the wife of Lot has her own name incidentally

(DROGHEDA cuts her off with a swift gesture of his hand. LOT laughs briefly…)

Naked even I must remain the wife of Lot the angel is a man then and takes a man's delight in wife-stealing often I am stolen Mr Drogheda but I remain Lot's wife this will frustrate you as in the end it frustrated all the others

(LOT goes to his wife and places his hands gently on her shoulders… DROGHEDA contemplates their complicity… the stricken WAITER crawls in, having made a fatuous and circular journey. In a spasm of resentment, DROGHEDA jumps off his chair and going to the WAITER, drags him half-upright.)

DROGHEDA: IF YOU ENTER MY SIGHT AGAIN

LOT: He's deaf

DROGHEDA: CRAWLING AND DRIBBLING AND

LOT: He's deaf Mr Drogheda

DROGHEDA: AND MAKING MOCK OF ME

LOT: You did it Mr Drogheda

DROGHEDA: *(Glaring at LOT.)* I DID IT YES AND SO WHAT IF MY ANGER STRIKES YOU AS CONTRADICTORY

(SVERDLOSK laughs, shaking her head. DROGHEDA looks at her. He lets the WAITER fall. He returns to his chair.)

Yes and certainly there is something nauseating about marriages like yours the darker aspects of which seem impenetrable as primeval forests but which we both know perfectly well are choked with nothing more exotic than self-interest and complacency this sordid encounter has delayed my departure but since you are determined to perish here I need not test God's patience any further I am in love with you but that is a fact which can be objectified and then abandoned as one abandons a chair as one abandons a table the table is a fact so what

(SVERDLOSK and LOT look at DROGHEDA, who does not move. DROGHEDA frowns. The WAITER, attempting to rise, trips and sprawls…)

So what

So what

(DROGHEDA stands as if to depart, but is hesitant…)

SVERDLOSK: Shall we go to a room?

(DROGHEDA is silent. His mouth moves in his crisis.)

We can go to a room but frankly that is not my way and in any case a room chosen by you will inevitably possess all those characteristics I found so distasteful in your choice of café an unaired bed a carpet so soiled I will hesitate to set a naked foot on it dead flies and threadbare curtains of course my foot need not be naked by all means let us make love in shoes but in my own home in my own home let us violate all those things conventionally described as homely and there are more shoes there not only red but black or blue

(DROGHEDA does not reply. His head turns in his discomfort…)

DROGHEDA: I have to say this and it will not I think come as a surprise God knows His own mind but speaking for myself I hate the pair of you

(SVERDLOSK laughs brightly…)

LOT: Shh

DROGHEDA: A hatred possibly more bitter because as we all three know I am in love with you in love with what however the miniature scale of your transgressions the pitiful collusion of your book-collecting husband the suffocating stench of an airless domesticity

(SVERDLOSK laughs again.)

LOT: Shh

DROGHEDA: Combine to make me shrink from you

SVERDLOSK: *(Standing up.)* Follow me

DROGHEDA: *(Pursuing his indictment.)* Sin or the idea of sin to be precise

(She brushes her suit with a gloved hand.)

SVERDLOSK: Follow me now

DROGHEDA: Excites you

SVERDLOSK: It is good to follow a woman is it not?

DROGHEDA: But what sort of sinner are you?

SVERDLOSK: Following and knowing?

DROGHEDA: No sinner at all

SVERDLOSK: Knowing she will be naked knowing that while she walks she trembles

DROGHEDA: But an imitation of a sinner

SVERDLOSK: Trembles with the thought of you

DROGHEDA: A copy a

SVERDLOSK: She marches and she throbs

DROGHEDA: A copy

SVERDLOSK: With fear and hope with hope and fear

DROGHEDA: A COPY I SAID

(The WAITER, trying to haul himself upright, pulls the table on top of himself. DROGHEDA, SVERDLOSK, even LOT, pay no attention.

With exquisite decision, SVERDLOSK goes to leave. DROGHEDA stands abruptly.)

I love you where are you going I love you

(SVERDLOSK stops, her back to DROGHEDA…)

LOT: *(Supremely complacent)* To the library

(DROGHEDA casts a withering glance at LOT.)

She is going to the library

(DROGHEDA's lip trembles with his resentment.)

To be naked in the library or a little naked in the library

(His gaze is unfaltering.)

To stand in the library in perfect nakedness or simply to disarrange her clothes as if the books were dead men gazing on her I don't know as if the intellectual character of the room pleaded for its violation I don't know as if as if

(He smiles thoughtfully.)

I really do not know and she leaves nothing after her so when I return to study there the library retains that air of sacred and impenetrable secrecy which the smallest relic of her presence a handkerchief a button even a single thread of her underwear would violate she knows this and is fastidious

(He heaves the table upright…)

Sodom is an ugly place but where else should I go Mr Drogheda I am in the library the library is in me a place of scholarship but not always scholarly nakedness and the book the book and nakedness ask God to forgive us I shall never find again the simplicity He demands of me and she has never in her life lifted a spade or planted a solitary geranium look at her Mr Drogheda her shoulders are more fragile than a child's does God seriously propose those

shoulders haul buckets out of wells does He do you Mr
Drogheda?

*(Pause. SVERDLOSK's head turns to DROGHEDA. Her look
commands him. She goes out. DROGHEDA stares at LOT, then turns
and looks after SVERDLOSK. He follows her. LOT is still. The WAITER
is silently turning on the ground like a dying insect. At last LOT
emerges from his meditation. He goes to the WAITER and takes both
his hands in his own. He hauls him up and edges him into a chair,
where he sits swaying, his head in his hands. LOT himself sits...)*

She wants him

(Pause.)

I could see that as soon as I came in you read the signs you
feel the feelings it could be in a look the way the hips slip
down the chair anyway she soon admitted it they must be
crossing the river as we speak as I speak you do not speak
obviously

*(Pause. The WAITER's hands comb the air. LOT takes one hand and
holds it...)*

Unless and I have often seen this done on bridges unless
she drifts to a standstill staring over the parapet one heel
a little raised and parked behind the other pensive so it
appears of course not pensive in the least as he draws
nearer sets off again that takes time all refinements take
time few have the patience for refinements turning
the corner she will look back conventional you say
conventional of course but in matters such as this the
conventional finds it apotheosis to innovate at this
stage would compromise the fragile and exquisite faith
which makes such extraordinary intimacies possible no
innovation comes later her key is in the look she lingers
pretending the door is stiff lingers until he arrives at the
bottom of the steps from his perspective her legs look oh
her legs look so the door swings open as we speak as I
speak you do not speak obviously and climbs the stairs she

leaves the door ajar and climbs the stairs the library is on the first floor only a little ajar these details are significant

(Pause. The WAITER's free hand gropes the air, discovers LOT's head and strokes it, pitifully. LOT does nothing to discourage him…)

She

(He smiles at the delicacy of the WAITER's touch.)

She

(He kindly removes the WAITER's hand and places it with the other, his own hand covering both.)

She walks directly to the table about a dozen steps the table not the desk the desk is heaped with objects any one of which could topple roll and smash minor accidents cause anguish in these circumstances out of all proportion to the value of the property no she avoids the desk she stands instead behind the table one hand idly posed on it the hand without the glove the ungloved hand pale in its nakedness the gloved hand she raises to her chest the gloved hand holding the glove do you follow and looks towards the door tilting her head so this first glance is dark conspiratorial a pact once this long and awful look has been exchanged she takes off the hat

(He stops.)

I think

I think she discards the hat and for this reason that their first kiss might be stripped of its magnificence if in his impatience he dislodged the hat not only that not only that

(Pause.)

In lifting both hands to remove the hat one to the pin the other to the brim a woman shows herself to immense advantage the light fails on her hair her undressed hair is it not a gift to him a promise even as we speak he as I speak you do not speak obviously he he he

(He stops, yielding to his meditation. His face expresses pain and ecstasy at once. At last he stands, depositing the WAITER's hands on the table. The WAITER is docile. LOT walks a little…)

Conceal yourself she said and from your hiding place observe me never have I done so and I must admit the proposition caused me some offence whilst acknowledging she extended this invitation as a testament of love it had the unfortunate effect of causing me to recognize the limitations of her sensibility to witness such a sacrament might well enthral me and I saw even to speak of it enthralled her but there is a greater place from which to sense the world a colder place cold but immaculate I was disappointed this was impossible to communicate to her there were other considerations for example would the fact of her husband being present and observing her cause her to act differently to exaggerate her feelings no there is an integrity in all encounters which has to be observed they're late

(He frowns. He bites his lip…)

Late and I am perfectly aware a couple returning from an intimacy how funny I do not like that word intimacy the word I do not think I ever have described these acts as intimacies I am both irritated and curious to know why I employed the word a couple walk more slowly from their union than they walked towards it I like union even less certainly they're late they're late whatever the word is

(He stares into the distance. He draws the back of his hand across his mouth. He sits in the chair. He stares at the ground. He frets. The immobile WAITER speaks.)

GOD: Lot

(Pause. LOT is uncertain if he heard his name. He lifts his eyes.)

Yes I spoke your name does it surprise you when God speaks through a dumb man's mouth?

(LOT shifts on his chair. He looks at the mask of oblivion that is the WAITER's face…)

LOT: No

No

No it is entirely predictable in God the wonderful is predictable any appearance of contradiction in that statement lies in the poverty of my understanding Mr Drogheda an angel is with my wife

(Pause.)

Naked with my wife that also is a contradiction only in so far as I fail to understand it he drew her skirt over her hips he took her from behind he he

(He closes his eyes in his agony…)

Her hat her gloves were on the table no not gloves one only one glove lay on the table the other she wore as he as he

(He stares at the ground…)

GOD: The angel does my will

(Pause.)

LOT: Does he? Does he do God's will?

(He bites his lip.)

Then neither his reluctance nor his fascination was sincere?

(He frowns.)

GOD: Lot's wife

LOT: Her name is

GOD: Lot's wife is Lot's property if she were not Lot's property she could not be stolen if she could not be stolen all that happens in his library would yield Lot no pleasure Lot's wife is therefore her whole identity

LOT: God knows us

(He works at his fingers in his anxiety.)

And because He knows us knows also the great dread that constitutes Lot's ecstasy the dread she

(He bites his lip.)

WHERE IS MR DROGHEDA?

(He stares into the adamantine face of the WAITER…)

It's cold I'm

(Pause.)

Evening's coming on we never

(Pause.)

My wife and I have solemnly agreed she never stays longer than

(Pause.)

Or I fret obviously

(Pause.)

Strangers however nice they seem to be are AND THIS IS SODOM

(He suddenly rises out of his chair.)

IF HE HAS HURT HER I WILL

HAS HE

HAS HE

(He goes to threaten the WAITER. He stops on a thought.)

No

No

It's worse

She loves him and she

(He half-laughs. He slumps into his chair)

HAS PACKED A BAG

(He stares, racked by imagination…)

A taxi to the station a train to the ferry and in their cabin an act which entirely excludes me

(He appears to dream…)

GOD: Sixteen times Lot's wife betrayed him

LOT: Sixteen is it I never counted them SIXTEEN I DON'T THINK SO can one betray a man who yearns for his betrayal who finds the very word exquisite SIXTEEN you are playing with me you are implying there have been occasions of betrayal to which I was not party authentic infidelity therefore not her not her not her SIXTEEN now you think me sentimental you think the idiot husband fawns upon his wife you

(He stops.)

Yes

Yes

(He frowns.)

Sixteen if you say it is

(He makes fists of his hands. He shakes his head)

Nothing spoils sin like giving sin permission

I ADMIRE HER

(He affects to laugh.)

ABUNDANT IS MY WIFE'S IMAGINATION HOW COULD SHE ALLOW HER INFIDELITIES TO BE POLICED BY ME IT'S PREPOSTEROUS SIXTEEN YOU SAY ONLY SIXTEEN ARE YOU SURE IT ISN'T MORE

I love her

I love her

How beautiful are the lies of Lot's wife how beautiful her truth

(His eyes fill with tears.)

Let her eyes look on me narrowed with their secrets how terrible it is to know all things I pity God I would not be Him

(The WAITER is still, then to LOT's horror he begins to weep. LOT stares…)

Forgive me

Forgive me my vast love my vast but mortal love of my own wife pitiful as it surely is

(GOD sobs. LOT's hands rise and fall futilely.)

Stop that

Stop that awful sound

(He covers his ears as GOD moans in his solitude. SVERDLOSK enters holding a packed bag. She looks at the WAITER.)

SVERDLOSK: Wasn't he dumb?

(LOT turns to his wife.)

Wasn't he deaf?

(LOT grasps his wife's hands and covers them in kisses. The WAITER walks away, faultlessly.)

Wasn't he blind the waiter?

(She looks down at LOT. With a profoundly loving gesture she places her gloved hands on his head and kisses him. LOT's gaze falls on the bag. At the same moment DROGHEDA walks in, sullen but patient. LOT's face is ghastly.)

LOT: You're leaving me

(SVERDLOSK frowns.)

You're leaving me and from some redundant sense of manners feel it necessary to perform this adieu and I imagined you already on the ferry petting as the throbbing engines churned the sea the gulls the fading cliffs or in your cabin yes straight to the cabin never mind the view clothes chasing clothes flung heaped chaotic hat gloves shoes entirely different from the library the library having been however breathless still discreet still constrained by etiquette and the moves few few moves in the library the effect of literature perhaps the sheer weight of philosophy moderating urgency and making both of you infinitely

SVERDLOSK: There is no library

(LOT stares at his wife.)

You know Mr Drogheda he

(Pause.)

Has tempers destructive tempers destructive not only to men also to property

(Pause.)

It's burned the library

(LOT cannot speak. DROGHEDA takes a chair and turning it, sits…)

DROGHEDA: Unhealthy place

LOT: Oh?

DROGHEDA: Menacing

LOT: Menacing?

DROGHEDA: *(Shooting a cruel look at LOT.)* It menaced me

(Pause.)

Up to a certain point I found it stimulating obviously
the shelves of arid argument and her naked arse the
meditations of the dead and her fingers searching me
gloved fingers incidentally then I lost my temper

*(DROGHEDA rocks on his chair, his eyes fixed on LOT…. LOT disdains
to quarrel… his horror subsides…)*

LOT: The angel does God's will it is a pity however that he
could not be satisfied to steal my wife perhaps I always
sensed this was a destiny and the books intended for my
consolation I am to have no consolation it appears

*(DROGHEDA stands and goes to LOT. He searches his face,
frowning…)*

DROGHEDA: What are you?

(LOT does not lift his eyes to DROGHEDA.)

LOT: A man more sensitive than God thought men could be

(Pause.)

No wonder He hates Sodom

(He lifts his eyes to DROGHEDA.)

No wonder he thinks the desert is the place for me

(He creates a smile.)

Churlish and arbitrary is God but my ordeal is obviously
necessary to me

(His eyes fall.)

I submit to His will

(He looks up again to DROGHEDA.)

Bookless and wifeless Lot will be

SVERDLOSK: Wifeless?

LOT: Under a bitter moon Lot will discover death or some other poetry than woman possibly

SVERDLOSK: How wifeless?

(DROGHEDA laughs brutally. SVERDLOSK turns on him.)

If I had heard that laugh even an hour previously never would you have visited me it is a dog's laugh the angel is a dog

DROGHEDA: Stroke your dog

SVERDLOSK: *(To LOT.)* The bag's for us

DROGHEDA: Stroke me

SVERDLOSK: Towels socks handkerchiefs

DROGHEDA: Don't stroke then it's a funny thing

(He drags the chair to himself and sits astride it.)

A funny thing the act of love I call it love I dignify the thing that has so many names it masquerades as a conclusion all that attaches to it confirms it is the end when all the time it begs for repetition hardly had I got to the foot of the stairs the smouldering stairs the stairs already thick with ash when the sight of her descending bag in one hand the other lifted to her tilted hat struck me with the force of an irresistible proposition it was as if we had completed one transaction only to discover this compulsion for another and that this also whilst seeming to be final would coerce us yet again into another and another and

SVERDLOSK: *(Discreetly.)* Shut up

DROGHEDA: As we struggled in the smoke-filled hall

SVERDLOSK: Shut up now

DROGHEDA: I sensed this was only the first instalment of a servitude

SVERDLOSK: Shut up I said

DROGHEDA: STROKE ME THEN

(He shrugs. He turns his shoulders away.)

SVERDLOSK: *(To LOT.)* Your razor I remembered but the soap I don't think I collected

DROGHEDA: NEVER STROKE ME AGAIN

SVERDLOSK: I was choking I could hardly see

DROGHEDA: NEVER NEVER STROKE AGAIN

SVERDLOSK: Use mine if necessary

(DROGHEDA smothers his head in his hands… LOT gawps at his wife. Suddenly DROGHEDA flings out of the chair.)

DROGHEDA: Leave by the East Gate if you have friends do not delay your departure by bidding them farewell they're dead and do not stop at Zoar pass through Zoar you may not exchange one city for another the life you have led here hurt God but still He pities you now give me one shoe you will find no use for high heels where you are going either will do

(SVERDLOSK removes one shoe and extends it to DROGHEDA. DROGHEDA studies it without taking it. He lifts his eyes to SVERDLOSK)

Exquisite perversity

(He seems to suffer. His hands open and close. He shakes his head.)

LOT: *(Kindly.)* Take it

(DROGHEDA is dark with resentment…)

Take it I understand how you

DROGHEDA: *(With a surge of rage.)* DO YOU DO YOU UNDERSTAND GOD IT MUST BE AND GOD ALONE STOPS ME BLINDING YOU

(His eyes return to the shoe, patiently held by SVERDLOSK.)

Preposterous and ridiculous refinement of a culture of depravity

(Pause. SVERDLOSK does not withdraw the shoe. DROGHEDA takes it.)

Hobble

(He smiles grimly.)

Hobble your absurdity will mock my idiot's infatuation

(The WAITER, crawling and slithering, enters as before, dumbly plucking at the air. DROGHEDA studies him.)

Pity the waiter

(LOT casts a glance at the man.)

Pity his writhing but is it more grotesque than yours?

(DROGHEDA walks out. SVERDLOSK watches his departure, then swiftly sits, unzipping her bag and deftly removing a pair of identical shoes. She selects the one necessary to restore her equilibrium. She stands. She saunters a little, as if before a mirror in a shop. LOT's eyes follow her practised moves…)

LOT: The desert

(He frowns, biting his lip in his longing.)

The desert I think might be

SVERDLOSK: The angel entered me

(She stops. Her look challenges her husband.)

Entered me and

LOT: We never discuss the

SVERDLOSK: Never discuss them no

LOT: The details never never

SVERDLOSK: No and having entered me or whilst inside me

LOT: Inside

SVERDLOSK: Inside me said

LOT: Inside

(LOT suffers.)

Inside you yes

Inside

Inside

(He runs his hands through his hair.)

Inside you

(He shakes his head)

Terrible words inside you inside you yes

(He exerts his concentration.)

Said what

Said what inside you?

(He aches.)

SAID WHAT?

SVERDLOSK: God wants me dead

(Pause.)

In order to save you

(She looks at the floor.)

Run away with me said Mr Drogheda not said he begged
and everything was just as you described it taxi train and

ferry the seducer is predictable and the seduced no less predictable she said I love my husband

(She laughs mildly…)

Which I do

(They look at one another, agonized and pitiful…)

I then went to the bathroom in the bathroom I smelled smoke

LOT: God works through Mr Drogheda

SVERDLOSK: I grabbed a bag

LOT: A wife would

SVERDLOSK: I grabbed a bag and packed it I did the thing I said I'd never do except I did not pack it I threw things in I threw whatever I

(LOT leans to the bag and opens with the fingers of one hand…)

LOT: Lipsticks

Stockings

Shoes

SVERDLOSK: *(Unreproached.)* Yes

Yes

And are they not the things most precious to you?

(LOT rises from his chair and embraces his wife, running his hands over her body with an insatiable possessiveness, at once sublime and pitiful. The WAITER, observing, is a sculptural tribute to their passion. LOT parts from SVERDLOSK. He takes the bag, and his wife by the hand. His attention is distracted by the WAITER.)

LOT: Can't take you

(He frowns. An urgency seizes him)

CAN'T TAKE YOU

(He draws his wife away. They hurry out of SODOM.)

*